NEW LEFT, NEW RIGHT AND BEYOND

New Left, New Right and Beyond

Taking the Sixties Seriously

Edited by

Geoff Andrews
Senior Lecturer in Politics
University of Hertfordshire

Richard Cockett
Lecturer in History
Royal Holloway College
University of London

Alan Hooper
Senior Lecturer in Politics
University of Hertfordshire

and

Michael Williams
Lecturer in Politics and Public Policy
University of Hertfordshire

First published in Great Britain 1999 by
MACMILLAN PRESS LTD
Houndmills, Basingstoke, Hampshire RG21 6XS and London
Companies and representatives throughout the world

A catalogue record for this book is available from the British Library.

ISBN 0–333–74147–1

First published in the United States of America 1999 by
ST. MARTIN'S PRESS, INC.,
Scholarly and Reference Division,
175 Fifth Avenue, New York, N.Y. 10010

ISBN 0–312–22035–9

Library of Congress Cataloging-in-Publication Data
New left, new right and beyond : taking the sixties seriously / edited
by Geoff Andrews . . . [et al.].
p. cm.
Includes bibliographical references and index.
ISBN 0–312–22035–9
1. United States—Politics and government—1961–1963.   2. United
States—Politics and government—1963–1969.   3. Right and left
(Political science)—History—20th century.   I. Andrews, Geoff,
1961–   .
E841.N44   1999
320.51'3'097309046—dc21   98–32036
                                                                CIP

This book is printed on paper suitable for recycling and made from fully managed and
sustained forest sources.

10   9   8   7   6   5   4   3   2   1
08   07   06   05   04   03   02   01   00   99

Printed and bound in Great Britain by Antony Rowe Ltd, Chippenham, Wiltshire

Contents

Acknowledgements

The idea for this book emerged from a course at the University of Hertfordshire, entitled Contemporary Political Movements and Ideas, which takes as its starting-point the legacies of the 1960s. Two public lecture series – 'Twenty-Five Minutes from King's Cross' (1997) and 'The Sixties and their Political Legacies' (1998) – helped to provide the impetus for the book and included earlier versions of contributions to this volume from Peter Saunders, Anne Showstack Sassoon, Richard Cockett and Paul Hirst.

We would like to thank Sandy McLean for secretarial support, Wayne Diamond for technical advice and support, and colleagues in the Social Sciences Department who participated in the staff seminar where many of these ideas were discussed. We are grateful to Rosemary Bechler, editor of *New Times*, for publishing an initial statement of our views and for allowing us to adapt an earlier version of Paul Hirst's piece which first appeared in *New Times*. *The New Statesman* has sponsored many of our events and we are grateful for their continuing support for our work. We would also like to thank our students for their interest, enthusiasm and tolerance of occasional reminiscence. Our colleague Vassilis Fouskas has been an enthusiastic supporter of our project and we are grateful to him for organising a seminar at the London School of Economics on our behalf.

Notes on the Contributors

Geoff Andrews is Senior Lecturer in Politics at the University of Hertfordshire and an Associate Lecturer at the Open University. He has written for a range of journals and newspapers, including *The New Statesman*, *The Times Higher Education Supplement*, *Renewal* and *Marxism Today*. He is the editor of *Citizenship* (1991) and co-editor (with Nina Fishman and Kevin Morgan) of *Opening the Books: Essays on the Social and Cultural History of the British Communist Party* (1995).

Richard Cockett completed his PhD at the University of London and is a Lecturer in History at Royal Holloway College, University of London. He has published several books, including *David Astor and the Observer* and *Thinking the Unthinkable*, on aspects of modern British history. He has also contributed to academic journals and is a regular contributor to the national press, especially *The New Statesman*, *The Economist*, the *Independent on Sunday* and *The Times Educational Supplement*. He lives in London and is too young to have any direct memories of the 1960s.

Marvin Gettleman is Emeritus Professor of History at Brooklyn Polytech, a member of the editorial board of the Marxist scholarly quarterly *Science & Society*, and a Staff Associate of the Veterans of the Abraham Lincoln Brigade. He was active in the Civil Rights and anti-Vietnam War movements, as well as the now-defunct New American Movement, precursor of the present Democratic Socialists of America. Author and editor of a dozen books, he is now at work on a historical study of the US Communist Party's educational work before 1957.

Paul Hirst is Professor of Social and Political Theory at Birkbeck College, University of London. His recent publications include *Associative Democracy* (1994), *Globalization in Question* (1996, with Grahame Thompson) and *From Statism to Pluralism* (1997). He is also Chair of the Council of Charter 88.

Alan Hooper is Senior Lecturer in Politics, University of Hertfordshire, and author of essays on modern British history and contemporary Brazilian politics.

Tariq Modood is Professor of Sociology, Politics and Public Policy at the University of Bristol. His many publications include (as co-author) *Ethnic Minorities in Britain: Diversity and Disadvantage* (1997), (as editor) *Church, State and Religious Minorities* (1997), (as joint editor) *Debating Cultural Hybridity* (1997) and *The Politics of Multiculturalism in the New Europe* (1997).

Peter Saunders is Professor of Sociology at the University of Sussex, and has held visiting academic positions in Australia, New Zealand, Germany and the United States. He is author of nine books and over fifty articles, most of them in the areas of urban sociology, political sociology and social stratification. His current research is on social mobility and meritocracy in Britain. He was an active member of the British Labour Party until the early 1980s, since when he has belonged to no party organisation, although he describes himself as sympathetic to the classical liberal position. He is currently on the editorial board of the Institute of Economic Affairs Health and Welfare Unit, and his most recent book is *Unequal but Fair?* (1996).

Anne Showstack Sassoon is Professor of Politics and Co-Director of the European Research Centre at Kingston University. She was educated in the United States, Italy and the United Kingdom. She has written widely on Gramsci, women's new socio-economic roles and, more recently, New Labour politics. A collection of her essays *Beyond Pessimism of the Intellect* is shortly to be published.

Tom Steele is a Senior Lecturer in Adult Education at the University of Glasgow. He was Organising Tutor for the WEA at the Swarthmore Centre in Leeds from 1973 to 1987 and Lecturer in Adult Education in the Department of Adult Continuing Education at the University of Leeds from 1990 to 1996. His previous publications include *Alfred Orage and the Leeds Art Club* (1990), *Learning Independence: a Political Outline of Indian Adult Education* (with Richard Taylor, 1995) and *The Emergence of Cultural Studies: Adult Education, Cultural Politics and the 'English' Question* (1997). He is currently working on a study of European popular education movements and popular knowledge.

Hilary Wainwright is editor of the journal *Red Pepper*, Senior Research Fellow at the Institute of Labour Studies, University of Manchester and Fellow of the Transnational Institute, Amsterdam. Publications include *Beyond the Fragments* (with Sheila Rowbotham and Lynne Segal) (1979), *Labour: a Tale of Two Parties* (1987) and *Arguments for New Left* (1992).

Wendy Wheeler is Reader in English at the University of North London, where she teaches English literature and critical theory. She has published many essays on literature, culture and politics, and is currently finishing her first book, *A New Modernity?* – on politics, identity, culture and science at the end of the twentieth century – for publication in 1999.

Michael Williams lectures in politics and public policy at the University of Hertfordshire and elsewhere. Before then he spent twenty years as a civil servant in what is now the Department of the Environment, Transport and the Regions. He has published papers on privatisation and the role of management consultants in shaping public policy.

Introduction
Alan Hooper and Michael Williams

Should we take the sixties seriously? People on the right often emphasise the frivolity and irresponsibility of the period – but they also insist on its baneful impact on society and culture. People on the left criticise the period for inflated rhetoric and negligible achievement. It can be seen as the climax of a short golden age of peace and prosperity, sandwiched between the extremes of earlier and later periods, and thus more occasion for nostalgia than for celebration or inspiration. Altogether the sixties can easily be dismissed as an era of bourgeois solidity tarnished only by occasional youthful or bohemian excess – mere froth upon the daydream.

But such an assessment would be to ignore other aspects of the period – those savage wars of peace in Algeria and Vietnam which still reverberate today; the wind of change that released most of Africa from European rule, the solid construction of the foundations of the European Union which can now be seen as Europe's greatest adventure since 1945. Might it not be that, as Marx observed of the 'so-called revolutions' of 1848, such 'poor incidents, small fractures and fissures' as, for example, the Berkeley Free Speech Movement or the London School of Economics gates incident when students tore down barriers separating two parts of the college (and countless similar manifestations), released 'oceans of liquid matter' which would subsequently 'rend into fragments' the 'hard rock' of complacency and placidity and precipitate the landslide of political dissolution and intellectual disarray of the century's last decades? (Fernbach: 279).

The essays in this volume seek to investigate this possibility through an exploration of the dialectic – dialectic of liberation, indeed – between those twin progeny of the period, the New Left and New Right, during subsequent decades. As such, they are concerned with the diffuse legacy of the sixties – social, political and cultural – and the way in which these contrasting but related political formations sought to channel the energies of the decade. The focus, therefore, is more upon the political appropriation of the period in ideological and organisational terms than upon its diverse expressions in subsequent 'new' social movements – though many of the essays are certainly informed by the link between the personal and the political which those movements sought to evoke. Equally, the editors have not sought to impose a single definition of either of the protean and diverse movements which constitute the New Left and the New Right.

1

Despite obvious differences, these two movements contributed to the erosion and ultimate dissolution of that mid-century stability which has been described – perhaps too easily – as the post-war consensus. That consensus was founded on a belief that the state had both the capacity and the need to plan social and economic development. It was that conviction that the New Left, riding the crest of wider social and economic changes, called into question in the name of participatory democracy. It was those questions to which the New Right – in the ensuing dialectic of liberation – delivered their own distinctive replies in the name of the supposed superior democracy of the free market.

Today the outcome of this dialectic is not so obvious as it might have seemed in 1990 at the climax of a decade of 'bourgeois triumphalism' (in Peregrine Worsthorne's memorable phrase). The 'emotional revolutionism' of the first phase of New Right militancy represented by Thatcher and Reagan faded and the faith became 'part of the conventional phraseology of political philistines' like Bush and Major (Weber, 1919: 125). John Redwood's and Newt Gingrich's attempt to revive the original insurgent impulse confirmed Hegel's remarks about tragedy and farce. Instead a suitably repackaged and chastened left has reoccupied the seats of what passes for political power in the global market-place that the Anglo-American right has bequeathed to the world.

This new left (deliberately uncapitalised) represents neither the old left nor the New Left but rather seeks to transcend both categories, and to leap beyond the old dichotomies accepted by New Right and New Left alike in a true *Aufhebung* – that untranslatable German word conveying both abolition and incorporation of contending opposites in a process of resolution in a higher plane – which Hegel saw as the third moment in the dialectic. This process has been described more prosaically (albeit with unconscious echoes of the triune dialectic) as 'triangulation' and a 'third way'. The project is as ambitious as it may be nebulous, with Blair seeking to join Clinton and other, more improbable, acolytes in an attempt to manage – from a 'centre-left perspective' – 'social change in the global economy'. As Blair put it: 'The old left resisted that change. The new right did not want to manage it. We have got to manage that change to produce social solidarity and prosperity' (Kettle, 1998).

The rhetoric echoes the concern of much American and certainly some British social theory in the 1990s with the danger of social disintegration. There is much controversy over the source of this development. The right, especially in the US, laid responsibility at the door of the sixties and an alleged over-emphasis on rights. Some on the left are disposed to see the development as the all-too-predictable outcome of the 'creative destruction' of unrestricted global capitalism celebrated by the right. Whatever the explanation the problem evokes a common response – on left and right alike – in terms of a concern with 'community'. However, this concern with community fails to answer the question of exactly what kind of community is being identified or proposed. Are we to conceive of community as some form of government-sponsored national cohesiveness with all its authoritarian implications and potential for intensifying division by stigmatising minorities, or some more pluralistic conception – of communities rather than community? Whatever the answer, the present concern about cohesion invokes the very concept of community which, however defined, was central to the New Left in the 1950s and 1960s – even though its critics today might be reluctant to agree.

Can we identify in these contemporary developments an emerging new consensus in which old divisions are healed and new understandings forged? Kondratiev's theories of long waves of capitalist development may point to the beginning of a new economic upswing arriving, on the dot, 50 years after the onset of the post-war boom. The current 'boom' of the Anglo-American economies has certainly encouraged some to hold out a prospect of sustained non-inflationary growth. Can we see a new institutional order in the making which will provide the necessary framework for the sort of sustained growth which, if it cannot restore the golden age from 1948 to 1973, will at least overcome the disruptions of the subsequent landslide and avoid the need for renewed shock therapy? Such is the formula widely propagated in the form of the 'Washington consensus' of free markets, civil societies and good governance – Yankee Hegelianism, perhaps. Thus far it has been mainly imposed on societies in Latin America and Africa – and more recently – east Asia that are unable to resist. How far the advanced capitalist countries – notably Japan and Germany – will be able – or indeed wish – to achieve a similar 'structural adjustment' remains to be seen.

For the moment the focus seems to be as much upon attitudinal as upon institutional change. Recent soul-searching by the likes of Michael Portillo or Peregrine Worsthorne, in which old racial or sexual chauvinism is renounced and new sympathies declared, does seem to point to a new 'era of good feelings' in inter-personal and inter-cultural relations. Here surely is evidence of the beneficial legacy of the sixties. Yet a common concern on the part of New Labour and New Democrat alike to reform the behaviour of the poor and dependent (while currying favour with the rich and glamorous) arouses echoes of an earlier age – and of the intervening Thatcher/Reagan era. Superficial associations with the sixties may disguise a harsher spirit, more in tune with the requirements of the 'Washington consensus', than with the more expansive and generous spirit of that time.

The chapters in this work explore the dialectic of New Right and New Left since the 1960s in a variety of ways. For Alan Hooper, writing about what he calls the long sixties – 1956 to 1976 – the popular insurgency of the time can be seen as a 'modernism in the streets' aroused by a modernising impulse from above which eventually evoked a repressive response. In a sense the crisis of the left of the 1970s represents an internecine (and intergenerational) conflict from which the right benefited and in which the New Left's search for community receded before market imperatives in a 'globalising' mode.

Tom Steele demonstrates in his chapter about the British reception of Gramsci that the Italian Marxist aroused such a strong response precisely because his broader conception of the role of the party complemented the concern with culture as community so characteristic of what has been called the first New Left around Edward Thompson and Raymond Williams. A fascinating example of an earlier dialectic between right and left can be seen in Williams' intellectual debt to T.S. Eliot who drew inspiration from Karl Mannheim – who in turn sat at the feet of the eminent Hungarian Marxist Georg Lukács who was 'rediscovered' by the New Left, first as a literary critic and then as a political theorist. For Lukács the Communist Party represented precisely such a recovery of lost community.

Wendy Wheeler picks up this theme in her discussion of the British counter-culture of the sixties. For her too the animating spirit of the movement lay in its search for a community of authenticity and principle in opposition to the atomisation of the market. Tony Blair as a child of this era can awaken a widespread response when he stresses the need for a new community of rights and obligations.

In his account of what he calls the three New Lefts in Britain, Geoff Andrews points to their common engagement with notions of culture and community. He argues that the third New Left (around *Marxism Today*) was attempting to engage with the consequences of the failure of their predecessors to recapture a lost commonality in the face of the wave of consumerism and individualism unleashed by the sixties and ridden so skilfully by their opponents.

Marvin Gettleman's chapter on the American New Left finds its animating impulse in a search for 'beloved community' which found more diffuse expression in the counter-culture – which has contributed its own distinctive strand to Silicon Valley-style capitalism and a proportion of the more soft-centred management theory of the 1980s and 1990s. Recent research has shown that increasing numbers of Americans feel more 'at home' at work than at home (Griffith, 1997).

Richard Cockett explores the central theme of a dialectic between New Right and New Left. He argues that the New Right may have won the economic battle but the New Left won the cultural battle. Tony Blair's New Labour can be taken to represent a synthesis of the economic liberation celebrated by the New Right and the personal liberation celebrated by the New Left.

Peter Saunders offers a rather different perspective on New Labour which points to a social liberalism which goes beyond a discredited social conservatism against which both New Left and New Right revolted and the liberal conservatism of the New Right itself which has been emphatically rejected by the electorate of both Britain and the US. Invoking Emile Durkheim, he sees the main thrust of New Labour as an attempt to overcome social fragmentation through a new social solidarity in which exclusion is overcome by 'welfare to work' and inequality justified by merit.

Michael Williams attempts to set Alan Hooper's long sixties in the context of the century as a whole by an examination of the work of two leading historians – Eric Hobsbawm on the left and Robert Skidelsky on the right – who have also played a prominent role in political debates since the 1960s. Despite very different points of departure both historians have made a significant contribution to New Labour – the one by stressing the need for a broad coalition against the right through themes of inclusion, and the other through policies designed to reconstruct the welfare state. The need to rebuild community has been a major theme of publications from the Social Market Foundation headed by Skidelsky.

Paul Hirst picks up the theme of community in his chapter on associative democracy. Against the authoritarian impulse lurking within the social liberalism discerned by Saunders, Hirst offers a more pluralistic conception which arouses echoes of the more generous, utopian impulses of the sixties. Hilary Wainwright explores another legacy of the sixties, investigating the extent to which the various movements that are associated with the Bennite left point beyond the twin antinomies of social democracy and stalinism – and thus, like Hirst, towards a new relationship between the institutions of state and market and popular social initiatives.

Tariq Modood advances another kind of pluralism in his discussion of changes in the conceptualisation of black identity in Britain since the 1960s. He argues for the existence of a range of identities and against a simple polarity of black and white. Like Hirst, Modood points to the problems of an imposed community – and of a single, over-arching community, however defined. Anne Showstack Sassoon shows the extent to which the first and second New Lefts in the 1960s were inspired by what one might call the 'heroic community' of the 1930s and 1940s. She also points to the need to transcend past heroics and embrace the search for a new settlement which New Labour claims to represent.

The chapters in this volume illustrate the diversity and eclecticism of the sixties themselves and the complex lineages of descent to today's uncertainties. Community is just one of the themes of the decade refracted through different lenses in the chapters that follow. They illustrate the contested nature of the concept while pointing towards some possible solutions. But they also touch upon a host of unresolved issues, broadly registered around the concern with 'modernisation' and cognate preoccupations with modernity and postmodernism, that may be traced back to that turbulent decade. The questions were first posed in their current form in the sixties themselves and until they have been resolved we shall need to take the decade as seriously as we can.

REFERENCES

Fernbach, D. (ed.) (1973), *Karl Marx. Surveys from Exile. Political Writings*, vol. II, Penguin.
Griffith, V. (1997), 'Satanic Mills', *Financial Times*, 7 May.
Kettle, M. (1998), 'The Next Step: a Blueprint for New Labour's World role', *The Guardian*, 7 February.
Weber, M. (1919), 'Politics as a Vocation', H.H. Gerth and C. Wright Mills (eds), *From Max Weber: Essays in Sociology*, Routledge & Kegan Paul, 1948.

1 A Politics Adequate to the Age: the New Left and the Long Sixties
Alan Hooper

The sixties continue to trouble friend and foe alike but while opponents are frequently intemperate in their criticism sympathisers often prove no more than lukewarm in their appreciation. Thus E.J. Hobsbawm considers the climacteric of the decade – 1968 – 'was neither an end nor a beginning but only a signal'. When we look for what it heralded, however, we are disappointed, Hobsbawm suggesting only that it cautioned past hubris – 'it served as a warning, a sort of *memento mori* to a generation that half-believed it had solved the problems of Western society for good' – rather than promised future hope (Hobsbawm, 1995: 286). If the message is largely a negative one it does highlight an important feature of the period, namely that those who invested their hopes in the sixties included not only the masses but also the ruling elites. Might Marx's comment on an earlier revolution, that it 'paralyses its own representatives and endows only its opponents with passion and forcefulness', apply to the later one as rulers seek to distance themselves from their own failures as much as to denounce the follies of their subordinates? (Marx, 1973: 171). What is crucial to understanding the sixties is a sense of the magnitude of what was at stake; the subsequent disdain heaped upon the decade by its opponents should be seen as evidence of the scale of its challenge rather than as confirmation of its futility.

It is just such recognition that informs Samuel Beer's analysis of the twin forces which expressed a 'culture of modernity' common to all western countries and resulted in 'a general transformation of political culture in Western countries' from the 1960s – a rationalistically inspired techno-cratic initiative from above and a rebellious and romantic populism from below. Beer describes the latter as a form of 'populistic democracy' but it is his characterisation of its goals as the 'quality of life, participation and decentralization' which is especially relevant for it is not unreasonable to describe them as a restatement of the historic formula of liberty, equality and fraternity (Beer, 1982: 111, 147). The sixties brought together many of the key challenges of the modern era – especially the possibilities of

7

democracy in a libertarian mode, culture in an egalitarian compass and community in a fraternal embrace – and tested their implications in a style that was as exhilarating in manner as it was problematic in outcome. This essay explores the way in which this engagement of the forces of the left with the modern condition unfolded in the 'long 1960s' in Britain and America. It begins with modernity's greatest challenge, the revolutions which were like a 'flash of truthfulness lighting up the world's political landscape', as Hans Konig observes in comparing 1968 with 1848 (Konig, 1988: 15).

The comparison of 1968 with 1848 is a telling one for, rather as 'all the doctrines developed after 1830 met their challenge in 1848', so too the aspirations of the sixties were put to the test in 1968; there was an *avant Mai* to match the earlier *vorMarz* and their illumination highlighted both past and future (Lichtheim, 1968: 61). Just as an 'unmistakable tang of modernity' emerged in 1848 so 1968 gave strong intimations of post-modernity (Elton, 1931: 138; Young, 1977: 93). As such, both compelled consideration of the significance of the 'modern': while the political aspect involved an engagement with the legacy of 1789 the social dimensions were no less significant. For 1968 came at the end of the greatest economic boom in the history of capitalism and a period of profound social change. As one observer noted in 1968, 'work has new meaning, personal space is compressed, leisure looms large, consumption has a different function' (Kopkind, 1995: 153). The changes involved the working-out of many of the issues first raised around 1848, in particular questions of 'culture', as an emerging 'post-industrial' society focused attention upon the consequences of information and education for the 'social individual'. The sixties represented an engagement with these changes not only by the left but also the hegemonic capitalist societies, Britain and the United States, whose rulers sought a liberal, as opposed to a revolutionary, solution to the democratic implications of social and political change. Their political strategies – the left drawing upon the revolutionary tradition of rights asserted by the masses in 1848, and the elites upon a liberal conception codified by T.H. Marshall a century later – unfolded in the shadow of the destructive rivalries of the Cold War as well as the liberating possibilities of an economic boom and gave to the period that peculiar mix of elation and desperation which came to a climax in 1968 (Cronin, 1996: 170–2; Nuttall, 1970: 20).

    The challenge of 1848 and 1968 was felt most intensely on the left whose need to define both the means to its goals and the identity of the popular sectors led to something like a 'revolution in the revolution'. There were, however, key differences in the answers, for while '48 simplified options by finding a focus for change in the state and an agency in the labour movement, '68 confirmed an increasing disenchantment with both by enlarging political perspectives to a point of indefinition as it sought to energise social forces in association with or even against the state and labour movement. As such '68 not only identified a 'forward march of labour halted' some ten years before the claim but also called into question the achievements of that march during its century of advance from 1848 to 1948. It did so in a spirit that owed as much to the 'communalism' of '48 and values – feminism, environmentalism and romanticism – which had blossomed with the growth of the early socialist movement, as the more influential communism which pushed such values to the margins in the social changes and movements of the following century (Lichtheim, 1968: 70–1, 75, 234, 243). If 1848 proved to be a culmination which presaged retreat, 1968 testified to the sixties rediscovery of what had been deferred and of what became an imperative, the search for fraternity.

For the rulers, and especially their intellectuals, it was the question of equality which emerged most powerfully from the two years. While 1848 held out the promise of the equalisation of cultural access, 1968 and the sixties seemed to signal its imminent realisation. In doing so they posed afresh the dilemma, analysed by de Tocqueville in *Democracy in America* and Matthew Arnold in *Culture and Anarchy*, as to whether democracy in its American/egalitarian mode would entail cultural levelling and debasement. It was a challenge which issued from the popular insurgencies of the 1830s and 1840s – Jacksonian and Chartist – and which lent urgency to the answers of both; by the second half of the nineteenth century, however, the question seemed to have been settled in a manner which accommodated popular aspirations while preserving elite privileges. Chartist goals were largely assimilated within Gladstonian liberalism, while Jacksonian ambitions were channelled into a capacious Republican party. While the energies of the 1830s and 1840s found powerful cultural expression in Whitman and Ruskin, cultural practice remained more restrained. Arnold's concern with the anarchy that would follow the 'Englishman's right to do what he likes' proved largely unfounded in his own century and his own country (Arnold, 1869: 231). When British workers did seek to do what they wished it was largely in private, in institutions of their own creation – co-operatives, friendly societies, pubs – and in a manner which left other classes largely undisturbed; the one exception being their trade unions but here too, though with significant periods of disruption, it proved possible to achieve long periods of national accommodation. The energies of an

American(ising) working class could be contained by that country's geographic and economic expansiveness during the second half of the century.

Arnold's 'grave question' concerning the 'tone' of a democratic society re-emerged in the twentieth century in the form of a modernist aesthetic which promised a revolutionary combination of political and artistic radicalism (Arnold, 1861: 113). Its first manifestation occurred in the opening decade of the century when, in John Berger's 'Moment of Cubism', it seemed that a 'transformed world (had) become theoretically possible and (that) the necessary forces of change could already be recognised as existing'. The conjunction of those 'necessary forces' was rarely achieved, however. In part this was a consequence of the political attitudes of the modernists themselves for, as Berger notes, '(t)he Cubists imagined the world transformed, but not the process of transformation'. But more important in the failure of the classic modernism of the early twentieth century were the wider political circumstances which conspired against the modernists' ambitions, the fortunes of the Bauhaus being emblematic of modernism's fate during the first half of the century. However, the material abundance of the 'affluent' societies like the US in the 1950s promised not only 'a peaceful, "evolutionary" transition to the new Utopia' but also a renewal of the radical energies and inclusive aspirations of early modernism (Berger, 1970: 145, 161; Fuller, 1980: 145). In short, an egalitarian culture to complement the democratic politics which, following fascism's defeat, had become a norm for the world's states.

Fulfilling democratic promise raised not only the issue of equality but also the question of the libertarian possibilities of a political community. Once again it did so in a manner which evoked 1848 and again it was the Anglo-American societies which faced the most urgent challenges. In seeking to reinforce their liberal credentials in the face of an expansive communism and to define their world role in a period when one had lost an empire and the other acquired one, the ruling class of both countries sought to renew their socio-political arrangements. In doing so they not only opened the door to the libertarian energies of the 1960s but called into question the very institutional arrangements created to close the phase of libertarian activity of the period around 1848. In both societies the second half of the nineteenth century witnessed a recomposition and rehabilitation of the ruling-elites following the mid-century turmoil (the 'hungry forties' in Britain; the civil war in the US) resulting in a set of institutions and practices which proved highly successful formulas of political rule until the middle of the twentieth century. In Britain there emerged that aristocratically-based 'Establishment' whose identity was recognised in the mid-1950s; in the US the corresponding elite were those patrician progressives whose presidential representatives, from Theodore Roosevelt to Franklin D. Roosevelt, guided the country from regional power to global hegemony (Harris, 1984: 38, 194; Lasch, 1974: 84, 87, 95; Hewison, 1997: 75–8; Blum, 1980: 17–19). Neither regime was without its exclusions, however. Such exclusions had been shaped by a mid-nineteenth century public/private divide which placed a predominantly male elite in the public sphere and 'minorities' – women, gays and blacks – in the private. In the mid-twentieth century 'personal troubles' arising from such exclusions became 'public' – even international – issues as a result of the Cold War. It was in seeking to redress these in the 1950s – by adding J.S. Mill's tolerance to Arnold's guidance – that both formulas and the elites who managed them were tested to something close to self-destruction in the 1960s. In the case of America this involved the most flagrant exclusion, the slavery which had tarnished the country's democratic credentials since its inception; in Britain's case the exclusions were more subtle and in so far as they bore a name it was the 'Victorianism' which censored or punished behaviour transgressing moral codes derived from that era. In both cases legal decisions signalled the search for a new settlement, the Supreme Court judgment of 1954 outlawing segregated schooling in one and the non-prosecution for obscenity of the publishers of *Lady Chatterley's Lover* in 1960 in the other (Marable, 1984: 17; Marwick, 1982: 151). The 1960s saw the Anglo-American democracies committed to fulfilling the libertarian potential of their democratic precepts as a way of overcoming exclusions which, in the context of the Cold War struggle for allegiance, had become an embarrassment or worse. With the egalitarian promise of expanding economies and the fraternal aspirations which emerged during the decade the 1960s promised a revolutionary agenda – whether it prompted a revolutionary response is the issue to which I shall now turn.

Defining the sixties is not simply a question of placing them in an historical perspective but also of establishing their duration. For just as 1956 was not simply a year but also, in Stuart Hall's words, a 'conjuncture' so too the 1960s cannot be understood if they are confined to their chronological limits; rather they can be seen as a period which was generational in scope, beginning in 1956 and ending with a set of events around the mid-1970s which we may fix in 1976 (Hall, 1989: 13). Such a periodisation helps to capture the content of the sixties by framing it in a span which was as distinctive as it was paradoxical. It highlights not only the manner in which the sixties brought together the challenges from the modern era but also how they were contested and contained. As such the period saw a complex interplay of the political and the cultural, of modernist aspiration and post-modernist critique, issues which can be approached through the most systematic attempt to define the nature and scope of the period, Frederic Jameson's essay 'Periodizing the 60's'.

'Modernism in the streets'. Such was the reported comment of Lionel Trilling concerning the youth movements of the 1960s and the 'adversary culture' of which they were an expression (Lasch, 1985: 200). It is an apt description in so far as it captures the insurgent nature of the popular forces of the decade but it misleads if it deflects attention from the modernism which was also to be found in the councils of the power-holders. For as Beer stressed, the sixties began as much with an elite-inspired 'assertion of the values of scientific rationalism' and of 'technocracy' as they did with popular insurgency; in a spirit of modernising renewal from above as well as modernist aspiration from below. Beginning in 1956 and continuing through to the mid-1960s power-centres with global pretensions sought to modernise their beliefs and practices to meet the challenge of the unfolding and apparently unending 'long boom'. For the cold war rivals – following Khrushchev's Twentieth Party Congress speech and Kennedy's New Frontier programme – this was especially urgent but left reassessment (in Crosland's *The Future of Socialism* and German Social Democracy's renunciation of Marxism) and right regimes (in the persons of Macmillan and de Gaulle) showed the extent of the imperative. Each sought to respond to the human and material possibilities of an expansive economy and, in the name of 'modernisation', to embrace a liberating science and technology which were to be directed to popular advantage by elites newly empowered by a faith in planning.

Stressing that the sixties were launched on a wave of elite renewal is not to underplay the popular energies that were decisive in the formation of the period. In identifying 1956 as the starting-point of the sixties I am not simply taking up a suggestion of a number of writers that the middle years of the fifties marked a watershed, but also pointing to a range of popular actions which caused that shift (Lukacs, 1990: 188; Barraclough, 1967: 36–8; Jameson, 1984: 180). Many are familiar and need no emphasis; they have been compellingly documented in Christopher Booker's *The Neophiliacs*. Two do need to be recalled, however, for they are central to my argument: first, and well-known, the emergence of the New Left from the twin international crises of Suez and Hungary; second, and less familiar, the first major exhibition of the group of artists called the Independent Group who together created Pop Art in Britain. The appearance of these two movements in 1956 points to the breadth and vitality of popular concerns in that year and also to an issue which was central to the prospects of the popular movements in the sixties, the renewal and possible combination of Marxism and modernism as expressions of political and aesthetic modernity.

This emphasis upon the western origins of the sixties and on the interplay between the political and the cultural as a central preoccupation contrasts with that of Frederic Jameson. He suggests that the decisive sources of the energies of the sixties derived from the anti-colonial struggles of the emergent Third World – with the civil rights movement in the US part of that de-colonising wave – and took the form of a cultural rather than political challenge in the west (Jameson, 1984: 180, 182–3). Neither claim is without plausibility but both capture only part of the story. Thus while it would be foolish not to recognise the crucial importance of events in the Third World – the emergence of the post-colonial world was the greatest revolution in the second half of the century – my claim would be that the sixties were a global phenomenon, not simply in the sense implied by Jameson that events in one part of the globe impacted upon the rest, but that societies, and especially the Anglo-American ones, were responding to a shared global challenge represented by the long boom and the competitive struggles between systems and ideologies which it entailed. Similarly, while recognising the centrality of the cultural in any definition of the sixties I would also stress the political character of the period, not only in identifying its origins in the elites' adoption of modernising strategies but also the manner of the period's closure and the reasons for its abrupt termination.

For while Jameson highlights a series of major political events during the years 1972–74 as marking the end of sixties – including the US withdrawal from Vietnam, the coup in Chile and the formation of the Trilateral Commission in 1973 – he places decisive emphasis, following Ernest Mandel, upon the 'world-wide economic crisis'. Thus he sees the sixties as a period characterised by linkages from economy to culture – the 'mechanization of the superstructure' involving, in a famous image, an 'immense and inflationary issuing of superstructural credit' in the form of popular energies – and from Third World to First as movements in the former inspired the mass culture of the latter. It is an analysis premised upon a view of the period as one in which the 'active political categories no longer seemed to be those of social class' (Jameson, 1984: 205–9). My claim is that the sixties not only began around 1956 with a class initiative – the elites' reformation – but that they ended around 1976 with a class defeat – of the masses' rebellion – and that both possessed fundamental political significance.

The manner in which the rebellion from below was checked and defeated will be examined later; given the importance of cultural issues to the sixties, however, it is vital to consider the cultural resources of the subordinate classes, in particular the modernism available for their purposes as the elites had defined a modernism for their needs. What was this popular modernism? For Beer it was a 'romantic revolt' imbued with radical-democratic ideas and a populist spirit in which the affinities between popular culture, especially pop music, and the political radicalism of the 1960s displayed the 'liberating spirit of modernity' (Beer, 1982: 139–40). Another expression of this was the Pop Art movement which began almost simultaneously in Britain and the US in the mid-1950s. It was the former that witnessed the first major public appearance of the movement at the 'This is Tomorrow' exhibition in 1956. A key exhibit on this occasion was Richard Hamilton's collage 'Just what is it that makes today's homes so different, so appealing?' which, with its images of modern man and woman surrounded by the objects and symbols of affluence in its industrial-capitalist mode, captured many of the concerns of the movement that was to flourish in the 1960s (Appleyard, 1989: 127; Hewison, 1981: 191). What did such a movement offer in the renewal of modernism and in relation to the aspirations of the masses?

The most positive aspect of Pop Art was its desire to embrace contemporary experience – 'simply to wake up to the very life we're living' as a related figure, John Cage, put it – thereby adding aesthetic dignity to what was socially popular. In so doing it connected with the concern of twentieth-century cultural and social modernism – from Freud to Trotsky – with the conditions of everyday life and with the nature of human experience in the context of industrialising, 'mass' societies. In seeking to express what Eduardo Paolozzi, one of its leading exponents, called the 'sublime of everyday life' it renewed the aspiration of early modernism to encompass the world of the masses and the 'real' and to end that divorce between the aesthetic and quotidian worlds which had afflicted modernism following its defeats at the hands of fascism and Stalinism. At its best Pop Art aspired to be inclusive and democratic and represented an heroic attempt to embrace the world and to put art at its service; together with '"serious" pop music and the "alternative" society' it expressed a 'conviction that old cultural distinctions were worthless and had to be replaced by a new acceptance of the totality of modern experience' (Russell, 1969: 21; Appleyard, 1989: 126, 131).

Such was the promise but it was not without its problems. One was a political innocence which it shared with classic modernism: though it was a movement which connected with popular energies – with the mass and above all the young – and could be seen as a 'resistance movement: a classless commando ... directed against the Establishment', it no more forged 'necessary' conjunctions with political radicalism than its early twentieth-century forerunner. The involvement of the Situationists or the Provos with what a key text of the former movement called *The Revolution of Everyday Life* (1963–65) and the explosive events of May 1968 did enable imagination briefly to seize power. Moreover the concerns of New Left figures like Raymond Williams and E.P. Thompson with culture, and especially the category of 'experience', pointed to the possibility of an 'integral lived politics' which would bring together the 'dissociated halves' of political and aesthetic radicalism which had frozen into 'Leninist' and 'avant garde' caricatures (Pinkney, 1989: 26). But a fusion of a renewed Marxism and a restored modernism proved problematic. For Pop Art's embrace of consumer society, its very non-judgemental quality, led to a mood of fatality rather than freedom before the universal reign of commodities. Williams had for some years expressed his reservations concerning modernism on the grounds not only of its tendency to self-regarding elitism but also because, in contrast to his preferred naturalism, it tended to be distant from 'experience ... within its real environment'. If he became more sympathetic to modernism's radical political potential it was not without recognition of how its potential for an 'innovatory inclusion of a diversity of voices' contrasted with the 'self-absorbed miming of others' or the difference between the 'everyday vernacular' and the 'Vox Pop'. It was precisely the inability of sixties aesthetic modernism to maintain this distinction between an open, democratic modernism and a closed, technocratic one that led Peter Fuller to break with his erstwhile modernist allegiance, based upon his sympathy for the writings of John Berger, and to move towards what would later be seen as recognisably post-modern preferences for the 'natural' and the 'spiritual' (Williams, 1989: 61–2, 79–80, 113; Fuller, 1988, 1990).

This move would become a fashion but it did highlight a growing doubt as to whether a renewed modernism could encompass an increasingly diverse social experience. Such doubts had been expressed at the beginning of the sixties when in 1959 three American observers, Peter Drucker, C. Wright Mills and Irving Howe, spanning the US political spectrum from conservative through radical to socialist, identified changes which pointed to a condition which tentatively they were calling 'post-modern' (Drucker, 1959: ix; Wright Mills, 1970: 184; Bertens, 1995: 22). By the late 1960s a sense of the dissolution of the modern – and with it the modernist project of social self-determination – was finding echoes elsewhere as the optimism of the early part of the decade gave way to the travails at its end. The writings of John Lukacs were especially striking in this respect. His *The Passing of the Modern Age* (1970) gave sophisticated expression to the vulgar conservative cry 'more will mean worse'. Identifying a process of generalised inflation or what he was later to call 'insidious devolution', Lukacs noted that whether 'it is money or books or degrees or sex, where there is more and more of something it is worth less and less' and that a 'decline of taste and judgement, of truthfulness and reason was inseparable from this devolution' in areas like politics and education (Lukacs, 1990: 265; 1993: 286). These views do more than prefigure the conservative cultural critique which has dominated recent American debate; they also connect with the post-modern sentiment that modernity, as a consequence of its own evolution and elaboration, has achieved a baroque complexity or 'involution' before which 'modern' solutions are doomed to be unavailing. As such it posed a clear challenge to the artistic and political radicalism of the sixties and to the attempt of thinkers like Wright Mills and Raymond Williams to define a politics adequate to the age. It is to that politics that I now turn.

The New Left shared with Pop Art not only its origins in the year 1956 but also its concern to deepen and make relevant ambitions which had atrophied over the course of the century; in its case, though initially at least more so in Britain than America, Marxism. The twin crises of 1956 in Suez and Hungary suggested the moral bankruptcy of a capitalism reformed in a social democratic guise and of a communism incapable of discarding its Stalinist habits. More fundamentally, however, and of continuing relevance to the critique of both systems as they entered their 'modernising' phases in the 1960s, was the sense that state-led and 'planned' industrial societies were not only incapable of addressing old grievances – especially those of race, sex and class – but that the solutions they could offer simply entailed patterns of social relations which were dispiriting and dehumanising. In this sense the New Left questioned modernity in its elite-led modernising mode, counterposing to its massification of society and its pluralist politics a more radical sense of the modern, involving the search for new forms of political community and popular participation. It was a search that proved to be as disruptive for the left as it was dramatic for society. By the end of the 1960s, the extremities of the period, the inadequacies of the left and a sense of the intractibilities of the modern condition, drove the movement into a phase of self-criticism whose destructive impact was only obscured by the buoyancy which derived from a period of wide-ranging working-class mobilisation. When this crumbled in the mid-1970s before the elites' counter-offensive, and opened the way to what proved a generation of New Right domination, the left was in full retreat.

At the outset the New Left was informed by a mood of intelligent pessimism offset by a conviction that creative optimism could achieve change. It was a mood which drew equally on critical detachment and pragmatic engagement, the balance of either reflecting the contrasting political legacies of the left in Britain and the US. Thus while the British New Left – at least in its ex-communist form around E.P. Thompson – sought the renewal of Marxism, Wright Mills in the US was disposed to question a central proposition of Marxism, what he famously called the 'labor metaphysic'. Nevertheless both movements shared a commitment to a sense of community and new forms of political action, seeking what Wright Mills called a 'community of publics' and Williams a 'knowable community', or what the Port Huron Statement, the 1962 testament of the US Students for a Democratic Society, described as '... a democracy of individual participation, governed by two central aims: that the individual share in those social decisions determining the quality and direction of his life; that society be organised to encourage independence in men and provide the media for their common participation' (Jacobs and Landau, 1967: 117; Wright Mills, 1959: 300; Williams, 1974: 13–14; Teodori, 1970: 167). Freed of its conventional gender – a freeing that was to be part of the left's subsequent, often anguished, self-discovery – it expressed a fraternity to inform both the left's more usual strategic concerns with equality and liberty and to guide its tactical choices.

That it was more than a pious aspiration was evident in the two great movements which gave the New Left political anchorage in the late 1950s and early 1960s – CND and the Civil Rights movement. Drawing on traditions of political mobilisation – pacifist and anti-slavery – whose roots were deep in the first half of the previous century, they also absorbed not a little of the religiosity that had inspired these movements, the personal witness of CND and its offshoots being matched by the search for 'the beloved community' amongst civil rights activists. The momentum of both carried them through to the mid-1960s with some sense of real achievement: the Test-ban treaty of 1963 and the Civil Rights Act of 1964 were testimony to their impact. Both, perhaps inevitably, fell short of their goals: the bomb was not banned and racism not eradicated and from the mid-1960s, in what are widely regarded as the decade's climacteric of 1965–68, disillusionment with Wilson's Labour Government and Johnson's Democratic Presidency, dramatised in both cases by the agony of Vietnam, drove the New Left in search of new responses (Burner, 1996: 155–7; Young, 1977: 157–9).

It was a search that proved as dramatic as it was destructive. Both were fully evident in the 'summer of love' of 1967, of hippiedom and psychedelia. Today the best remembered, and easiest mocked, phase of the sixties it was the most assimilable to the imperatives of capital accumulation. Nevertheless, it arose from the same impulse as movements, of which black power was the first, which were concerned to explore the relationship between self and society and which produced one of the most famous slogans of the period, the 'personal is political'; its legacy was not simply the cultivation of lifestyle but also the emergence of the feminist and gay movements. A second and related response in these years was the establishment of communes for living or collectives for service-provision. Such (anti) institution building drew upon traditions which had been nurtured in Europe in the years before 1848 and often found a lasting home only in the United States during the nineteenth century; it was there that they received the greatest support and perhaps their lasting achievements. Often representing an attempt to rethink the nature of professional practice – as in moves to establish centres of artistic, psychiatric and academic provision in Britain by Wesker, Laing and Cooper – their more exploitable energies could be commodified by capitalist entrepreneurs as in Silicon Valley. Equally, the same region, perhaps the leading centre for such communal experiment, could also nurture a gay community which, if it could not create an alternative society, did sustain a sense of alternative values (Hewison, 1986: 17–18, 138–9, 155–6; Berman, 1996: 166–8; Roszak, 1988: 161–4).

The most dramatic attempt on the part of the left to meet the challenge of the explosive mid-1960s period, however, came in movements which sought to look outwards rather than inwards and to give an encompassing meaning to the notion of community rather than one based upon individual or group identity. As a sense of crisis intensified, above all in the US but also in a wave of military coups in the Third World and the unravelling of Stalinism in Czechoslovakia and Gaullism in France, so the left looked to total explanations and solutions. A desire for 'sweeping summations' has been noted as a feature of the period and by the latter part of the decade, and especially around 1968, this reached a peak. It was as evident in the writings of newly discovered gurus like Marshall McLuhan and Buckminster Fuller as it was in the practice of artists like Stockhausen and Cage; politically it found its clearest expression in the revival of interest in the Marxism of Lukacs and the humanistic analysis of the French and British New Left (Appleyard, 1989: 203, 213). It represented an attempt to engage with the 'totality' of socio-political circumstances facing societies transformed by the long boom and apparently experiencing an equally comprehensive crisis, revolutionary in its ramifications and in the response it seemed to require.

'1968' was that response. It took place at a time when the 'organised' forces of the New Left, the SDS and the May Day Manifesto initiative in Britain, were entering a deep and terminal crisis (Young, 1977: 87, 160). Nevertheless, spontaneous organisation, as in France in May, seemed both adequate to the task and more in keeping with the spirit of events whose spread was as rapid as it was unpredictable. Moreover, the events seemed to reveal that fusion of culture and totality whose dimensions the New Left had sought to define. The spirit was captured in much of the art produced during the turmoil but we also possess, in the accounts of Tom Nairn and Henri Lefebvre, compelling witness to what was at stake. Thus Nairn noted the actuality of totality: '(1) ate capitalist society is infinitely more united than the conventional categories allow for, and this unity (because the system remains divisive at the same time) is itself an omnipresent contradiction', while Lefebvre identified the cultural dimensions of the crisis – 'a certain conception of learning ... a certain rationality ... is disinte-grating' – and saw as the solution 'self-management' not just of 'learning' but 'of the totality of social life' (Nairn, 1968: 162–3; Lefebvre, 1969: 140–1). Such eloquence testifies not only to the revolutionary spirit of the May 'events', but also suggests their character as an attempt to realise that fraternal embrace, egalitarian culture and libertarian democracy which was the historic significance of the sixties. That they failed will come as no sur-prise to those for whom goals of this magnitude are bound to seem as delu-sive as the forces seeking their realisation were nugatory. In turning in the final section of this chapter to the defeat of the left I want to suggest that the manner of the defeat is itself testimony to the enormity of the challenge posed by the movements of the long 1960s and that it is in defeat that we learn as much about the character of the period's aspirations as in success.

The defeat of the left, and with it the close of the sixties, seems so easily accounted for that it might be described, in a word that reverberated throughout the left in the 1970s, as 'over-determined'. Such an interpreta-tion runs the risk of failing to give adequate attention to left opportunities because of an only-too-easy temptation to accept right inevitabilities. To do so would be to ignore the very real sense of crisis which afflicted western political economies in the mid-1970s, one expression of which was the 'crisis of democracy' literature of the period (Crozier *et al.*, 1975). Because that crisis has now been resolved, for the moment at least, the left's insurgency at the time looks both implausible and insignificant. In seeking to document the left's failure it is necessary to avoid a narration which makes defeat appear pre-ordained. Only by giving back to the period a sense of the possible can we restore to the sixties and to the left a sense of their continuing significance.

By the late 1960s there was clear evidence that the energies of the decade were in danger of self-destructing. I have noted the crisis of the New Left organisations which, paradoxically, co-incided with the climax of mass mobilisation in 1968; equally, however, there was a sense of waning cultural confidence. The promise of an aesthetic modernism was called into question not simply from the right but also from the left, from Peter Fuller as well as John Betjeman. The urban environment, key to any modernist artistic and political project, was the focus. Already in the early sixties, in a text that can now been seen as a precursor of the post-modernist turn, Jane Jacobs had warned of the destructive effects of comprehensive urban planning; the fate of the high-rise blocks at Ronan Point, East London and Pruitt-Igoe, St Louis in 1968 and 1972 respectively, quickly becoming symbols for the failings of an overweening modernism. It was an unfair charge, for it conveniently ignored the political and economic constraints on both architect and planner, but it was one which stuck. Modernism had failed to connect with popular sensibilities: an international style attuned to national sensibility, of the sort proposed by the 'arch-modernist' Nikolaus Pevsner, was not achieved (Appleyard, 1989: 122–5; Curtis, 1996: 499).

A similar dissociation of the modern and the popular, the cosmopolitan and the local, afflicted Marxism. The political equivalent of the New Brutalism in architecture was the Althusserianism that swept the Anglo-American left in the 1970s. Not only did it marginalise what was now increasingly called the 'old' New Left – Thompson and Williams being rejected for their 'romantic populism' – but it also had adverse political consequences for the left as a whole. A key legacy of 1968 was, as we have seen, the discovery of new social identities which blossomed into the new social movements that came to dominate much left politics in the 1970s. This could be seen, at the very least, as a necessary development for the left, remedying its own exclusions – of blacks, women and gays – of the past century and reconnecting with the diverse concerns and romantic energies of the era of 1848. However, in its Althusserian inflection it countenanced, if it did not actively encourage, the fragmentation of the left and, as Jameson has noted, a 'semi-autonomous cultural politics'.

This development, understandable in so far as it reflected the surge of energies of movements engaged in what were increasingly perceived as struggles against millenial-long oppressions, took a heavy toll on the left's confidence. For not only did the 'centrifugal force of the critique of total-ity' lead it to 'self-destruct', in Jameson's words, but the avowed anti-humanism of Althusser and his epigones identified the left, fairly or not, with the anti-democratic, technocratic and inhuman features of moder-nity against which the New Left impulse had first emerged. With the counter-culture increasingly identifying such forms of 'modernity' with the Enlightenment the way was open for a veritable surge of post-modernist 'spirituality': Thompson's bitter polemic and Berger's embarrassed retrac-tions could not stem a tide which made Prince Charles the defender of the values of community and drove Peter Fuller in search of the 'lost illusions' of Nature and God (Jameson, 1984: 191–2; Thompson, 1978; Jencks, 1988; Dyer, 1986: 139).

This disarray among the left assumed epidemic proportions in the 1980s for by then the countervailing force of an insurgent working-class was in decline. For the early 1970s had seen a wave of labour militancy of a sort that many on the New Left had thought a thing of the past; a product of the crisis of the western political-economies which unfolded between 1968 and 1973, and perhaps of the student 'signal' of 1968, its political reper-cussions were felt in the crisis of governability in Britain and the United States – the miners' strikes and the Watergate crisis respectively – and throughout Western Europe in the form of Eurocommunist advance and the crisis of the dictatorships – Italy and Portugal being the key instances. A full narration of these events is beyond the scope of this essay but two fundamental political consequences may be noted. First, the development of the New Right. As a political formation its emergence may be dated from the election of Margaret Thatcher in May 1975, its American annun-ciation following with Ronald Reagan's unsuccessful campaign for the Republican Presidential nomination in 1976. Both were to achieve preemi-nence in the 1980s when their versions of free market liberalism, reinforced where necessary by reactionary moralism and aggressive militarism, estab-lished the supremacy of an Anglo-American version of capitalism whose global extension proved to be one of the most remarkable features of the latter part of the century. Second, and related to the emergence of the New Right, was the role of the 'old left' in the mid-1970s crisis. For if the New Right were the ultimate beneficiaries of the end of the post-war era it was the old left that oversaw its initial death-throes. It was Wilson and Carter who guided Britain and the US through the 'present danger', seeing off the challenge of those imperfect embodiments of New Left energies, Benn and

McGovern, while the course of the 'transition' crises in Europe were decisively influenced by left politicians – communist and socialist – in Italy, Spain and Portugal (Pimlott, 1993: 659–63; 1995: 243–4). While the old left claimed to be defining a new popular settlement, the outcome was not only a disabling of left organisations and energies but an opportunity for an emboldened New Right to seek an 'irreversible shift in the balance of wealth and power' to the possessing classes.

Writing five years after 1968, of a different but not unrelated conjuncture – 1945 – E.P. Thompson noted that the reforms of that year and those which followed 'if sustained and enlarged by an aggressive socialist strategy, might well have affected such a cancellation of the logic of capitalism that the system would have been brought to a point of crisis'. So far so familiar perhaps but then he added: 'a crisis not of despair and disintegration but a crisis in which the necessity for a peaceful revolutionary transition to an alternative socialist logic became daily more evident and more possible' (Thompson, 1978: 144). Was it not 'despair and disintegration' which set in from the mid-1970s and which has gathered apace for the socialist left thereafter? And was there not an absence of 'aggressive socialist strategy' which could have carried forward the energies of the sixties and at least have challenged if not cancelled the 'logic of capitalism'? Instead that logic has assumed new and perhaps unprecedented momentum in what is now called 'globalisation'. It represents a stark contrast to the ambitions of the sixties left for, as George Katsiaficas has put it, '(p)eriods of revolutionary crisis bear little resemblance to crises produced by economic breakdown' for while the latter have their roots in the irrational organization of the economy and the state ... general strikes and revolutions are essentially attempts to provide rational alternatives', so that while economic breakdown eventuates in a reassertion of the 'blind hand of change' resting solely 'on the internal development of the economy' revolutions seek a process by which Nature becomes History (Katsiaficas, 1987: 10, 96). Was it not just such a reconciliation of that which the New Right sought to sunder – the 'natural' and the 'cultural' – that was sought by the New Left in theory and by the sixties in practice in their quest for 'totality' and 'community' and are we not living with the consequences of their failure in a world from which the values of libertarian or participatory democracy, egalitarian cultural practice and, above all, fraternal social relations are absent? Let the last word – of modernist aspiration to set against post-modern dissolution – come from the founding statement of the American New Left which is even more relevant today than it was then: a 'new left must transform modern complexity into issues that can be understood and felt close-up by every human being. It must give form to … feelings of helplessness and indifference, so that people may see the political, social and economic sources of their private troubles and organize to change society' (Teodori, 1970: 172).

REFERENCES

Appleyard, B. (1989), *The Pleasures of Peace. Art and Imagination in Post-War Britain*, Faber & Faber.
Archer, R., Bubeck, D., Glock, H. *et al.* (eds) (1989), *Out of Apathy. Voices of the New Left Thirty Years On*, Verso.
Arnold, M. (1861), 'The Popular Education of France' in *Matthew Arnold: Selected Prose* (ed. P.J. Keating), Penguin, 1970.
Arnold, M. (1869), 'Culture and Anarchy' in *Matthew Arnold: Selected Prose* (ed. P.J. Keating), Penguin, 1970.
Barraclough, G. (1967), *An Introduction to Contemporary History*, Penguin.
Beer, S. (1982), *Britain Against Itself. The Political Contradictions of Collectivism*, W.W. Norton.
Berger, J. (1970), 'The Moment of Cubism' in *The Look of Things* (ed. N. Stangos), Penguin.
Berman, P. (1996), *A Tale of Two Utopias. The Political Journey of the Generation of 1968*, W.W. Norton.
Bertens, H. (1995), *The Idea of the Postmodern*, Routledge.
Blum J. Morton (1980), *The Progressive Presidents. Theodore Roosevelt, Woodrow Wilson, Franklin D. Roosevelt, Lyndon B. Johnson*, W.W. Norton.
Booker, C. (1970), *The Neophiliacs. A Study of the Revolution in English Life in the Fifties and Sixties*, Fontana.
Burner, D. (1996), *Making Peace with the 60s*, Princeton University Press.
Cronin, J.E. (1996), *The World the Cold War Made. Order, Chaos and The Return of History*, Routledge.
Crozier, M.J., Huntington, S.P. and Watanuki, J. (1975), *The Crisis of Democracy*, New York University Press.
Curtis, W.J.R. (1996), *Modern Architecture since 1900*, 3rd edn, Phaidon.
Drucker, P. (1959), *The Landmarks of Tomorrow*, William Heinemann.
Dyer, G. (1986), *Ways of Telling. The Work of John Berger*, Pluto Press.
Elton Lord (1931), *The Revolutionary Idea in France, 1789–1871*, Edward Arnold.
Fernbach, D. (1973), *Surveys from Exile, Political Writings*, vol. 2, Penguin.
Fuller, P. (1980), *Art and Psychoanalysis*, Writers and Readers Publishing Co-op.
Fuller, P. (1983), *Aesthetics after Modernism*, Writer and Readers Publishing Co-op.
Fuller, P. (1988), *Seeing through Berger*, Claridge Ltd.
Fuller, P. (1990), *Images of God. The Consolations of Lost Illusions*. Hogarth.
Hall, S. (1989), 'The First New Left: Life and Times' in *Out of Apathy. Voices of the New Left Thirty Years On* (ed. R. Archer), Verso.
Harris, J. (1984), *Private Lives, Public Spirit: Britain 1870–1914*, Penguin.

Hewison, R. (1981), *In Anger. Culture in the Cold War 1945–60*, Weidenfeld & Nicolson.

Hewison, R. (1986), *Too Much. Art and Society in the Sixties, 1960–75*, Methuen.

Hewison, R. (1997), *Culture and Consensus. English Art and Politics since 1940*, Methuen.

Hobsbawm, E.J. (1995), *Age of Extremes. The Short Twentieth Century 1914–1991*, Abacus.

Jameson, F. (1984), 'Periodizing the 60s' in *The 60s Without Apology* (ed. S. Sayres), University of Minnesota Press.

Jacobs, P. and Landau, S. (1967), *The New Radicals*, Penguin.

Jencks, C. (1988), *The Prince, the Architects and the New Wave Monarchy*, Academy Editions.

Katsiaficas, G. (1987), *The Imagination of the New Left: a Global Analysis of 1968*, South End Press.

Keating, P. (1970), edited and introduced, *Matthew Arnold: Selected Prose*, Penguin.

Konig, H. (1988), *1968. A Personal Report*, Unwin Hyman.

Kopkind, A. (1995), *The Thirty Years' War. Dispatches and Diversions of a Radical Journalist, 1965–1994*, Verso.

Lasch, C. (1974), *The World of Nations. Reflections on American History, Politics and Culture*, Vintage.

Lasch, C. (1985), *The Minimal Self. Psychic Survival in Troubled Times*, Pan.

Lefebvre, H. (1969), *The Explosion. Marxism and the French Upheaval*, Monthly Review Press.

Lichtheim, G. (1968), *The Origins of Socialism*, Weidenfeld & Nicolson.

Lukacs, J. (1990), *Confessions of an Original Sinner*, Ticknor & Fields.

Lukacs, J. (1993), *The End of the Twentieth Century and the End of the Modern Age*, Ticknor & Fields.

Marable, M. (1984), *Race, Reform and Rebellion: the Second Reconstruction in Black America*, Macmillan.

Marwick, A. (1982), *British Society since 1945*, Penguin.

Marx, K. (1973), '18th Brumaire of Louis Napoleon' in *Surveys from Exile, Political Writings*, vol. 2 (ed. D. Fernbach), Penguin.

Mills, C. Wright (1959), *The Power Elite*, Oxford University Press.

Mills, C. Wright (1970), *The Sociological Imagination*, Penguin.

Nairn, T. (1968), 'Why it Happened' in *The Beginning of the End. France, May 1968* (eds A. Quattrochi and T. Nairn), Panther Books.

Nuttall, J. (1970), *Bomb Culture*, Paladin.

Pimlott, B. (1993), *Harold Wilson*, Harper Collins.

Pimlott, B. (1995), *Frustrate their Knavish Tricks*, Harper Collins.

Pinkney, T. (1989), 'Introduction' in *The Politics of Modernism. Against the New Conformists*, Verso.

Quattrochi, A. and Nairn, T. *The Beginning of the End. France, May 1968*. Panther Books.

Roszak, T. (1988), *The Cult of Information. The Folklore of Computers and the True Art of Thinking*, Paladin.

Russell, J. (1969), 'Introduction' in *Pop Art Redefined* (eds J. Russell and S. Gablik), Thames & Hudson.

Sayres, S. (ed.) (1984), *The 60s Without Apology*, University of Minnesota Press.

Stangos, N. (1970), edited and introduced. *The Look of Things*, Penguin.

Teodori, M. (ed.) (1970), *The New Left: A Documentary History*, Jonathan Cape.

Thompson, E.P. (1978), *The Poverty of Theory and Other Essays*, Merlin.

Williams, R. (1974), *The English Novel. From Dickens to Lawrence*, Paladin.

Williams, R. (1989), *The Politics of Modernism. Against the New Conformists*, Verso.

Young, N. (1977), *An Infantile Disorder? The Crisis and Decline of the New Left.* Routledge & Kegan Paul.

2 Hey Jimmy! The Legacy of Gramsci in British Cultural Politics

Tom Steele

The legacy of Gramsci in the British New Left is both profound and puzzling. It's now almost 50 years since the first translations of Gramsci's work were made but still the 'war of position' and the 'organic intellectual' read as enigmatic metaphors rather than political realities. In the absence of a proletarian revolutionary party, or 'Modern Prince', which was central to Gramsci's project, the cultural struggle initiated by the New Left has only fitfully grounded itself in any social movements. Despite an impressive body of solid cultural analysis, the caricature of academic cultural studies as looping psychotically between mandarin theoretical discourses and an uncritical populism, is not without some truth. Such a grounding in political economy and social movements, which was the aim of the old New Left, has yet to be made. The moment may have passed. Class as an organising myth of solidarity has given way before the claims of gender, ethnicity, sexuality, disability and a variety of issue-based politics, much of which, it has to be said, have been made visible by the new forms of cultural analysis. Academic cultural studies, indeed, ushered in the politics of New Times in which post-Marxists so successfully deconstructed their own foundations, that they left themselves without party or central direction. Failing to materialise, the 'rainbow coalition' faded into the dull blur of New Labour. But, not to be too gloomy, there are what Raymond Williams called 'resources of hope' here. The desubordination of women has profoundly affected everyday life in the post-1960s decades through making the politics of the personal central to 'family' life and increasingly unavoidable at the workplace. Older forms of industrial struggle, as the 1984–85 Miners' Strike graphically displayed, were transformed into struggles for lives and communities by the critical engagement of women – culture as a form of life. What the new politics have also shown moreover is the importance of place and locality rather than the abstractions of state and nation. Beginning with demands for quality of life, cultural struggle is centrally about here and now.

'Hey, Jimmy! Huv ye nae heer't o' Gramsky?' In February and March, 1968, the *Scotsman* published an angry correspondence between two old comrades which announced a new star in the night sky of the British Left. The Scottish poet, Hugh MacDiarmid, responding to a reference his friend, Hamish Henderson, had made to his brief flirtation with fascism in the 1920s, wrote that it was amusing that Henderson should have used 'the great name of Gramsci' to confute him. Henderson's rebuke was that if MacDiarmid had a wanted a true political hero why, instead of Il Duce, did he not contemplate the career of Antonio Gramsci. MacDiarmid replied that of course he already knew about Gramsci, who 'dealt primarily with the 'superstructure' – the whole complex of political, social and cultural institutions and ideals – rather than its 'economic foundations' (quoted in Henderson, 1997: 167). MacDiarmid was remarkably familiar with Gramsci's ideas:

> Gramsci believed that 'cultural' problems were especially important in periods following revolutionary activity, as in Europe after 1815 and again after 1921. At such times, he said, there are not pitched battles between classes: the class struggle becomes a 'war of position' and the 'cultural front' the principal area of conflict. But a 'cultural' battle was not easy: Marxism had retained too many elements of materialism, determinism and economism.' (Henderson, 1997: 168)

He then quoted a rather puzzling paragraph about something called 'the philosophy of praxis' and revealed just how it was that he knew so much about a long-dead Italian communist of whom few, outside of the minuscule British New Left, had heard:

> The quotation is from Gramsci's *Quaderni del Carcere* – as perhaps Mr Henderson knows, since he told me about twenty years ago that he had been entrusted with the translation of Gramsci's works into English – a project of which, so far as Mr Henderson is concerned, nothing quite characteristically has been heard since. (Henderson, 1997: 168)

Twenty years! And thirty years since 1968. Yet looking back, without 'Gramsci' the shape of the British New Left would have been almost unimaginable. He was placed in the vanguard of what was to become a significant stream of European Marxist intellectual influences, invoked by the New Left to restore the intellectual deficit at the heart of British culture, the famous 'absent centre' described by Anderson in 1967, and to repair the theoretical defects of Marxism itself (Anderson, 1991).

In the 'New Left' an entirely new politics had been conjured up to deal with, by the end of the 1960s, an increasingly prosperous and markedly unrevolutionary British working class, easing comfortably into the post-war welfare state; a Communist Party in terminal decline from its war-time high water mark of 60 000 members; a Labour Left abruptly disaffected from Harold Wilson's 1966 government and, stemming from the expansion of the Robbins Report, a rebellious libertarian student population.

But, despite MacDiarmid, it was in large part Henderson's proselytising that brought Gramsci to the attention of the notoriously insular British Left. During the latter part of World War Two he had served in Italy with the partisans and, on his return to Britain, his friend Amleto Micozzi sent him the volumes of Gramsci's writings as they appeared in Italian, which included the 'Letters from Prison' in 1947, 'Historical Materialism and the Philosophy of Benedetto Croce' in 1948 and 'Notes on Machiavelli, Politics and the Modern State' in 1949. Henderson 'began the translation of them straightaway, as a labour of love, and without (at first) a thought of a publisher' (Henderson, 1997: 168). No publisher was immediately forthcoming. The newly founded Instituto Gramsci had also approved Louis Marks to make a translation of selections from the prison notebooks and he discussed the problems of translation with Henderson. Lawrence and Wishart eventually published them as *The Modern Prince* in 1957, effectively the first text of Gramsci's in English to get a thorough airing. Extensive extracts from Henderson's translations were however published in 1959 in successive numbers (9 and 10) of the *New Reasoner* which Edward Thompson and John Saville were then publishing from Yorkshire.

THE OLD NEW LEFT AND SOCIALIST HUMANISM

Thompson and Saville had begun the *New Reasoner* as a critical organ within the Communist Party but after Khrushchev's public exposure of Stalin's crimes and the suppression of the Hungarian uprising in 1956, they left the party. Tentatively, they made contact with the group of former Oxford University students, which included Stuart Hall and Raphael Samuel, who ran the *Universities and Left Review* (Dworkin, 1997: 66). The resulting collaboration produced *New Left Review* which became the primary intellectual organ of the emergent British New Left. The *New Reasoner* was explicitly a journal of 'Socialist Humanism', the guiding rationale of which was a trenchant critique of the Stalinised economistic marxism which characterised the ideology of the Communist Party of Great Britain (CPGB). In effect it opened the cultural front within British Marxism itself. While the issue of culture had never been entirely absent from the CPGB, until the end of the war it had been more or less marginalised to the party's intellectual groupings. Although intellectuals and writers were encouraged to form sections for literature, writing, history and so on, they were not expected to engage with the political decisions taken by the party's central committee.

One of the British Communist Party's more congenial aspects for intellectuals had been precisely its cultural activity (Croft, 1995). The party was indeed a source of patronage and education for young writers during the 1930s, for whom it could offer publication in literary journals and introduction to left publishing houses like Lawrence and Wishart. At the same time its most energetic historians' group, under Dona Torr and Christopher Hill, was attempting to reconstitute a British social history along marxist lines and based on popular sources (here it paralleled the more social democratic social history of R.H. Tawney, G.D.H. Cole and others whose centre was in adult education) (Steele, 1997). It also enabled a cosmopolitan atmosphere into which other European refugees from Nazism could discuss non-Soviet European Marxism, like that of the Lukács group, so long as they were discreet about it. The party acted both as a club and mentor group. Dissident intellectuals and writers were attracted to it in part because it provided alternative arenas for serious cultural debate to those commanded by Bloomsbury and the aesthetic elite but also offered a partisanship with working people. Although, between the World Wars, the party adopted a relatively laissez-faire approach to its cultural groups and allowed them considerable rein, later disputes between the groups and the party leadership grew bitter. With the onset of the Cold War, in 1947, however, the leadership began to realise the growing political significance of culture and established a National Cultural Committee, under the chairmanship of Emile Burns, to 'co-ordinate' the work of the ten specialist cultural groups, including the Writers' Group. The Cold War in Britain was, inevitably, given the overdetermined influence of 'English' writers in the national culture, shaping up on the literary high ground – as exemplified by Crossman's *The God that Failed* – and the party's view increasingly was that culture was too important to be left to intellectuals (Croft, 1995).

As orthodox Marxist models of economic determinism came increasingly under attack from defenders of the 'open society', the party had become more sensitised to the power of ideologies and representations in forming class consciousness. Moreover, inspired by the Chinese Revolution in 1948 and the importance given to the cultural struggle in the writings of Mao Tse Tung, the Twenty-Second Party Congress called for a cultural front alongside the political struggle. 'The British Road to Socialism', the party's new political programme, which stressed the independent national dimension, had to be supported by some more developed understanding of what Britishness, or Englishness, actually was. Under the auspices of *Arena*, the most important of the party's cultural journals, a seminal series of conferences on aspects of culture were held, to which many of the party's intellectuals contributed, including the young Edward Thompson.

These conferences were important for mapping the ground on which the cultural struggle should be fought. In tune with growing anti-colonial movements, they attempted to construct an alternative sense of national identity to that associated with imperialism and oppression, which revalued the radical tradition of Paine, Cobbett and Morris. It was clear that, in these conferences, the idea of a militant 'class' culture was strategically giving ground to that of a national 'common' culture. George Thomson, the classicist and one of the party's most respected intellectuals, argued that it was wrong to think of 'culture' as class-bound only since, in Britain, so-called bourgeois culture was also the heritage of socialism. Tommy Jackson, the proletarian philosopher, argued that it was even a revolutionary culture and English literary realism, as Gorky had said, was 'pioneering' in its ability to lay bare the injustices suffered by working people. However, at this stage, George Thomson's ambitions for the cultural struggle were relatively limited. He wanted the party to encourage 'worker-writers', so that writing was seen not simply as a class-bound activity. He encouraged intellectuals not only to unite with the workers but be tempered by them and he also wanted intellectuals to interpret the British cultural heritage in the light of Marxism–Leninism.

But, by quoting from the heretical communist literary critic of the 1930s, Christopher Caudwell, that the struggle should 'drag the past into the present and force the realisation of the future', Thomson seriously offended the party leadership. They, in turn, drummed up a fierce debate in the pages of the party's journal *The Modern Quarterly* during 1950–51, intended to bring dissident party intellectuals into line. This had the opposite effect on Edward Thompson who was inspired into re-thinking the role played by culture in the class struggle. He was completely persuaded by Caudwell's refusal of the reduction of consciousness to passive reflection and mechanical materialism and of the galvanic power of poetry (Thompson, 1977). This broke with the conventional Marxist base and superstructure analogy and allowed a much more flexible interpretation of cultural determinants to be developed.

In his own contribution to the *Arena* conference on 'The American Threat to British Culture', Edward Thompson made perhaps his first major intervention into the party's cultural debate with a talk called 'William Morris and the Moral Issues of Today'. Here, he argued that party could not wait until a new kind of 'socialist man' appeared after the revolution: 'We must change people now, for that is the essence of all our cultural work' (Thompson, 1951). Morris's 'moral realism' was clearly in his sights at this time and the significance of the talk is that he interpreted the political project of the party as in major part to be achieved through educational and cultural objectives. Thompson's work as a university staff tutor in adult education at the University of Leeds, in the West Riding of Yorkshire from 1948 to 1965, gave him a base for putting this policy into practice. Here he produced two seminal works which were to create new mental maps for the emergent new left, *William Morris. From Romantic to Revolutionary* in 1955 and *The Making of the English Working Class* in 1963 (this last was to attract a truly popular readership only when it was published by Pelican in 1968).

While the CPGB's strategy was to reconstruct a radical vision of Britain primarily through new historical narratives, Thompson had long known that orthodox marxist economism had little to offer. Thus *The Making* pursued the Caudwell heresy in implying a relative autonomy of the cultural sphere. The working class was not just passively shaped by economic forces, it shaped itself. In Thompson's account, it moved, through its own agency, from being a class in itself, in the Hegelian sense, to being a class for itself. 'William Morris' became a key sign, which signalled the power of culture to inspire both anti-stalinist and anti-capitalist energies in the political struggle, through what Thompson called 'moral realism' and 'socialist humanism'.

Thus in part the New Left began to emerge in Britain through the invocation of significant writers on culture and centred in the practice of education, particularly adult education. The seminal texts such as *The Making of the English Working Class*, Richard Hoggart's *The Uses of Literacy*, Raymond Williams's *Culture and Society* and *The Long Revolution*, were all written during the ten to fifteen years that their authors worked in university adult education. It is important to emphasise that these works were not isolated events but were nested in a widespread culture of experiment in adult education which had begun with the debates over arts and literature teaching in the mid- to late-1930s (Steele, 1997). In one of his last essays Raymond Williams noted:

> when I moved into internal university teaching, when at about the same time Richard Hoggart did the same, we started teaching in ways that had been absolutely familiar in Extra Mural and WEA classes, relating history to art and literature, including contemporary culture, and suddenly so strange was this to the Universities they said 'My God, here is a new

subject called Cultural Studies'. But we are beginning I am afraid, to see encyclopaedia articles dating the birth of Cultural Studies from this or that book in the late 'fifties. Don't believe a word of it. That shift of perspective about the teaching of arts and literature and their relation to history and to contemporary society began in Adult Education, it didn't happen anywhere else. (Williams, 1989: 162)

Williams believed that the basis for a New Left politics was the constituency of working-class and lower middle-class students who came to adult education classes and he envisaged a new culturally based left politics. Williams's own short-lived journal, *Politics and Letters*, and a companion volume called the *Critic*, were attempts to engage in that arena which Williams increasingly saw as the 'decisive' world for his political work: 'Virtually every WEA tutor was a Socialist of one colour or another. We were all doing adult education ourselves. So we saw the journals as linked to this very hopeful formation with a national network of connection to the working-class movement. If there was a group to which *Politics and Letters* referred, it was the adult education tutors and their students.' (Williams, 1979: 69) Although he was familiar with members of the Communist Party's Historians Group, especially Eric Hobsbawm, Williams had only briefly been a member before the war and was never a committed Marxist. Indeed, precisely to displace Marxism (to use Stuart Hall's term derived from Gramsci) from the centre of his intellectual work, he had all but constructed his own radical tradition in the Tawney mode, which he called the 'Romantic critique of capitalism', which was the burden of his epochal book *Culture and Society*. Paradoxically, Williams almost certainly gained his understanding of the significance of this kind of cultural political work, not from any left theorist but from F.R. Leavis and from T.S. Eliot's recently published *Notes Towards a Definition of Culture*, which he rather admired. For him, Eliot was a conservative for whom radicals should be grateful. (But, in an interesting intellectual loop, Eliot in his turn was indebted to the work of Karl Mannheim, with whom he had regularly come into contact in Oxford Christian Socialist networks.)

While the contemporary significance of William Morris and the adult education constituency had been where Williams and Thompson and the old New Left met, it was of no interest to the young turks who, in the early 1960s, ousted the founders of *New Left Review* from the editorial board, and this signified a conceptual break in the notion of the cultural struggle. The project for this new New Left then became less one of 'nostalgically' rehistoricising Britain, national identity or a new Englishness, than of

'Europeanising' the Left and constructing marxist intellectual cadres. Perry Anderson and his colleagues on NLR were convinced that the intellectual hardware for conducting the cultural struggle could not be resurrected from domestic sources. They embarked on an ambitious programme of translating European marxist, revisionist and post-marxist theorists, while simultaneously dumping the non-theoretical and popular cultural issues of the journal into the out-tray. Of Anderson, Thompson wrote: 'we found we had appointed a veritable Dr. Beeching of the socialist intelligentsia.... Old Left steam engines were swept off the tracks: way side halts ("Commitment", "What Next for C.N.D.?", "Women in Love") were boarded up; and the lines were electrified for the speedy traffic from the marxistentialist Left bank.... Finding ourselves redundant we submitted to dissolution' (Thompson, 1978: 35).

As we have seen, Thompson had already published some of the first translations of Gramsci by Henderson in the *New Reasoner*. But there were other important European precursors. As immigrants to Britain in the 1930s, Jewish intellectuals on the run from nazi persecution had by the mid-1950s, by and large, secured for themselves academic appointments and were publishing significant 'cultural' sociology in English: for example, Karl Polanyi's *The Great Transformation*, Karl Mannheim's *Ideology and Utopia* and Arnold Hauser's *Social History of Art*. Although Norbert Elias's *Involvement and Detachment* was published in 1956, most of his work had to wait until the last twenty years to be read in English despite his position in an English university (Kilminster, 1993). Adolf Löwy was another refugee from the 'other' Frankfurt to gain intellectual influence in Britain (Pels, 1993).

However, what characterised this group of European intellectual was their indebtedness to German philosophical idealism, the Hegelian–Marxist dialectic and Weberian sociology. This group prepared the way for the reception of George Lukács, translated and published during the 1960s by the Merlin Press, one base of the old New Left (see also Watnick, 1962). While many years earlier in the Budapest *Sonntagkreis* his *History and Class Consciousness* had stimulated Mannheim's engagement with the sociology of consciousness, it now resonated strongly with Thompson's re-examination of working-class consciousness. Goode remarks that the translation of Lukács's work was an important precursor for the reading of Thompson's and that 'Thompson's concept of consciousness as historical agent teaches us more about the actual behaviour of literary texts in history than most of the analyses of the behaviour of signifiers' (Goode, 1990: 190).

While the younger New Left took a considered interest in this strand of Euro-marxism, it became fascinated by the more radical Frankfurt School of Benjamin, Horkheimer and Adorno. Many in the student movement took up Herbert Marcuse with relish because they read his dialectics of liberation as implying that students now replaced the working class as the agents of revolution and 'Students of the World Ignite!' became the slogan which sparked off campus occupations across Britain. But its main preoccupation was with what Thompson called the 'marxistentialist Left Bank', ie Parisian theory. Initially this centred on Sartre's later work, particularly *The Problem of Method*, which was sharply critical of Lukács, and the *Temps Modernes* writers such as André Gorz. But, in his turn, Sartre was critiqued and translations of Louis Althusser and Jacques Lacan followed, along with a turn towards structuralist and linguistic methods. Although Deleuze had announced in *Nietzsche et la philosophie* (1962) that the labour of the dialectic must be replaced by the play of difference, the widespread English dissemination of French deconstructionist and post-structuralist writers did not take off until more than a decade later – and then on the rebound from the United States.

FROM LEAVIS TO GRAMSCI: THE BIRMINGHAM CENTRE FOR CONTEMPORARY CULTURAL STUDIES

Without doubt, however, the seminal institutional innovation in the project of advancing the cultural struggle was the foundation by Richard Hoggart in the mid-1960s of the Centre for Contemporary Cultural Studies at the University of Birmingham. A shoestring post-graduate set-up, castigated by some of his elitist colleagues as 'Hoggart's line in cheap hats', the Birmingham Centre produced some of the most acute cultural criticism and analysis of popular culture yet to appear in Britain. Significantly, the centre grew from Hoggart's less politicised pre-occupation with working-class and popular culture, much of it based on reflecting on his own background in, and emigration from, the urban working class. It was determined much more by Hoggart's engagement with literary criticism, particularly Leavisite methods, a reading of Orwell's radical journalism, and marked by an explicit hostility to Marxism, which he regarded as methodologically too crude to deal with cultural questions. Ironically, Hoggart did not see this work as political but, if anything, anthropological, or an extension of literary critical methods into an analysis of popular culture already begun by Orwell. He was sceptical of socialist utopian claims and unhappy with Williams's term 'common culture' (Corner, 1991). He put this down to the difference in their understanding of the value of their class background despite the apparent identity of being 'working-class'. In a conversation with Williams, Hoggart confessed,

> I felt from your book [*Culture and Society*] that you were surer, sooner than I was, of your relationship to your working-class background. With me, I remember, it was a long and troublesome effort. It was difficult to escape a kind of patronage, even when one felt one was understanding the virtues of the working-class life one had been brought up in – one seemed to be insisting one these strengths in spite of all sorts of doubts in one's attitudes, (Hoggart and Williams, 1960: 26).

However, he recruited Stuart Hall from *New Left Review* to increase the sociological edge of the new centre. Hall may have been glad to escape the feuding on the journal's editorial board but clearly had a different agenda from that of Hoggart and, although he followed the emphasis Hoggart placed on working-class culture as resistance, he gradually dislocated it from Hoggart's vision. What Hall did was to bring a sociological perspective and a personal determination to explore non-Soviet and revisionist marxist theory for ways round the utterly disabling base-and-superstructure metaphor.

His rediscovery of Gramsci in the early 1970s, even more than Althusser – 'this profound misreading, this superstructuralist mistranslation, of classical marxism' (Hall, 1996: 266) – was a breakthrough. Gramsci, he said, radically displaced some of the inheritances of marxism in cultural studies; his work was a necessary detour around the blockages to a marxist study of culture. From Gramsci cultural studies in the British context learned 'immense amounts about the study of culture itself, about the discipline of the conjunctural, about the importance of historical specificity, about the enormously productive metaphor of hegemony, about the way in which one can think questions of class relations only by using the displaced notion of ensemble and blocs' (Hall, 1996: 267). So more than two decades after Hamish Henderson's initial attempts to translate and publish Gramsci in Britain, he finally arrived.

Hall's project at the Birmingham Centre fitted somewhere between the Thomson/Williams 'long revolution' of an educated democracy with a socialist consciousness and the Anderson/*New Left Review* attempt to create an elite of marxist theoreticians who could act as the storm troopers of the cultural struggle in the long march through the institutions. Hall was struck in particular by Gramsci's conception of the 'organic intellectual'. Even though they were not sure what it would mean, 'there is no doubt in my mind that we were trying to find an institutional practice in cultural studies that might produce an organic intellectual' (Hall, 1996: 267).

For him, the crucial aspect of this kind of intellectual was her or his align-ment with an emerging historical movement. But where was it to be found? After over a century, the 'working class' or 'labour' movement was hardly emergent any longer and seemed to have fossilised into a set of bureau-cratic institutions concerned with what Gramsci would have called defen-sive economico-corporate positions, whereas what the Centre was looking for were the building blocks of Gramsci's ethico-political.

Despite the absence of an obvious social movement with which he or she should be aligned, the organic intellectual must work on two fronts simultaneously. It was essential both to be at the forefront of intellectual theoretical work and to engage in educational work. The organic intellec-tual had the responsibility of transmitting those leading ideas to those who did not belong to the professional class of intellectuals. Without those fronts operating at the same time, Hall argued, the project of cultural stud-ies was fatally flawed, because you might get enormous advances on the theoretical front without any engagement at the level of the political pro-ject. Hall confessed that the intellectuals of the Centre never connected with 'that rising historic movement' and had to content themselves with operating with it as a metaphor and 'as if'.

For Hall, the second major irruption into the cultural struggle and cul-tural studies was the women's movement and feminism. But was this not precisely the connection between the organic intellectuals (of feminism) and the rising historic movement (of women), Hall was seeking? The his-tory of women's studies in Britain demonstrates great debts to the educa-tional activity of women in self-help groups and in adult education where the connections between theoretical understanding and political practice could at times be close and effective (Rowbotham, 1989: xiv). The boys' club of the New Left suddenly came under sustained assault and 'a thief in the night, it (feminism) broke in; interrupted, made an unseemly noise, seized the time, crapped on the table of cultural studies' (Hall, 1996: 269). Hall had no doubts about the impact of this turn: it demanded the politics of the personal; expanded the notion of power to the non-public sphere; centred gender and sexuality alongside, or instead of, class; opened up the question of the subject and the subjective; and reopened the closed frontier between social theory and psychoanalysis. Thus while Gramsci had effec-tively displaced orthodox marxism from cultural analysis, feminism all but dispensed with conventional constructions of class, power and the subject. Cultural politics therefore took a quantum leap from the modest proposals of the CPGB of the early 1950s to reinvent a national identity and the old New Left of the late 1950s to recreate a common culture. Hall's third irruption, that of ethnicity and race, effectively opened the cultural struggle on the front previously occupied largely by the right. Here too theory could connect swiftly with a social movement and organic intellectuals might find themselves with a political function beyond the academy. Significantly, the initial energy for both feminists and black consciousness came from the United States, where both the women's and black movements were more angry and more assertive than in Britain and Europe. Yet the ultimate connection between theoretical work and social movements seem not to have happened in the way that Hall wanted. Why not? Hall implies that the crucial tension between textual or theoretical practices and social affiliations was either broken or never fully established. Despite the dazzling theoretical contributions made by cultural studies, no corresponding advance was made in cultural politics. In America cultural studies appears to have broken completely free from social movements and become both fully institutionalised and isolated within the academy. In Britain the tension still exists but the moment of profound danger which for Hall is represented by institutionalisation has been recognised by those, like Angie McRobbie, who have striven to become 'organic intellectuals', as a crisis in cultural studies (McRobbie, 1991). McGuigan insists that cultural studies has lost touch with political economy (McGuigan, 1992) and has instead tended to bifurcate between, at one extreme, a celebratory populism in which anything goes, so long as it comes from the people and, at the other, mandarin (or should we say Martian) theoretical discourses which make no concessions to the intelligent layperson.

Recognising this, Hall makes the point that, although they might abut and even overlap at times, academic work is not the same as intellectual work. The movement for cultural politics has not achieved an 'organic intellectual political work' 'which does not try to inscribe itself in the overarching meta-narrative of achieved knowledges, within the institutions' (Hall, 1996: 274–5) – and language like that perhaps explains why. In other words, in Gramsci's terms, the new knowledge has not translated itself into the new common sense, but has been content to remain trapped in the political economy of academic institutions. Whole careers have been made from it.

How much is Hall's pessimism conditioned, despite his best intentions, by a metropolitan outlook? Do the marginal spaces hold out any hope? Hall's colleague at the Open University, Angus Calder, has argued consistently that Scottish cultural politics and intellectual work cannot simply be incorporated into the English hegemony and has subtly resisted the more arcane elements of current cultural theory. Calder annoyed many of his colleagues in the early 1980s by suggesting that many of the new Emperors of Theory were not in fact wearing any clothes and that the debate over popular culture in English left-wing circles represented 'a compound of displacements' (Calder, 1994: 238). In the first place many of the translations from French cultural theory simply failed to resonate in English and carried little specific purchase. Secondly, the very heavy theoretical superstructures which were deployed to deal with elements of popular culture such as James Bond films or Coronation Street were frequently comic. Perhaps the worst indictment Calder makes, however, was the displacement by many academics of genuine political practice by theoretical argument. Some colleagues managed to convince themselves and their students that doing cultural theory was, somehow, politics. On the whole, Calder argues, precisely because of Scotland's marginality, even provinciality, the discussion of fashionable French thinkers has been severely limited.

In England, certainly, the dislocation during the last two decades, between academics and social movements, has been such that Raymond Williams could argue that the project of cultural studies no longer recognised the social formation to which it belonged (Williams, 1989). Despite the undoubted fecundity of contemporary Cultural Studies, what began in the late 1950s as a movement for a new left politics and a popular democratic education, threatens to become, in the 1990s, deeply pessimistic of rational political intervention, obsessed with style and frankly conservative in its aspirations. Fewer practitioners engage with social movements or even accept their existence, even to what might have been the hope of the new politics, the women's and ecological movements. Instead, as Rowbotham notes, 'The women's studies courses which emerged out of argument and struggle have now begun to grow into a little knowledge industry of their own' (Rowbotham, 1989: xiv).

The role of public intellectuals has of course changed significantly. While Debray noted the rise of the intellectual as smooth television commentator, Bauman has argued the drift from the nineteenth century of the intellectual as legislator to that of interpreter. Intellectuals in effect have been mostly reduced to the role of supervisory academics overseeing a multiplying plethora of paper qualifications within a system whose drastically declining unit of resource threatens to deprive them of even the most cursory contact with their students, let alone a wider public. The decline in academics' pay relative to other professional groups graphically states their fall in status and the new vocationalism of qualifications recognises the deep suspicion of liberal and humanistic learning in governing circles.

WORK, PLACE, PEOPLE AND PLAY

In 1996 I moved from Leeds '24-hour City' to Glasgow 'City of Culture'. While Leeds seemed to be taking off culturally, Glasgow already seemed to be in decline. 1997 saw the last Mayfest, Scottish Opera losing its orchestra, museums shut one day weekly and widespread accusations of city corruption. Leeds on the contrary, under its squeaky clean New Labour administration, now has Opera North, a vibrant West Yorkshire Playhouse under Jude Kelly, the Henry Moore Sculpture Centre, several excellent dance companies, a great club scene, street cafés and a postmodern lighting scheme in the shopping centre. I used to think that the strength of Leeds's cultural scene was really its underground as in the avant-garde Nietzschean group the Leeds Arts Club and subsequent societies (Steele, 1990), the punk and Gothic art house bands of the 1970s and 1980s and alternative presses. With the greater visibility of official culture this may have changed but clearly many more people can simply enjoy living in the city than ever before.

Even in decline, however, Glasgow is much richer culturally. It's not just the six theatres offering a brilliant range of productions, Scottish Opera, the Scottish National Symphony Orchestra, avant-garde chamber music at the Royal Scottish Academy of Music and Drama (RSAMD), the Glasgow Film Theatre, the Celtic Connections Festival, the wealth of art galleries and museums including the Burrell Collection, Mackintosh's School of Art, the People's Palace, etc., etc. though they mark an institutional valuation of culture few other cities of comparable size could match. But there is something about the life of the town itself in its multitude of clubs, bars and cafés where talk and music are endless. Even contemporary bands sing songs about Glasgow in a way that rarely happens elsewhere and there seems to be a powerful commitment in the vibrant musical and literary scene of musicians, writers and singers to the place itself. Yes, this is provinciality, but it is an extraordinarily productive and resonant provinciality which makes metropolitan culture seem limp and regressive. It respects Patrick Geddes's mantra: 'Work, Place, People' to which Pat Kane, the cultural commentator, might add 'Play'.

I don't know whether this is to do with a resurgent Scottish nationalism and an instinctive anti-metropolitanism or a shrewd political intervention by a now discredited city boss, but it is surely the product of a still-serious attitude towards learning and living, intense enjoyment of a sense of place, and feel for social justice and historic struggle, which is a form of cultural politics. All this is powerful and persuasive and produces a fine quality of life for all those with disposable income. However, as in Leeds, the inhabitants of the windswept 1960s council estates and unfashionable tenements get little value from it. Cultural politics has left them without a politics. Calder notes that a Glasgow colleague found the pronunciation of 'hegemony' that came easiest off the tongue was 'Hey Jimmy!' – and Gramsci, of course, had to be Gramsky.

The cultural turn in politics has been vital and has produced incisive critiques of the dominant culture (its own invention) which left an older Marxism and socialism tongue-tied. So successfully has it opposed the base and superstructure metaphor, however, that it has all but disconnected from political economy and loosed culture theory into the stratosphere. Abandoned by New Labour and the culture of labour all but destroyed, the inhabitants of the estates and the tenements have discovered other diversions, which have required them to be heavily policed (see 'Trainspotting' and the TV drama series 'Jo Jo'). Intellectuals and cultural theorists will be positioned once more in the nineteenth-century role of colonial missionary and explorer in order to gain the consent of the oppressed to new forms of governance. Alternatively, they could begin to build a new educational movement and offer their collective services, free, to whatever groups are seeking humane, democratic and socialist solutions for their situations. Fifty years of 'Gramsky' has to have its uses.

REFERENCES

Anderson, P. (1966), 'Socialism and Pseudo Empiricism', *New Left Review*, 35, pp. 2–42.

Anderson, P. (1991), 'Components of the National Culture', *English Questions*, Verso.

Calder, A. (1994), *Revolving Culture, Notes from the Scottish Republic*, I.B. Tauris.

Corner, J. (1991), 'Studying culture: reflections and assessments. An interview with Richard Hoggart', *Media Culture and Society*, Vol. 13, 1991, pp. 137–51.

Croft, A. (1995), 'Authors Take Sides: Writers in the Communist Party, 1920–1956' in *Opening the Books: New Perspectives in the History of British Communism*, Kevin Morgan, Nina Fishman, Geoff Andrews (eds), Pluto Press.

Dworkin, D. (1997), *Cultural Marxism in Postwar Britain*, Duke University Press.

Eliot, T.S. (1948), *Notes Towards a Definition of Culture*, Faberand Faber.

Goode, J. (1990), 'Thompson and the Significance of Literature', Harvey J. Kaye and Keith McClelland (eds), *E.P. Thompson, Critical Perspectives*, Polity Press, pp. 183–203, p. 190.

Gramsci, A. (1971), *Prison Notebooks* (eds) Q. Hoare and G. Nowell Smith, Lawrence and Wishart.

Hall, S. (1996), 'Cultural Studies and its Theoretical legacies' in (eds) David Morley, Kuan-Hsing Chen and Stuart Hall *Critical Dialogues in Cultural Studies*, Routledge.

Hall, S. (1990), 'The Emergence of Cultural Studies and the Crisis of the Humanities, October, 53, 1990, pp. 11–23.

Henderson, H. (1997), *The Armstrong Nose, Selected Letters of Hamish Henderson* (ed.) Alec Finlay, Polygon Press.

Hoggart, R. (1957), *The Uses of Literacy*, Pelican.

Hoggart, R. and Williams, R. (1960), 'Working-Class Attitudes', *New Left Review*, No. 1, Jan/Feb 1960, pp. 26–30.

Kaye, H.J. and McClelland, K. (1990), (eds), *E.P. Thompson, Critical Perspectives*, Polity Press.

Kenny, M. (1995), *The First New Left British Intellectuals After Stalin*, Lawrence and Wishart.

Kilminster, R. (1993), 'Norbert Elias and Karl Mannheim; Closeness and Distance, *Theory, Culture and Society* Vol. 10, No. 3, August 1993, pp. 81–114.

McGuigan, J. (1992), *Cultural Populism*, Routledge.

McRobbie, A. (1991), 'New Times in Cultural Studies', *New Formations*, 13, Spring.

Pels, D. (1993), 'Missionary Sociology between Left and Right: A Critical Introduction to Mannheim', *Theory, Culture and Society*, Vol. 10, No. 3, August 1993, pp. 45–68.

Rée, J. (1984), *Proletarian Philosophers*, Clarendon Press.

Rowbotham, S. (1989), *The Past is Before Us, Feminism in Action since the 1960s*, Penguin.

Steele, T. (1990), *Alfred Orage and the Leeds Arts Club, 1893–1923*, Scolar Press.

Steele, T. (1997), *The Emergence of Cultural Studies 1945–65: Adult Education, Cultural Politics and the English Question*, Lawrence and Wishart.

Swindells, J. and Jardine, L. (1990), *What's Left, Women in Culture and the Labour Movement*, Routledge.

Thompson, E.P. (1951), 'William Morris and the Moral Issues Today' in *The American Threat to British Culture*, Arena Publications, pp. 25–30, p. 30.

Thomson, E.P. (1955), *Romantic to Revolutionary*, Lawrence and Wishart.

Thompson, E.P. (1968), *The Making of the English Working Class*, Pelican.

Thompson, E.P. (1977), 'Caudwell' in Socialist Register 1977, J. Saville and R. Miliband (eds), Merlin Press, pp. 228–76, p. 244.

Thompson, E.P. (1978), 'The Peculiarities of the English' in *The Poverty of Theory and Other Essays*, Merlin Press, p. 35.

Watnick, M. (1962), 'Relativism and Class Consciousness: Georg Lukács' in Leopold Labedz (ed.), *Revisionism Essays on the History of Marxist Ideas*, pp. 142–65.

Williams, R. (1958), *Culture and Society 1780–1950*, Penguin.

Williams, R. (1961), *The Long Revolution*, Pelican.

Williams, R. (1979), *Politics and Letters*, Verso.

Williams, R. (1989), 'The Future of Cultural Studies', in *The Politics of Modernism*, Verso.

3 Stars and Moons: Desire and the Limits of Marketisation

Wendy Wheeler

KISSING THE WORLD BETTER

Sometime in the 1960s, my mother – advocate of the unlikely mix of Freudianism and astrology which produced the intense sixties interest in the work of Carl Jung – took me, excitedly (because here was evidence of a new, popular and marketable, interest in the esoteric ideas which she considered important), to a new bookshop in Camden Town. This bookshop – Compendium – sold and thus released upon the market *ephemerides* (plural of *ephemeris* – the annual book of tables detailing the movements of the planets which are used by astrologers to erect astrological charts) which had, previously, only been available via very limited specialist outlets.

Compendium bookshop is still there – astrology and alternative everything at the back; heavy critical theory downstairs. In the sixties, its exterior – including the whole house above it – was covered in a sort of hippy, flower-power, mural. By the mid to late sixties, the whole of north Camden Town, focusing on the open-air market by Camden Lock, and the Roundhouse at Chalk Farm, was a celebration of alternative sub-culture and entertainment. People living alternative life-styles made what they could by selling (gorgeous) second-hand clothes, or home-made hippy candles, or stuff brought over from India in the wake of the obligatory guru-pilgrimage of the period. Stars and moons and fairies were everywhere. Almost everyone read Tolkien's *Lord of the Rings*.

Twenty-five or so years later, in 1993, I went down to Compendium for some books I needed (downstairs department) and, afterwards, wandering around Camden Town in the leisurely way that is only possible for an academic on sabbatical, I realised that the shops (Camden Lock market having been replaced by a bricks and mortar version) were full of stars and moons again. The old hippy candles were back, supplemented this time by candles and candle-stands of a more frankly medieval and ecclesiastical sort, of the kind once only available from church outfitters in Victoria. India was well represented again also – in jewellery, incense, and clothes.

The difference was that what we had once thought of as the stuff of an alternative culture – alternative to capitalism, you understand – was now very obviously commodity. What, I asked myself, was going on?

For a brief while – exemplified in the golden summer of 1967 when anyone wearing a kaftan and beads was your friend, man – me and kids like me really believed that we would be able to love the despised world of the adults, of the 'straights' in their suburbs and suits, and of the West with its wars and murderous nuclear hatreds. Joannie Mitchell sang 'By the time we got to Woodstock, we were half a million strong'; the British contribution to the first global TV link-up was the Beatles, with a studio crammed full of friends, singing 'All You Need is Love'; and, a little later, if memory serves, John and Yoko would have bed-ins and bag-ins, and all the other forms of love-in through which we flower children pursued our liberatory credo.

In 1993, and subsequently, it seemed to me that the commodification of the sixties marked the desire to retrieve that brief and youthful hope when we went about trying to kiss everything, and everyone, better. It is often said these days that the young are depoliticised, or that they express their 'politics' in different ways – single-issue campaigns, rebellious celebrations of drug culture, green politics, and so on. But, in the main, we were no different. Party politics were where the 'straights' were; going on CND marches did not, for most, lead to joining the Labour Party; taking illegal drugs (it was in the sixties that Release – an alternative culture law service for people who had been 'busted' – was set up in a rundown area of Notting Hill) was for personal enlightenment and to put two fingers up to the Establishment; tree-hugging (usually when stoned) affirmed both different ways of experiencing living things, and also an alternative way of valuing life on earth.

ESCAPING COMMODIFICATION

The stars and moons in Camden in 1993 (and, still in 1997, more or less everywhere, with the late addition of kitschy Christian iconography, and decorated utility articles such as calculators with multi-coloured plastic jewels for buttons) speak to a desire for symbolic enrichment and a rejection of the dominant utilitarian and neo-economic-liberal culture of the post-1979 period. The predominant gesture of the mid to late 1960s was the search for spiritual and cultural authenticity, for a place that capital couldn't reach. The commodification of the 1960s which began in the early 1990s, implicitly makes that gesture again – rather sadly, this time, by commodifying an earlier site of attempted resistance. All that the commodification of hippiedom in the 1990s can do is to express, via the obscure desires of the market, the fact of a hopeless desire for that earlier moment, and especially for what it signified; it cannot be made real again, but it can be made, and then sold.

The problem, as Marx foretold, is that the inexorable logic of capitalism is to commodify – that is to marketise – everything. As became very evident on the night of May 1st/2nd 1997, very many people believed that something in what Tony Blair said, and stood for, might allow us to escape – even if only a little – from the debasing worship of the market, and from its accompanying devaluation and degradation of ethical life; that is to say that, in the 1997 General Election, what was expressed was some form of desire for a way of living in which the good life is not reducible to possessions, greedy getting, or simple self-interest, but in which other, not strictly accountable, things might also be seen to have value. For clearly, it is in non-accountable things – things which cannot be priced – that resistance to the ethically enfeebling rule of money is to be found. Political commentary, criticism and gossip since the election has really revolved around the question of authenticity and principles. Does the Blair government have integrity at its core (pictures of Tony and Cherie on their knees at church on Labour Party Conference, Sunday 1997), or has Blair simply understood, much more clearly than Margaret Thatcher even, that politics is a commodity too – to be packaged and sold (New Labour, endlessly spun to the punters)?

But, of course, commodification is always caught up in desire. The lure of the commodity does not lie simply in its utility (although very often that it a part of its attractiveness), but in the way in which it stands in for something that seems perpetually to elude us. Where there was once danger and magic in the world, or something magically transforming in our direct and labouring engagement with the world, with modernity there has been disenchantment and reason. The commodity, like any fetish, has an auratic quality; in it we glimpse, all unknowingly, the power of an identity which seemed once to be in the world, and which now seems estranged from it and hopelessly fragile.

An earlier generation of Freudians had believed that the expression of desire in non-violent forms – full and natural self expression (including, of course, sexual self-expression), existential freedom, and so on – would be the undoing of the world of bourgeois repressions, and all the other forms of psychical and physical violence associated with capitalism. Thirty years on from the 'liberation movements' of the 1960s, the manifest untruth of this seems incontestable. Bourgeois society may have

classically produced neurotics, but various critics, and many psycho-
analysts, have noticed a steady increase this century in patients suffering
from the unresolved narcissisms of the so-called 'borderline' personality
(the borderline is between normality and psychosis) in whom desire is dis-
organised, and affective life deadened. The classic background to borderline personalities is not too much repression and too much (irrepressible)
affect, but too much affectlessness; the borderline personality has suffered
from a lack of relatedness and an emotional deadness in early (usually
maternal) care. In other words, desire must be organised. That means pro-
voked, enjoined and constrained. Desire is not desire unless it is organised.
Just as much as gravity and topography make possible the great force of
a mighty river, so desire is nothing without the forces which contain
and channel it, no matter how much it is in continual 'conflict' with them.
The great question about desire for twentieth-century critics (Adorno, for
example) sceptical of 'liberation of desire' theories such as those associated with the work of Marcuse or R.D. Laing, was that of describing a
form of constraint, or 'mastery', which is not experienced as a violent
objectification.

The most compelling answers – psychoanalyst D.W. Winnicott's, for
example – take us directly back to one of the things which was also
directly articulated in sixties flower-power: the matter of love. For
Winnicott, the non-violent excitation/containment of desire is found in
what he called 'holding': holding is a form of emotional containment
which is endlessly reciprocal and adaptive. It certainly implies one who
holds and one who is held, but it also includes the idea of mutual
exchange and learning, and mutual transformation. As all good enough
parents know, the emotional space which is marked out by the child–
parent relation is not simply about the authority of the one who holds;
it is about authority as responsibility; that is: continually readjustive
responsiveness. Typically this relationship also marks the space – what
Winnicott called the 'transitional' space which is filled with 'transitional
objects' – where the infant first creatively invents his or her own forms of
symbolic life. Note that meaning is not 'violently' imposed here; there is
negotiation, eccentricity, waywardness, and a to and froing of the labour
upon the symbols being created, bartered, and exchanged. Containment –
or 'holding' – is achieved through a mixture of anarchic devotion to the
miracle of human creativity and development, and an understanding
of the importance of limits as the recognition of safety and trust in the
reliability of others. It is quite clear that, for Winnicott, these creative
transitional spaces of holding and making are the model of the conditions
of the good life.

THE LIMITS OF MODERN RATIONALISATION AS MARKETISATION

What does this have to do with the question of the politics of desire as that was widely and popularly raised during the 1960s? Then, bourgeois life was seen as deadeningly oppressive to human creativity and relationship. One of the results of the intervening 30 years has been a significant lessening of stifling conventionality. Nonetheless, the unbinding forces of capital – increasing and intensifying marketisation – have taken over the disciplining effects of convention; where once we were subject to the disciplines of moral convention, now we are subject to the disciplines of the market. What is still lacking – and what born-again Christians, new agers, cultists of various sorts, and purchasers of stars and moons still seek – is a space for an experience (call it what you will: spirituality; creativity; love) which cannot be bought. This cannot be a fantasised space of absolute freedom of desire. As I have suggested above, desire is precisely what is called into being and channelled; 'free' desire is not desire at all, but rather its opposite: affective deadness and psychotic-like amorality. If a playful and creative space – something like Winnicott's transitional space – offers a model of possible sites of resistance to the claustrophobic grip of the commodification of all human experience, what would the implication of this understanding of desire be for politics, political action, and policy?

Tony Blair's call to modernisation remains problematic. Markets do not provide for all human needs: there can be no market of true affections, no market of the inexplicable things that move us and which make life worth living. If modernisation means more investment in the production of skills, and in education, then it is still the case that, there too, not everything in the relationship between a teacher and a learner can be reduced to a simple checklist of aims and objectives. Mysterious things happen in relationships between individuals whose minds and abilities are bent on the same task. Such things effect transformations upon all those involved – and these transformations, by which new things can come about, and in which cultural life and knowledge are truly renewed, are not susceptible to strict calculation. The Oxbridge colleges wish to preserve the economic privileges which make the one-to-one tutorial possible because they understand very well the transformative and educational power of close human contacts. Modernisation as rationalisation has its limits. Rational conduct – simply understood – is neither creative, nor productive, nor, actually, how our most pressing personal and political problems are solved. Here, for example, is Thomas Powers, describing the transcripts when reviewing *The Kennedy Tapes: Inside the White House During the Cuban Missile Crisis* (eds Ernest May and Philip Zelikow) in the *London Review of Books* (Powers, 1997, p. 18ff):

> This exchange is elusive; its exact meaning seems to hover just out of reach. Other passages are simply incomprehensible as Kennedy's advisers converse with each other in a semi-coherent shorthand of sentence fragments, truncated questions, vague allusions, swallowed words, repetitions, deferential nods and shrugs and miscellaneous noises of objection, assent, qualification, emphasis. There are pages so opaque and unrecoverable that it seems one could evolve a whole new perspective on spoken language as depending less on grammar and syntax than on a kind of emotional semaphore.
>
> What becomes clear in the course of these often tedious discussions is that men in groups don't so much try to figure things out – an intellectual process depending heavily on articulation – as feel things out: to weigh what they are planning to do, and their reasons for doing it, by consulting their gut.

Here we see, in the most critical and pragmatic situation of the postwar period imaginable – when World War 3 seemed imminent – just how very much some of the most central actors were not, thank God, constrained by some idiotic and limited idea of rationality. And here is the lesson for Blair's continuing commitment to Thatcher's market neo-liberalism: the absolutely managed life-world – the life-world in which everyone jumps to the supposedly 'rational' tune of markets and commodification – is dangerous because inhuman. Fully human processes and negotiations – such as those recorded at the White House during the Cuban missile crisis in which a third world war was averted – are rather like, as Powers notes, the human negotiations within a good marriage:

> Such crises, routine at home, are rare among nations. Kennedy did not live to write his account of the lessons learned from the Cuban missile crisis, but it would probably have sounded very much like the sort of thing marriage counsellors say every day to marriage partners at the breaking point: 'leave your anger in the office, decide what you want, if you want to make up say so; if it's over, say that; draw the line and make it clear, set your limits, stick to your guns'.

Powers's drawing of the affective domestic parallels to political relations seems right. If you want to raise a good society, it is necessary to make spaces for affective, 'gut', work; over-rationalisation and over-management are deadly to creative problem-solving and real progress; toleration of the creative messiness of emotional semaphore is essential. What the

Kennedy Tapes expose is the extent to which good political judgements rely upon the apparent incoherences of transitional spaces where people can feel their way to creative solutions.

ECOLOGIES OF MIND

All this may seem a hundred light year's away from the pragmatic concerns of politicians and policy, yet Geoff Mulgan, since May 1997 installed in the Policy Unit at Number 10, has – in his 1997 book *Connexity* – made an extended version of the argument offered here (Mulgan, 1997). 'Soft' knowledges, emotional literacy, and all the forms of human relationship skills which are, strictly speaking, non-calculable, are increasingly important in contemporary societies. In a chapter entitled 'Ecologies of Mind', Mulgan concludes by saying:

> In a modern liberal society we see ecologies of mind as somehow outside the realm of politics and of conscious choice. The choosing individual is sovereign. But in densely populated societies, this is not a sustainable perspective. We depend on the minds of others, on their being healthy and well-intentioned. The implication of taking these ecologies seriously is that every institution is open to judgements: it becomes legitimate to ask what mentalities they tend to create, whether they leave those who come into contact with them stronger or weaker, more able to bear responsibilities or less so, ethically fluent or ethically stunted. If they drain, suppress, destroy the human spirit then it is legitimate to ask them to make up the cost they impose on everyone else. (Mulgan, 1997: 144)

For Mulgan, such ecological 'mentalities' (understood in the broadest sense) constitute 'social capital'; but the term may be misleading since such 'social capital' cannot in fact be bought, only acquired through time and affection. Significantly, Mulgan himself turns to the parent–child relation as the model of good or bad 'mentalities': 'The starting-point for understanding mentalities is childhood. It is at an early age that we learn to make connections with others.' (Mulgan, 1997: 132)

Tony Blair has said that people expect too much of governments; yet it is clear – eighteen years of Thatcherism made it obvious, and New Labour's 1997 Election Campaign made it central – that one thing which governments can do is to set a certain tone which then spreads out into all aspects of society at large. Thatcherism elevated individualism and markets above all else; Blair campaigned on anti-corruption and integrity (which is why the November 1997 Formula One tobacco advertising exemption, following upon a million pound donation to the Labour Party by the Formula One Chief Executive Bernie Ecclestone, caused such a furore). The idea that a government could promote the importance of emotional competence, and the importance of the non-calculable things which nurture such competence, is not far-fetched.

THE LEGACY OF THE 1960s AT THE END OF THE
TWENTIETH CENTURY – RE-ENCHANTMENT

We have come a long way since the 1960s. Then, the question of human desire and self-expression was first widely raised as a political question. Hippiedom sought to resist the most dehumanising aspects of bourgeois commodity culture and the disenchanted world. It didn't succeed, but it did put in train, and popularise, a way of thinking about the world which has not only not disappeared but which, thirty years later, is being expressed with even greater force – albeit, very often, in commodified forms. Alongside this, perfectly serious and realistic people (in the humanities and in the sciences) have begun the processes of thought, research and publication which feed into what is increasingly a mainstream, and perfectly level-headed body of work which returns us to the roots of counter-cultural concerns. These roots lie in the perception that what is most valuable about human beings – their creative communicative souls – can never be a commodity upon the market because the labour of love and relatedness that makes it is absolutely incalculable.

In talking about the cultural importance of protected 'held' creative spaces, I mean, of course, both science and art; not all research or thought must be money-profit or ends directed. But in these market-god times, perhaps a special plea needs to be made for the humanities – for the liberal arts. Only totalitarian regimes seem fully to appreciate the subtle effects of the arts; democracies often seem inclined to think them peripheral, or at least, not as sources of real knowledge (which position, it is popularly believed, only science can attain). Yet when we think about the most profound social and cultural changes of the second half of the twentieth century, a substantial part of these – the gender revolution and the black and gay consciousness movements – have neither come from the 'hard' sciences nor, barely, been articulated by them at all. It has been from the social sciences and from the arts – not from the hard sciences and business – that a substantial part of our changing self-perceptions in the contemporary world have arisen.

What the 1960s put in train on a wide and popular scale was the possibility of thinking human goods differently. What this meant was that enchantment and love were 'in the air', as something resistant to the affective violences of bourgeois life, because uncommodifiable. Capitalism will try to commodify the soul – witness the presence in the shops of kitsch Catholic iconography on candles, keyrings, and so on – and the wisest among us will try to resist it. This is not because the cash nexus is simply evil – capital is immensely inventive and creative in its own ways – but because, as with Louisa Gradgrind and James Harthouse in Dickens's *Hard Times*, it turns the heart to ice. The coup de grâce of capitalist commodification will lie in obliging it to recognise non-Faustian space – the unpurchaseable place – and thus in obliging it to recognise the unquantifiable, that is, the priceless, value of its absolute 'other': the spaces which escape commodification. Here, the logic of commodification would reach its limits, and would reach something like Hegel's attained community of mutual recognition in which the absolute other cannot be mastered, but can only be – must be – simply acknowledged as absolutely other – and absolutely valuable on that account.

REFERENCES

Mulgan, G. (1997), *Connexity*, Chatto & Windus.
Powers, T. (1997), 'And after we've struck Cuba?', *London Review of Books*, Vol. 19, No. 22, November 13, 1997.

4 We Didn't Know It Would Be So Hard: the Short, Sad, Instructive History of the US New Left

Marvin Gettleman

Of all the western countries in which something like a new left appeared during the 1960s, probably that in the United States exhibited the most stunted sense of historical continuity with earlier movements both in the US and abroad (Caute, 1988; McDermott, 1997). Part of the reason was cultural, rooted in the romantic American illusion of having escaped from history into a realm of pure voluntarism. But the virtual disappearance in the preceding decade of a viable Communist old left did deprive the New Left of a generation of elders who might have passed along some much-needed political wisdom and historico-internationalist perspective. But by the beginning of the 1960s, the CP/USA had become a moribund dogmatic sect, its once-extensive praxis destroyed by government repression during what has been called the McCarthy era (Schrecker, 1983, 1993, 1998). New leftists saw little to admire in what was left of American communism, ideologically tethered to its increasingly unattractive Stalinist political orientation. The Port Huron Statement, the New Left's major early ideological manifesto flatly stated that 'we are in basic opposition to the communist system' (Miller, 1987, p. 350; cf. Weinstein, 1970, Ch. 7). For their part the Communists contemptuously dismissed the new leftists as troublesome anarchists, while the independent Marxists around *Monthly Review* magazine ignored them (Green, 1971; Miller, 1987, p. 162).

Yet subtle organic ties linked these two generations of American leftists. For one thing many new leftists were 'red diaper babies' with parents who were, or who had been, in the CP/USA. Whatever doctrinal and tactical disputes separated these generations, the young folk sometimes prodded their discouraged relatives back into political action (Isserman, 1987, Ch. 5; Gitlin, 1987, pp. 67–77; Breines, 1982, Ch. 4) and to fruitful inter-generational political discussions. Another less wholesome and even more complex link derives from the Communist old left's uncritical admiration of the Soviet Union, which the New Left justifiably repudiated. But in a few short years, significant portions of the American New Left would come to embrace strategies drawn from third world liberation movements of no less dubious relevance to circumstances in the US. (Here the difference between the British New Left, which included a number of distinguished former Communist intellectuals, as well as an active Ban The Bomb movement, whose praxis had considerable impact, is instructive.)

Some early new left activists did seek political guidance as they began to plan their assault on the all-too-evident faults in American society, and although a few individual old leftists played an advisory role, that whole generation of trusted, experienced elders from whom these activists might have learned more, was no longer available. Pacifists contributed as much as any group, especially on the level of demonstration tactics (DeBeneditti, 1990, *passim*). Of the old left groupings, the Trotskyist Socialist Workers Party (SWP) probably had the best working relationship with the New Left, because of its occasionally acrimonious but generally responsible work in the Vietnam era anti-war movement – bringing needed good sense into a movement that was constantly in danger of breaking out into ultra-left fantasies (Halstead, 1978). Progressive Labor (PL), although it only emerged in the 1960s, was definitely old left in orientation, ideology and agenda. Its aim was to replace the CP/USA as the keeper of the flame of Stalinist orthodoxy, and also to infiltrate and take over the major New Left youth organisation – Students for a Democratic Society (SDS). As we shall see, by 1968 PL had succeeded in this aim, revealing what was by then the New Left's volatile vulnerability, and its already precipitous decline.

Could the collapse of the New Left have been averted? Or to pose the counterfactual question in a narrower form: what lessons might the New Left have drawn if it had available a more respected and credible set of political ancestors? For one thing New Left radicals might have been diverted from the naive but tempting analysis that the major problem of the era was America's moral failure to live up to its ideals. A more nuanced and realistic approach, less parochial, focusing instead on Marxist categories of economic interests that had to be overcome in the hoped-for transformation to a brave new world. Such a perspective could have helped counter the debilitating despair (and its attendant tactical consequences) when the inevitable discovery came – that neither the US nor any other country invariably lives up to its announced ideals. Contact with trusted elders might also have militated against the romantic fascination about revolutions elsewhere (and their dashing heroes) that impeded sober appraisals of actual conditions in the US.[1] Nor, as will be mentioned later, was the potentially useful wisdom of Antonio Gramsci yet available to American radicals.

Even so, the US New Left, undeterred by hostility from old left spokespersons, and not yet stalked by PL, managed to produce a movement of great vitality in the early and mid 1960s. A Civil Rights movement, a student movement, an anti-war movement and a women's movement were considerable achievements, even if not all of these can be credited solely to the new left. Furthermore, these radical projects at first developed with the characteristic North American sense of near-limitless possibility. This illusion that these students and other young people could remake the world reflected a giddily optimistic mood American of the 1960s that many of us later came to look back upon with wonder – and some shame. Why didn't we know it wouldn't be so easy? What attenuated our realism and tragic sensibilities?

The New Left's initial improvisational and non-ideological approach derived in great measure from the example of young black protestors in the upper south who courageously challenged segregation. The spark was struck at Greensboro, North Carolina, in early 1960 when students at the local Agricultural and Technical College refused to leave a segregated Woolworth's lunch counter and immediately inspired imitators all through the region. Out of this wave of lunch counter sit-ins would eventually emerge the main New Left civil rights organisation – the Student Non Violent-Coordinating Committee (SNCC), which, along with the Congress of Racial Equality (CORE), galvanized young people white and black all over the country.

When white college radicals in the north began demanding an end to segregation and racial oppression, and themselves joined SNCC or SNCC-support groups, the New Left was born. Racial injustice, along with the threat of nuclear annihilation and the prevalence of bureaucratic insensitivity to injustice (and later, when it became possible to utter the words, imperialism and sexism too), became the perceived by-products of a debased American liberalism. The University of Wisconsin-based journal, *Studies on the Left* (1959–1967), which along with SDS's *New Left Notes*, became the closest approximations of theoretical journals of the New Left, also helped focus the nascent movement's ideological energies on 'Cold War Liberalism', deemed the New Left's main ideological enemy (Weinstein and Eakins, 1970; Buhle, 1990, Ch. 10). The colleges became the initial incubators for the upsurges of both black militancy and the closely linked white struggle that comprised much of the early New Left, as well as for the anti-war and the women's liberation struggle that eventually emerged, but whose outlines were taking shape earlier (Matusow, 1984, pp. 321–5; Evans, 1979; Echols, 1989).

The *ur*-text of the New Left, containing some of its most compelling ideas, as well as its unresolved dilemmas (the woman question is totally absent from its pages) was Tom Hayden's 1962 SDS manifesto, the Port Huron Statement. The Students for a Democratic Society had its roots in the obscure, moderate leftist Student League for Industrial Democracy, which in order to reinvigorate itself, in 1960 hired University of Michigan graduate student Al Haber as Field Secretary. Haber's vision was of a radical organisation that seeks the 'root causes' of the 'inadequate society of today' and pursues solutions 'with vigor, idealism and urgency, supporting our words with picket lines, demonstrations and even our own bodies ... '. The conservative older LID leadership fired Haber, but then reluctantly re-engaged him in chastened recognition that only his new youthful enthusiasm (or that of someone like him) would enliven the near-moribund parent organisation and its student offshoot. Haber hired Tom Hayden, a recent Michigan graduate, who had studied the writings of dissident Columbia University sociologist C. Wright Mills, and then travelled around the country (making contact with SNCC activists in the South). Debating with critics who attacked the vague utopianism of his draft manifesto and retaining much of Mills's influence, Hayden revised the position paper he was planning to present at the SDS convention scheduled for June, 1962, at Port Huron, Michigan (Sale, 1973).[2]

The final version of the Statement adopted at Port Huron was, as the historian of SDS put it, 'unabashedly middle class' (Sale, 1973, p. 50). Although sympathy for the poor and suffering pervaded the document, it spoke not primarily for the downtrodden masses but for 'university people ... bred at least in modest comfort', who were uneasy about the world they were about to inherit. Two immediate situations shaped that unease: the struggle against racial bigotry, which 'compelled most of us from silence to activism'; and the 'common peril' of nuclear annihilation, which similarly challenged us to take active personal responsibility 'for encounter and resolution'. To Hayden, who on this matter voiced the common views of an entire political generation, the threshold for effective action comes with the escape from 'subjective apathy' into active citizenship, a sundering of 'shell of moral call[o]us' that deadens sensitivity to human suffering, even our own. The prevalence of such apathy within the American population allows the dominant business community to eviscerate democracy, while hypocritically rhetorically upholding its tenets. The notion of active democratic citizenship along with its correlate, 'participatory democracy', was the main theme of Port Huron. And it soon became the core idea of a vast reborn student movement that did not long remain only on campus.[3]

Interspersed with its hard, analytical passages (on overseas investment, trade unions, nuclear deterrence strategies, automation and military–industrial politics), SDS's new-minted ideological manifesto also contained naive quasi-anarchist visions of 'inherently good men and women liberated from hierarchic institutions and living in decentralized communities where the individual counted' (Breines, 1982; Sale, 1973, Chs. 7–9). What is remarkable is that in its early years the New Left actually created approximations of such communities, one of which even took shape at SDS's bureaucratic centre – the National Office in New York City. Dedicated teams of new leftists elsewhere, especially in the segregated south, in northern ghettos, and at anti-war coffee houses set up around US military bases, were able for a time to create little 'beloved communities' of radical activists which, in their internal relations, prefigured the good society they were attempting, but never quite managed, to build.

Before the final, partially self-inflicted total defeat of the new left, there were also interim defeats (as well as occasional victories). 1963–64 saw the advent of SDS's Economic Research and Action Project (ERAP), which dispatched mostly white students to such northern and upper south cities as Philadelphia, Louisville, Boston, Cleveland, Trenton and Newark. A tactical shift away from campus organising, ERAP seemed like white, missionary social work ('romantic Narodnikism', the historian of SDS put it), paternalistic in its very striving to avoid paternalism. Years later Todd Gitlin conceded that ERAP 'was based on [white] guilt' (Sale, 1973, pp. 143, 161). By 1965, its cadres unsure of what they were supposed to do in these mostly black communities, and under attack from advocates of what would come to be called 'black power', ERAP disbanded.

Alongside the failure of ERAP there were victories, none more spectacular than Berkeley in 1964–1965. When University of California students (some of whom had spent the previous 'Freedom Summer' working in the south with SNCC and other civil rights' organisations) returned to the Berkeley campus in the fall, they found that university administrators had banned political activity and fund-raising on a strip of the campus where it had previously been allowed. SDS did not play a prominent organisational role in the struggle that followed. Campus civil rights groups took the initiative in contesting a ban they felt (with considerable justification) was directed against them. Just as they had battled oppression in racist Mississippi they did so again right on the Berkeley campus. When a CORE member was arrested for setting up a table and soliciting funds on the proscribed strip, students surrounded the police vehicle and in effect held the arresting officers captive. Within a short time thousands of students joined what had become a spontaneous sit-in and an open forum against what Mario Savio, a leader of the Free Speech Movement, termed 'the greatest problem of our nation – depersonalized, unresponsive bureaucracy'. When fraternities threatened violence, the crowd sang to bolster its confidence. This experience of a community that had instantly come into being, and was shaping its own collective life, became a classic new left epiphany. The scenario might have come right out of the Port Huron Statement, as could Savio's famous speech in early December, before the Berkeley administration capitulated:

> There is a time when the operation of the machine becomes so odious, makes you so sick at heart, that you can't take part: you can't even passively take part, and you've got to put your bodies upon the gears and upon the wheels, upon the levers, upon all the apparatus and you've got to make it stop. And you've got to indicate to the people who run it, to the people who own it, that unless you're free, the machine will be prevented from working at all.

Police arrests on campus rallied moderates, and the faculty 'roused itself to endorse the demands of the students' (Matusow, 1984, pp. 317–18; Rorbagh, 1989; Kitchell, 1990). Victory over the Berkeley administration and trustees energised the new left there (and all throughout the country) for the next obvious crusade: to end the war in Vietnam.[4]

African-Americans and white new leftists, willing to fight domestic oppression in the name of racial justice and democracy, also came to see the war in Vietnam as a conflict in which the US was supporting the wrong side. At first, few would follow the logic of this position and come right out and say they were in favour of victory of the Communist-led forces. Even Martin Luther King Jr., who, a year before his murder, ascended the pulpit in New York's Riverside Church with apologies for not having spoken out earlier and more forcefully against that war, would not go that far. But in his 1967 sermon King offered a far more truthful position on the conflict in Indochina than had a series of US presidents and governmental spokespersons.[5] King saw the Americans as 'strange liberators' in Vietnam, supporting the post-war restoration of French colonialism there, and later blocking unification of the country, land reform and genuine independence. Still striving to preserve the image of a legitimate American aims in Vietnam, he pointed to the 'cruel irony of watching Negro and white boys on TV screens as they "kill and die together for a nation that has been unable to seat them together in the same schools".' In Vietnam, the US was 'wrong from the beginning', exhibiting 'the deadly Western arrogance' that undermines the stated goals of 'revolution, freedom and democracy'. King lamented the racial oppression at home and 'violence and militarism' abroad as poisoning America's soul (King's 1967 Sermon, in Gettleman, 1995, Reading 46). Even earlier, SNCC had reached a similar, if not so eloquently stated, position on the war (SNCC,

1966; Carson, 1981, pp. 183–90), while the National Liberation Front for South Vietnam (NLFSV) was clever enough to post notices on Vietnam battle fields specifically directed to 'Negro army men', who were told that they were 'committing the ignominious crimes in South Vietnam that the KKK [Ku Klux Klan] is perpetrating against your family at home' (Young, 1991, illustration facing p. 242).

Appeals like these eventually undermined morale in the American armed forces among both black and white troops. Many soldiers who originally supported or went along with their country's war changed their perspective once they arrived 'in country'. The new leftists, who led the early opposition to the war, planned their campaigns mainly for the civilian home front, and only sporadically connected with these largely working class 'grunts' in 'Nam (Appy, 1993). By the late 1960s largely spontaneous opposition to the war among US armed forces, along with the continued unpopularity among growing numbers of Vietnamese for the US-backed military governments there, became serious problems for Washington war managers (Gettleman, 1995, Readings 30, 48, 49; Gibson, 1986). The image of antiwar protest taking place only among pampered youth seeking to escape conscription was one of the most persistent myths of the Vietnam war era. At first, before the draft calls increased but with the war greatly intensifying, students and old pacifist activists from the War Resisters' League and other organisations sponsored major 'actions', the seasonal demonstrations – a spring March in Washington, then another in the fall – more or less coordinated with local events of a similar kind. SDS's planned demonstration on April 17, 1965 attracted over 20 000 people to Washington DC, the largest peace march in American history (Sale, 1973, Ch. 11). No one dreamed that it would go on for yet another decade, extend into the Nixon years, and include invasions of Laos and Cambodia. A complex political and social choreography ensued in which US government escalation prompted shifts to ever more radical (but not necessarily more realistic) oppositional strategies within the US – all played out against the apparent backdrop (but really the main arena of struggle) of Vietnam and the neighbouring countries of southeast Asia.[6] US escalation of the war prompted ever more bold and daring Vietnamese military responses, they also seemed to demand escalation of efforts in the US to end it – moves from mere protest to militant, even ultra-militant, resistance.

Charting in proper sequence the major steps of this three-sided escalation cannot be attempted here, but as the war dragged on the domestic American advance from mere demonstration and protest to active resistance came to include burning draft cards, refusing induction, attempting to halt troop trains, breaking away from legal demonstrations to engage in illegal actions.[7] Beyond what these civilian antiwar militants did were the steps of resistance taken by US military personnel – sometimes spontaneous acts (fragging, i.e. killing their own officers by means of a grenade), or refusals to go into action, or outright desertion. Some of these were undertaken collectively, and may have reached some outer boundary when the soldiers in and around the Marxist group Workers' World attempted to organise a Servicemen's Union (Cortright, 1975). The ambiguous heading under which many of these actions took place was 'bringing the war home'. Some antiwar and black power militants, along with guilt-drenched white radicals, interpreted this to mean the obligation to reproduce the Vietnam war on the streets of such American cities as Berkeley and Chicago, with them playing the heroic role of the Vietnamese insurgents (Farber, 1988). Gone was the 'speak truth to power' sentiment that animated the earlier, peaceful 'teach-in' phase of anti-war protest.[8] As it turnedout, what was hard to accept both by new leftists and right-wing American defenders of the war in Vietnam, was that the conflict in Indochina might be resolved in the way it eventually was – by the successful military and political efforts of the Vietnamese themselves at long last to liberate their country, which they did by 1975.

Despite their consistent opposition to US aggression in Vietnam, the main task of leftists in the US were domestic – combating racial oppression, gender discrimination and poverty. But internal fissures, some with deep historical, cultural and political roots, rendered unified action, and eventually any effective action, on these matters increasingly difficult. The civil rights movement, once the common interracial commitment of the entire New Left, by mid-decade became contested political terrain. Former allies (white and black civil rights activists) divided sharply on both tactics and strategies. On one level it was a replay of SDS's failed ERAP programme – sending white volunteers into the black ghettos of northern cities to facilitate community action. Similar problems came up as Freedom Summer 1964 approached.

The Freedom Summer Project brought 700 white college students to Mississippi. Segregationists greeted the Freedom Summer pilgrims with the same savage hostility that had shown to local black civil rights militants. Three civil rights workers – James Chaney, a black Mississippian, Michael Schwerner a white CORE member from New York City, and Andrew Goodman, a student at New York's Queens College – were brutally murdered near the town of Philadelphia (Carson, 1981, pp. 114–15). Working under harrowing danger, the Project volunteers also experienced tensions internal to the movement, especially what was perceived as the contradiction within an effort to empower poor southern blacks that also needed to call upon whites to carry out their plans. Another was the delicate problem of interracial sex, especially between white women and black men, which became a divisive one among the beleaguered civil rights communities under constant assault.

The effort that summer to organise a Mississippi Freedom Democratic Party (MFDP) that would unseat the segregationist delegation at the Democratic Party's national convention in that tense election year was blocked, and the disenchantment of blacks with what they considered, with considerable justification, as a betrayal, contributed to the growth of black separatism (Carson, 1981, Ch. 9). By the end of the summer the racial coalition had begun to unravel; despair, discouragement and pessimism soon led to the appearance of the divisive programme of 'black power'.

The complicated roots of the black power tendency cannot be extensively explored in this chapter, but it had profound effects on the New Left, greatly hastening its dissolution. A 1966 SNCC paper argued that after '400 years of oppression and slavery', blacks in America had good reason to feel intimidated by whites 'no matter what their liberal leanings are'. Therefore, since the racial problem in the US is far more a white problem – even a colonial problem – whites should battle racism where it mainly exists, in white communities. To help preserve the group identity and organisational integrity of black communities, the work that hitherto was done by interracial teams, would be handled by blacks alone (Carmichael and Hamilton, 1967; Carson, 1981, Ch. 14). Soon it was made clear to whites in SNCC and CORE that their presence was no longer wanted. Also contributing to this separatist trend was the growth of the Nation of Islam and the Black Panther Party, which on the basis of its revolutionary programme, demanded leadership over the entire New Left (Matusow, 1984, Ch. 12).

Partially independent of these developments in the black movement, and in the white New Left, but affecting both, was the amorphous set of Dionysian impulses that are collectively termed the counterculture of the 1960s. Loosely uniting rock 'n' roll enthusiasts with advocates of sexual freedom, drug use and 'far out' gestures, a segment of the counterculture became allied with a segments of the anti-war and black power movements that celebrated and even practised revolutionary violence. This was the movement's anarchist fringe, followers (most unknowingly) of Mikhail Bakunin and practitioners of 'propaganda of the deed' (Carr, 1961). Many in the counter-culture remained non-violent flower children, pacific distributors of free food, macrobiotic vegetarians and erotic experimenters.

But in such locales as San Francisco's Haight-Ashbury, an unstable, 'far out', drug-crazed fringe 'became willing cannon fodder for the increasingly violent demonstrations' planned by New Left leaders (Gitlin, 1987, Ch. 13; Matusow, 1984, Ch. 10). Having abandoned rationalism and embraced mindless ultra-radicalism, these final new leftists (Weathermen and the other splinter groups thrown up when PL took over SDS in 1968–69) were ready to bring about the violent end of a vulnerable 'Amerika' of their imagination. One such group in early March 1970 were preparing explosives in an elegant borrowed house in New York's Greenwich Village when it blew up, killing three of them (Sale, 1973, pp. 3–5). Since the Vietnamese were actively and successfully challenging the US by armed defence of their country, it seemed that the only way for Americans to be 'true revolutionaries' was to emulate the Vietnamese by picking up a gun, or making bombs – to bring the US closer to its deserved and destined apocalyptic extinction.[9]

Contributing to this embrace of violence in the New Left was a heightened sensitivity to the media, and the temptation offered by media coverage to stage spectacular but ephemeral spectacles instead of pursuing serious political strategies. The laid-back counter-culture contributed greatly to the impatience with serious activity of any kind, political or otherwise. Former SDS leader Todd Gitlin has analysed the temptation to become 'celebrity leaders' before TV cameras, and to conform to the gaudy image of what the news media assumed radicals 'had to be'. Humdrum work of non-charismatic rank and filers was not 'news' (Gitlin, 1980). While internal forces in the movement and in the surrounding society undoubtedly did more than media distortions to shape the New Left's downward trajectory, it is a factor that must be acknowledged.

As both antiwar and civil rights wings of New Left collapsed, another movement arose, phoenix-like, out of the political ruins of the late 1960s – the woman's movement. Its intellectual and political core took shape around the recognition of male oppression of female comrades, and it broadened to a general theory of patriarchy. Going far beyond Betty Friedan's poignant critique of the oppressive domesticity that affected white middle-class women (Friedan, 1963), movement women began tentatively, and then more forcefully, to protest not only against imperialism and racism, but against sexism as well – including the attitudes and behaviour of male comrades. As early as 1964 a SNCC position paper credited women as being the crucial cohort 'that keeps the movement running on a day-to-day basis', but are excluded from policy-making (SNCC, 1964). The following year two white women working in SNCC raised the question within SDS (Hayden and King, 1965). The New Left's male 'heavies' did not like to hear of this new internal protest in the ranks, and fought against it as a 'diversion' from more important matters, like ending the Vietnam war. Eventually, in ways that Sara Evans and Alice Echols have made fairly clear (Evans, 1979; Echols, 1989; cf. Gitlin, 1987, Ch. 16), an independent women's movement did grow out of the New Left, forming at first those 'beloved communities' that neither SDS or SNCC were able to sustain. But even this new movement was not able to escape some of the splits and internecine feuds similar to those that affected the New Left itself – and a few original ones as well. Few of the other New Left organisations and publications survived the 1970s, and thus the New Left's major institutional creation within civil society is the woman's movement.

The importance of the creation of such institutions to contest oppressive social hegemonies is of course a central part of the legacy of Antonio Gramsci, which unfortunately was not available to American new leftists in their brief and troubled history.[10] Had his 'Lettere dal Carcere' been translated earlier into English or had his ideas been given wider, earlier currency by the US Communist movement, there might have been a stronger collective voice raised against several of the more bizarre and unfortunate forms of sectarianism that marked the American New Left's precipitous decline, and its almost total subsequent effacement from the US political scene. Some pockets of 1960s radicalism still survive under the leaky umbrella provided by a few academic institutions in the US. And as has been noted, there still exists a woman's movement of sorts. Few of the great battles the New Left entered were won, and some of them (race relations, poverty, just to name two arenas of struggle), despite a decorative veneer of reform, remain in as critical a state and as far from satisfactory solution as ever.

What newer historians of the New Left are now stressing is that, even as leftists were waging their battles of the 1960s, there was forming beneath the surface of American life a deep popular current of anti-revolutionary sentiment and a resurgent hegemonic value system virtually deifying 'the market' (Farber, 1994c). Proponents of triumphant post-cold war global capitalism have met some of their most vehement opponents on the loony fringes of the American right, people who are also the left's enemies. Clearly if a 'newer' American left were to emerge, there are many lessons about sectarianism, about political unity, about clear-sighted political realism, about media distortions and about the use of tact in trying to win people over, that will have to be pondered. When the present doldrums experienced by the left have ended, when appropriate praxis is developed, there will be many texts – not the least of them Gramsci's writings – to be studied and discussed. Historical amnesia will then be, as it was in the 1960s, a costly error that must be overcome.

NOTES

1.   Of all the third world radicals revered by the New Left, probably the most universally admired was Che Guevara, but as Allen Matusow has observed, few of his American disciples heeded the wisdom in his 1961 book, *Guerrilla Warfare*: 'Where a government has come into power through some form of popular vote, fraudulent or not, and maintains at least an appearance of constitutional legality, the guerrilla outbreak cannot be promoted, since possibility of peaceful struggle have not yet been exhausted.' (Quoted in Matusow, 1984, p. 326).

2.   Beside Mills, another academic loner whose ideas influenced the New Left was University of Wisconsin historian William Appleman Williams. See Buhle, 1990, Ch. 28 and Abelove, 1983, pp. 123–46.

3.   There had been a vibrant earlier student movement that terminated when the 1939 Nazi-Soviet Pact broke up the Socialist-Communist alliance that underlay it (Cohen, 1993).

4.   By no means the last student uprising of the 1960s, or of the new left era, Berkeley had a sequel four years later, when the Columbia University campus erupted over the decision to build a University gymnasium on public parkland in the adjoining black Harlem community. The gym was never built (Sale, 1973, pp. 430–41; Avorn, 1969).

5.   Compare, for example, President Ronald Reagan's ludicrously inaccurate 1982 account of the genesis of the Vietnam conflict (Reagan, 1982) with King's sermon in Gettleman, 1995, Reading 46.

6.   During the Nixon years, in a strange response to and inversion of the new left fantasy of 'bringing the war in Vietnam home', the President's advisers acted out a counter-fantasy, setting up spring and fall 'war rooms' in the White House to direct the battles against anti-war protesters, as if it were a real war. This fantasy became something of a self-fulfilling prophecy. The behaviour of Nixon and his entourage is well-brought out in an otherwise undistinguished volume (Wells, 1994), far inferior to the best book on the antiwar movement: DeBenedetti, 1990. Another bizarre distortion (not totally unrelated to the behaviour in the Nixonite White House) crept into the American discourse on Vietnam, in which the shadow conflict in the US became inflated and the indigenous Asian nature of the war tended to downplayed. In Gettleman 1991, I call this Cartesian imperialism ('we invade you, therefore you are').

7.   Women had no draft cards, since they were not (and are not) subject to conscription. Thus, as the antiwar movement progressed new left women, who were asserting themselves against sexism throughout

the movement, felt they were being reduced to subordinate roles in the antiwar struggle as well. This was one of the factors that gave rise to the women's liberation movement (Echols, 1989, Ch. 1).

8. To 'speak truth to power' constituted the motivation for much of the intellectual antiwar activity. The naivete of this notion was clearly revealed in 1970 when Daniel Ellsberg and Anthony Russo, antiwar militants within the US government, 'liberated' and publicized the Defense Department's twelve-volume history of the war known as The Pentagon Papers (for bibliographical data on the three published versions of The Pentagon Papers, see Gettleman, 1995, p. 541). Although confirming the main points that antiwar scholarship was striving to establish at the time (that Vietnam was one nation, not two; that the Communist leader Ho Chi Minh was a justly revered Vietnamese patriot; and that the US bore major responsibility for supporting post-World War 2 French colonialism, and primary responsibility for the post-1954 phase of the conflict), The Pentagon Papers also showed that Washington's war managers knew everything we did, but discounted it!

9. The belief that 'Amerika' was on the verge of extinction reflected the ultra-militant New Left's inability to distinguish its own desires from actual real-world possibilities. Having abandoned rationalism, rejected the peace movement, this group that became dominant just as the New Left disappeared of course repudiated anything that could be construed as conventional 'bourgeois' thinking. Hence it could not recognise that the greatest of all apocalyptic threats, nuclear war, was being held in abeyance by a tacit US–Soviet Cold War agreement.

10. This is not the place for any extended discussion of Gramsci's ideas, or their impact in America. One of the earliest books on Gramsci is still perhaps the best guide (Cammett, 1967, and the follow-up, Cammett, 1991).

REFERENCES

Abelove, H., ed. (1983), *Visions of History* [a publication of MARHO – the Radical History Organization], Pantheon Books.
Appy, C. G. (1993), *Working-Class War: American Combat Soldiers & Vietnam*, University of North Carolina Press.
Avorn, J.L. and members of the *Columbia Daily Spectator* staff (1969), *Up Against the Ivy Wall*, Atheneum.

Belfrage, S. (1965), *Freedom Summer*, Fawcett Crest.

Bloom, A. and Wini Breines, eds (1995), *'Takin' it to the Streets': a Sixties Reader*, Oxford University Press.

Breines, W. (1982), *Community and Organization in the New Left, 1962–1968: the Great Refusal*, Praeger.

Brown, M., R. Martin, F. Rosengarten and G. Snedeker, eds (1993), *New Studies in the Politics and Culture of U.S. Communism*, Monthly Review Press.

Buhle, M.J., P. Buhle and D. Georgakis, eds (1990), *Encyclopedia of the American Left*, Garland Publishing Co.

Buhle, P., ed. (1990), *History and the New Left: Madison, Wisconsin, 1950–1970*, Temple University Press.

Cammett, J. (1967), *Antonio Gramsci and the Origins of Italian Communism*, Stanford University Press.

—— (1991), *Bibliografia Gramsciana, 1922–1988*, Fondazione Istituto Gramsci [an ongoing series of annotated bibliographies].

Carmichael, S. and Hamilton, C.V. (1967), *Black Power*, Penguin.

Carr, E.H. (1961), *Bakunin*, Vintage Books [first published, 1937].

Carson, C. (1981), *In Struggle: SNCC and the Black Awakening of the 1960s*, Harvard University Press.

Caute, D. (1988), *The Year of the Barricades: a Journey Through 1968,* Harper & Row.

Cohen, R. (1993), *When the Old Left Was Young: Student Radicals and America's First Mass Student Movement, 1929–1941*, Oxford University Press.

Cortright, D. (1975), *Soldiers in Revolt: the American Military Today*, Doubleday Anchor.

DeBenedetti, C. and Chatfield, C. (1990), *An American Ordeal: the Antiwar Movement of the Vietnam Era*, Syracuse University Press.

Echols, A. (1989), *Daring to be Bad: Radical Feminism in America*, University of Minnesota Press.

Evans, S. (1979), *Personal Politics: The Roots of Women's Liberation in the Civil Rights Movement and the New Left*, Vintage Books.

Farber, D. (1988), *Chicago '68*, University of Chicago Press.

—— (1994a), *The Age of Great Dreams: America in the 1960s*, Hill and Wang.

—— ed. (1994b). *The Sixties: From Memory to History*, University of North Carolina Press.

—— (1994c), 'The Silent Majority and Talk About Revolution', in Farber (1994b), pp. 291–316.

Freidan, B. (1963), *The Feminine Mystique*, W.W. Norton.

Gettleman, M.E., ed. (1965), *Vietnam: History, Documents and Opinions…*, Fawcett Books.

—— (1991), 'Against Cartesianism: Three Generations of Vietnam Scholarship', in D. Allen and N.V. Long, eds, *Coming to Terms: Indochina, the United States, and the War*, Westview Press, Ch. 11.

—— J. Franklia, B. Franklin and M. Young, eds (1995), *Vietnam and America*, Grove Press.

Gibson , J.W. (1986), *The Perfect War: Technowar in Vietnam*, Atlantic Monthly Press.

Gitlin, T. (1980), *The Whole Word is Watching: Mass Media in the Making and Unmaking of the New Left*, University of California Press.

Gitlin, T. (1987), *The Sixties: Years of Hope, Days of Rage*, Bantam.

Grant, J., ed. (1968), *Black Protest: History, Documents, and Analyses 1916 to the Present*, Fawcett Books.

Green, G. (1971), *The New Radicalism: Anarchist or Marxist?* International Publishers.

Halstead, F. (1978), *Out Now! A Participant's Account of the American Movement Against the Vietnam War*, Monad Press.

Hayden, C. and King, M. (1965), 'Sex and Caste: A Kind of Memo', in *'Takin 'it to the Streets': a Sixties Reader* (A. Bloom and W. Breines, eds), Oxford University Press, New York, 1995, pp. 47–51.

Horowitz, D. (1996), 'Rethinking Betty Friedan…', *American Quarterly*, 48 (March).

Isserman, Maurice (1987), *'If I had a Hammer…': The Death of the Old Left and the Birth of the New Left*, Basic Books.

Kitchell, M., producer & director (1990), *Berkeley in the 1960s*, First Run Films.

Lipset, S.M. and Wolin, S. eds (1965), *The Berkeley Student Revolt: Facts and Interpretations*, Doubleday Anchor.

Matusow, A.J. (1984), *The Unraveling of America: A History of Liberalism in the 1960s*, Harper & Row.

McDermott, J. (1997), 'On the Origin of the Present World in the Defeat of "the 60s"', *Socialism and Democracy*, XI (Fall).

Miller, J. (1987), *'Democracy is in the Streets': From Port Huron to the Siege of Chicago*, Simon and Schuster.

Moody, A. (1968), *Coming of Age in Mississippi*, Dell Laurel.

Port Huron Statement (1962), See Miller, James (1987), Appendix.

Race, J. (1972), *War Comes to Long An: Revolutionary Conflict in a Vietnamese Province,* University of California Press.

Raskin. M.G. and B.B. Fall, eds (1965), *The Viet-Nam Reader*, Random House.

Reagan, R. (1982), *Statement on the Vietnam Conflict* (1982), Public Papers of the Presidents of the United States: Ronald Reagan, 1982, Washington DC, 1983), I, pp. 184–5.

Rorbagh, W.J. (1989), *Berkeley at War: the 1960s*, Oxford University Press.

Sale, K. (1973), *SDS*, Random House.

Schrecker, E. (1983), 'The Missing Generation', *Humanities in Society*, VI (Spring/Summer).

—— (1993), 'McCarthyism and the Decline of American Communism, 1945–1960', in *New Studies in the Politics and Culture of U.S. Communism* (eds M. Brown, R. Martin, F. Rosengarten and G. Snedeker).

—— (1998), *Many Are the Crimes: McCarthyism in America,* Little Brown.

SNCC (1964), 'Women in the Movement', in *'Takin' it to the Streets': a Sixties Reader* (eds A. Bloom and W. Breines) pp. 45–7.

—— (1966), 'Statement on Vietnam', in Grant (1986), pp. 416–18.

Weinstein, J. and Eakins, D.W., eds (1970), *For a New America: Essays in History and Politics from Studies on the Left*, Random House.

—— (1975), *Ambiguous Legacy: the Left in American Politics*, New Viewpoints/ Franklin Watts.

Wells, T. (1994), *The War Within: America's Battle over Vietnam*, University of California Press.

Young, M.B. (1991), *The Vietnam Wars, 1945–1990*, HarperCollins.

5 The Three New Lefts and their Legacies

Geoff Andrews

'We were all still on the escalator Progress, the whole world ascending towards prosperity. Did anyone challenge this happy optimism? I don't remember it. At the end of a century of grand revolutionary romanticism; frightful sacrifices for the sake of paradises and heavens on earth and the withering away of the state; passionate dreams of utopias and wonderlands and perfect cities; attempts at communes and commonwealths, at co-operatives and kibbutzes and kolhozes – after all this, would any of us have believed that most people in the world settle gratefully for a little honesty, a little competence in government?' So writes Doris Lessing in *Volume Two of My Autobiography 1949–1962* (Harper Collins, 1997: 368).

If it wasn't apparent before then the 'revolutionary' year 1989 seemed to mark the final end of the dreams of the New Left. Other moments, such as the failure of the left to benefit from the economic crisis of the mid-1970s and the rise of the New Right were already down as markers. The significance of 1989 however was far-reaching. Wrongly seen by many on the left as a mere escape from Stalinism, it signified the emergence of a quite new global politics which threatened to undermine traditional left–right polarities that had been consolidated around the capitalism–socialism divide in the framework of the Cold War and under the shadow of which the New Left developed. The different utopias of the New Left which attempted to revive the socialist idea such as 'libertarian socialism', 'creative Marxism', Althusserian structuralism, 'Socialist Internationalism', 'Marxist–feminism', 'Eurocommunism', appeared themselves as almost relics from another age. Together they became incorporated as the 'old socialism' – or indeed, paradoxically 'Old Left' – whose end projects were now thought unachievable. If further confirmation of the demise of the New Left were needed, then it seems one only has to look at the contemporary fortunes of some of its leading protagonists; those who helped to shape the aspirations, reading groups and demos of the period have either long departed the scene or else have been reincarnated as media pundits, born-again liberals or (arguably worst of all) career academics.

However to see the sixties and indeed the wider influence of the New Left as either irrelevant or its protagonists merely political fall guys for the New

Right is to misunderstand the contribution the ideas of this 'movement' continue to pose for contemporary politics. Moreover to see all the ideas, aspirations and cultural concerns of the New Left as having been replaced by the harsh realities of global capitalism or having no purchase on the contemporary shifts in economies, cultures and politics of western societies merely gives credence to postmodern cynicism as well as preventing us from learning from history in a reflective, non-dogmatic way.

It is certainly important to recognise the crisis of the grand narratives, that is the inability of those emancipatory projects of the western enlightenment – liberalism, social democracy and Marxism – to organise people's belief systems in the conditions of late modernity. In the wake of the 'post-isms' which increasingly shape the debate about the future of politics, the 'big issues' related to the emancipatory projects of the grand narratives are, rightly, interrogated; what remains from them, what still holds good in the reinvention of politics, gets much less attention. Yet if we look more carefully we find that the reinterpretation and application of older currents in new configurations will continue to inform political debate.

My main argument here therefore is that while the New Left, in what I see as its three moments, is no longer around to organise a new utopia, or bring about a new mass politics, or provide a global alternative to capitalism, released from its totalising ideological frameworks, it contains, in different ways, important comments on the direction of contemporary societies. Specifically what is common to the New Left which relates closely to current dilemmas are the projects of what I would call 'radical modernisation'. Radical modernisation included the need to democratise culture, a particular concern of the first New Left; to confront in different ways the new forms of power, strategy and control and the rise of new social movements that were taken up by the second New Left, and an engagement with the 'new times', the main concern of what I see as a third New Left.

Common defining features which united and distinguished the New Left can be summarised as follows. Firstly, the New Left developed as an alternative 'third way' between Stalinism and social democracy. Although never an organised movement, it sought political space outside orthodox political structures. Indeed in doing so it helped to redefine politics itself, providing a broader understanding of culture, and the importance of the autonomy of political movements. Secondly, it took as a starting-point the need to analyse and confront new forms of capitalism, which included at different times, the mass consumer society and technocratic managerialism, imperialism and latterly post-fordism. Thirdly, there was a need to move away from the state and to turn towards the sphere of civil society for solutions. Fourthly, the New Left rejected vanguardism and democratic

centralism; indeed it rejected most forms of centralised political organisation. 'Only connect', a phrase used as a criticism of the first New Left,
could now be seen in a more positive light to prefigure the looser political
structures that were becoming characteristic of contemporary societies.

Thus the history of the New Left in many ways illuminates some of the
major cultural, political and economic dilemmas of the 'long 1960's' as a
whole. This engagement with modernity I will argue should be seen as a
major organising theme that ran through the different projects of the New
Left. The underlying principle which gave expression to this was agency.
This was conceived in quite different ways. In the first New Left, for
example, which takes as its defining moment the period of 1956 and the
break with Stalinism as well as the onset of mass consumerism, it was the
cultural terrain which was seen as providing a new focus for emancipation.
For the second New Left, whose moment was '1968', the belief in agency
was emphasised by the concern with analysing new forms of state and
economic power and the need for the autonomy of the new social movements that grew in civil society. It was this sphere, independent of the
state, which was thought to be decisive for those movements such as
CND, the anti-Vietnam War movement, the feminist and workers control
movements of the 1970s and given theoretical justification in the works
of Marcuse, Althusser, Gramsci and Foucault for whom in different ways
the manufacturing of consent, and the 'relative autonomy' of ideological
struggles were the decisive areas of politics. For the third New Left, which
takes 1979 as its starting-point as a recognition of the crisis of the left and
the rise of the right in the late 1970s, the focus was on the 're-making
of the political', a broader concept of politics rooted in the multiple identities of individuals and the need to 'reconnect' the left with the diverse aspirations and activities of the people that were characteristic of 'New Times'.

These then are the themes which will organise my argument. I accept
that the New Left was a movement with a strong international flavour and
that the focus here will be limited to the British traditions. I also realise in
making this argument that some of the interesting complexities and rup-
tures between the different elements of the New Left may be underplayed;
this is not to deny them or to assume a coherence and continuity that didn't
exist, but to draw out what I believe to be the lasting legacies, written from
a position of hope and optimism.

THE FIRST NEW LEFT

The first New Left was characterised by an eclectic range of influences. It
combined the labour movement ethos of the dissident communists who

left in 1956, such as E.P. Thompson and John Saville, based in the North of England, with a more cosmopolitan and metropolitan chic of writers and university students (including Stuart Hall and Raphael Samuel) who met in places such as the Partisan Coffee House and Jimmy's Restaurant in Soho or student houses in Oxford. Its journals, *Universities and Left Review* (later *New Left Review*) and *The New Reasoner*, brought together a creative, humanist brand of Marxism, which distinguished their objectives from both the statist ideologies of orthodox Leninism and social democracy. As Peter Sedgewick, a left critic of the first New Left suggested, they 'brought ... an explicit commitment to class struggle, an iteration of the role of human agency as against impersonal historical process, be it gradual or cataclysmic, a devotion to relatively punctilious work' (Sedgewick, 1976: 135).

This emphasis on agency was apparent in many of the key texts of the time. In *Out of Apathy*, written in 1960, E.P. Thompson felt that the new consumer-driven affluence of contemporary capitalism, while maintaining the old inequalities, had encouraged new forms of apathy, resignation and political expediency. This needed to be met by a moral revolution which would release the capacity for 'democratic self-activity', a greater participation in decision-making and popular democratic control of the economy. He explicitly rejected forms of state monopoly, in the form of either the bureaucratic or technocratic features of social democracy or the dictatorship of the proletariat, while advocating the decentralisation of political power to the locality, abolition of the House of Lords, and reform of the House of Commons. His humanism extended to international affairs where he argued for the democratic self-determination of the third world. (Thompson, 1960; Chun, 1992: 47–51). The campaign for Nuclear Disarmament which had recently formed was to Thompson, in *The New Reasoner*, an 'assault against fatalism' (p. 5, quoted in Archer *et al.,* 1989: 7).

The necessity for working people to take control over their lives was further expanded by Thompson in 1963 in his *The Making of the English Working Class* in which agency rather than structure was recognised as being at the root of working class formation and development. In his Workers' Educational Association classes, which provided the backdrop to his work, Thompson challenged the empiricism and economism of orthodox scientific socialism which said nothing about the human and moral aspects of working-class experience. Thompson's interest in the work of William Morris reinforced the view that the ethical critique of capitalism should be at the heart of socialist values. This preference for the moral critique of capitalism over a more developed analysis of the economic system was recognised as a distinguishing feature by other members of the first New Left in retrospect as well as the basis for conflict with their immediate successors (Samuel, 1989: 46).

In a much publicised dispute with the theoreticists of the second New Left, who took over the editorship of *New Left Review* from 1962 – notably Perry Anderson – Thompson's work was regarded as a provincial and untheoretical contribution which made no attempt to interrogate contemporary forms of British capitalism. Anderson did not share Thompson's view of a native Marxist tradition and was not enthused by the traditions of the English labour movement. Thompson was involved in a 'moral protest' rather than a theoretical engagement, guilty of a 'messianic nationalism' in his attempts to redefine a progressive concept of Englishness. The battle here became one of structure and agency. Thompson, it was argued, had not addressed the structural questions that needed to be at the heart of any analysis of British society. In particular this included the backward and deferential political culture that had prevented the development of the political maturity of the working class. Anderson and his colleagues on the other hand, according to Thompson, had shifted towards theoretical abstraction and dogma and had separated theory from practice. While there were clear theoretical differences between the two that were taken further throughout the 1960s, following the growing influence of Althuserian structuralism, there was also a question of the difference in political allegiance and culture of the protagonists. The socialisation of Thompson *et al.* by the Communist Party of Great Britain (CPGB), as well as their links with the labour movement, were quite distinct from the more aloof and elitist postures of Anderson. On the other hand, the latter's interest in theories of power helped to provide a context for the later theoretical debates between Marxists in the 1970s, between for example Poulantzas and Miliband (Chun, 1992: 61–4).

The importance given to agency by the first New Left was further reflected in the political role attributed to intellectuals and as the basis for renewing the left at different moments. The first New Left was crucial in delivering a new concept of the intellectual, one closely resembling the organic, public, critical type associated with Gramsci (even though the latter's work was yet to become fully available). This was closely related to the 'organic' links between first New Left intellectuals and adult education. It was an explicit recognition of the new opportunities available to working people to achieve personal fulfilment. This encouragement of self-realisation and autonomy was rooted in an alternative philosophy of education, exemplified by the particular commitment to adult education made by members of the first New Left. Indeed as Tom Steele has argued the creation of the new discipline of cultural studies which reflected many of the academic concerns of New Left thinkers – most obvious in the Centre for Contemporary Cultural Studies, set up by Richard Hoggart – was a result of the struggles and alternative philosophy that had taken place in adult education; it was the outcome, Steele argues, of a 'political project of popular education amongst adults'. (Steele, 1997: 15). In addition to Saville and Thompson's work for the Workers' Educational Association, Raphael Samuel embarked on a 30-year association with Ruskin College, the college of the labour movement, and helped set up the History Workshop; Raymond Williams spent his early teaching time in extra-mural departments and took much of his inspiration for his work on culture from this and Richard Hoggart was succeeded by Stuart Hall as Director of the Centre for Contemporary Cultural Studies. Hall, a figure who appears in all the phases of the New Left, went on to become Professor of Sociology at the Open University. The importance then of being a committed and organic intellectual, linking intellectual work to popular movements, a phenomenon almost anathema to contemporary academic life, was a defining feature of the first New Left.

What this illustrated was the importance given by the first New Left to the way in which history was made by working people through their own experiences and contributions. The interrogation of popular culture was a further example of this and given much prominence as the route for emancipation. Indeed this sphere produced a pioneering and exceptional contribution from the first New Left thinkers. This approach found its way into a far-reaching analysis of the changing nature of post-war British society, the dangers as well as opportunities that modernity was bringing, the breaking down of the barriers between 'high' and 'low' culture; ultimately an interrogation and redefinition of the concept of culture itself. Michael Kenny identifies three reasons for this new attention given to culture. These were firstly the need to respond to the narrowness of Stalinism and Labourism when it came to cultural questions. Culture was inevitably reduced to the economic sphere, 'either as an appendage to more important considerations or as a purely epiphenomenal entity'. The second reason, according to Kenny, was the 'novelty' and 'specificity' of what was a period of tremendous cultural change. The third reason were the changes in popular culture which were transforming the landscape of societies (Kenny, 1995: 87).

This new emphasis on culture was taken up in the work of Richard Hoggart in *The Uses of Literacy* and Raymond Williams in his seminal works *Culture and Society* and *The Long Revolution*. Their concerns were with the implications of the major cultural transformations underway in western societies in what Eric Hobsbawm has termed the 'golden decades'.

For Hobsbawm working class consciousness had reached its peak by the end of the second world war yet by the 'golden years' of the 1960s and 1970s had been 'undermined' by 'the combination of secular boom, full employment and a society of genuine mass consumption (which) utterly transformed the lives of working class people in the developed countries and continued to transform it' (Hobsbawm, 1995: 306).

Hoggart's work is an attempt to come to terms with the effect of cultural changes on the lives of working-class people, the dilemmas brought by this onset of mass culture, such as the 'danger of reducing the larger part of the population to a condition of obediently receptive passivity, their eyes glued to television sets, pin-ups and cinema screens' (Hoggart, 1957: 316). He saw contradictory tendencies emerging. On the one hand, the breaking down of old class barriers had provided new opportunities, while on the other new types of conformity and degeneration were produced by the shift towards the commercialisation and standardisation of mass culture. Hoggart perceived a conflict between an 'earnest minority' who sought a critical engagement with the new mass culture, and a cynical working class majority.

Raymond Williams was also worried about the 'visible moral decline of the labour movement' (1983: 32). However, Williams remained optimistic about the prospects of change that cultural transformation could deliver. According to Williams we were engaged in a long-term struggle against the alienation of a consumer society from which the possibilities of a more democratic culture needed to emerge. Cultural expansion could enable not only the fulfilment of individual aspirations and talents, as an 'empowered learning community' but it also reinforced the need for democratic control of cultural institutions (Rustin, 1989: 118–28).

This particular engagement of the first New Left led them into a wide ranging debate on socio-cultural questions, including the debate with the Croslandite revisionists over the implications of changes in the post-war class structure, where it was argued crucially that the working class should not always be seen as on the 'receiving end of transmissions from an alien agency, whether as the objects of survey research, the beneficiaries of welfare and planning proposals, or the consumers of shoddy cultural goods' (Sedgewick, 1976: 137–8). The 'new classlessness in culture' therefore had brought positive and negative aspects. These were the negative aspects; however there was also evidence of what Hoggart referred to as a 'good classlessness' (Hoggart, 1957: 137) and the possibility of a common culture breaking down traditional divisions and forms of elitism, a situation made possible by more access to cultural forms such as the cinema, the extension of educational opportunity and more consumer power.

The legacy of the first New Left then remains the way in which aspects of modernity encouraged the ability of working people to intervene and extend control over their lives. They left many forms of power and control untouched and their concept of culture while addressing the 'personal' and 'subjective' in very specific ways (such as working class 'lived experience'), did not for example account for the significance of gender. Indeed Hoggart's concepts of community while containing a strong emphasis on the role of working class women, did not question in any depth the extent of inequality and patriarchy. With the exception of isolated examples such as Doris Lessing's *The Golden Notebook* the position of women got scant attention in the first New Left, nor even in 'The May Day Manifesto', a political intervention from a reunion of first New Leftists published in 1967. It was one example of an absence of theories of power, an omission developed by the second New Left.

THE SECOND NEW LEFT

The second New Left differed sharply in its view of the impact of capitalist modernisation. Indeed its approach grew out of the critique of the historical, 'populist', 'moralist' and 'culturalist' (as it saw it) perceptions of Thompson and others. The second New Left, which was initially characterised by the new generation of intellectuals who took control of *New Left Review*, was quite a different grouping; younger, more privileged backgrounds, less assimilated into – indeed, at times openly hostile to – the political culture of British socialism and less connected to the organic movements that had helped shape the priorities of their predecessors. Their inspiration was from theory rather than history and more European rather than 'native' English. The second New Left, however, was much broader in scope and it is difficult to establish close points of contact; it is better to see them as a looser set of groups who had some defining features. These derived from the new analyses of capitalism and in particular the renaissance in new forms of western Marxism – notably the works of Althusser, Marcuse, Gramsci and Foucault. Although there was a rise of Trotskyist groups during this period, with the exception of the International Socialists (particularly at its most productive and creative period around 1967–68), these reverted to more orthodox Leninist forms of organisation. The movements that were inspired by these thinkers included the second wave feminism, the students' movement, the workers' control movement and Eurocommunism and it is these that I will consider.

These movements' view of radical modernisation stemmed from their analysis of the power structures of modern capitalism, which in different ways threw up important 'contradictions'; for example the extension of liberal rights and social democratic welfare reform had failed to address the position of women, let alone alleviate poverty and social inequality, while the rise of consumerism had brought new cultural and technocratic forms of control and alienation. The state itself had become bureaucratised and its legitimacy increasingly open to question. What was the nature of power relations in contemporary (or 'late') capitalism? Was the state still the instrument of a particular class or did it operate with 'relative autonomy'? How, in a society characterised by mass culture and an extension of civil society, was consent 'manufactured'? What other forms of power do modern capitalist societies produce and what are the terrains and positions, in which this power is to be exercised? And, fundamentally, what social forces and movements exist to be organised as a challenge to these power structures? These were the questions that dominated this part of the New Left, given of course greater focus and optimism by the 'moment' of 1968, in which 'revolution' was once more on the agenda. There were many different responses to these questions which reflected different sections of the second New Left and which often found themselves in conflict with each other, for example, between the group around *New Left Review* (such as Blackburn, Ali, Anderson and Nairn) and others such as the younger generation of communists in the CPGB.

The important analysis which pre-occupied the group around *New Left Review* was the deep-seated conservative culture of Britain's class society. According to this 'Nairn–Anderson thesis', the lack of a hegemonic bourgeoisie (and specifically a bourgeois revolution) had sustained deference and forms of social hierarchy that preserved a backward and antiquarian political system and culture. In addition the lack of an effective British Marxism had meant that the working class, despite having been 'made' earlier than in other European countries, was unable to accede to its historical mission. Instead it was shaped by a variety of reformist ideologies compatible with the development of capitalism and given credibility, it was argued, by E.P. Thompson's romanticism. The working class had shown all the signs of a deferential culture, with no motivation for revolution, a condition reinforced by the reformist, parliamentarist, labourist and corporatist ideologies of the left which Tom Nairn and others spent much time analysing. As Anderson put it: 'a supine bourgeoisie produced a subordinate proletariat' (Anderson, 1964: 39).

As is evident from the conflict between Thompson and Anderson alluded to above the differences between the approaches of the two New

Lefts in this context is quite clear. The somewhat elitist and obscurantist (and certainly less engaged) approach of the second New Leftists around *New Left Review* took it away from the humanist, activist elements of the first New Left. This shouldn't suggest that it was completely isolated from movements; indeed in the aftermath of 1968 the analysis shifted towards what were becoming 'new social forces'. Tariq Ali's autobiographical reflections, *Street Fighting Years*, reads as a left-wing adventure story of the times. What changed things of course were the events of 1968. 'Be realistic; demand the impossible', may not have been on the lips of all student activists and political movements of the time, but it illustrates the change of mood. Students in particular were at the forefront of activities at the LSE – as they were to a higher degree in France in the same year and Italy a year later – while the Prague Spring was the defining moment for an emerging generation of (Euro) communists (Andrews, 1995).

New analyses of 'student power' saw students as a new social group that had benefited from the expansion of higher education and who had not been conditioned to the same extent by the mass culture. It was not only the militancy of the student movement (and its Red Bases, occupations and demos) it was a wider self-confidence of an emergence in the political generation. The era of the 'counter course' provided a theoretical critique of the nature of power in higher education, taking further some of the concerns of Hoggart's 'earnest minority'. Reading groups brought dynamism and an overlap of study and politics, a development extended to a much higher degree in the Communist University of London which met from 1969 until 1981. The Eurocommunist-led Broad Left took control of the National Union of Students, and delivered a new form of pluralism and an alternative to careerist Labour students.

The new spirit of optimism and activism was reflected in other 'new social movements' such as feminism. The revival of feminism in its more militant and creative forms in the late sixties was a consequence of changes in the socio-economic structure and in particular the greater freedom that had come from the pill, abortion and the rise in women's employment. The theoretical input of Marxist thinkers like Althusser who provided a 'structuralist' analysis of women's position, or Gramsci who gave specific attention to non-class forms of oppression within ruling hegemony, gave feminism new frameworks for challenging power inequalities. More grassroots movements, including that of the History Workshop, gave a voice to women, the first women's liberation movement conference being held at Ruskin College in 1969. The transformation that was taking place within the left itself offered new opportunities for women. As Sassoon has argued, feminism posed a real challenge to the left to modernise and transform its structures, 'to recast its own ideological framework, abandoning the unspoken axiom that the socialist movement was a movement of men which women could join on men's terms and, in exchange, receive men's support. This new movement of universal emancipation required a demasculinised politics; a socialism for women and men' (Sassoon, 1996: 422). The publication of Juliet Mitchell's 'Women: The Longest Revolution', in *New Left Review* (*NLR* 40, Nov–Dec 1966) probably the first defining second-wave feminist text, was important in taking the project of the second New Left forward.

The Institute For Workers Control provided the focus for another social movement concerned with strategies for power. It had some roots in the first New Left where democratic control of industry, based on alternatives to bureaucratic nationalisation, was put forward in the debate over Harold Wilson's plans for modernisation. The Workers Control Movement identified a new route to power and a way of challenging capital by labour. It took on a new significance with the greater bargaining power of the trade unions and the victory of the left within the biggest unions from the late sixties, aided by movements such as the Liaison Committee for Defence of Trade Unions. The sit-ins at the Upper Clyde Shipbuilders in the early 1970s and at Lucas Aerospace in the late 1970s gave it more impetus and helped create the conditions for the Bullock Report on Industrial Democracy (1977), though ultimately little came of this. It would be naive to link these developments with later interest in stakeholding, except to say that there was a continuity in the belief in workers' ability to participate in decision-making as a way of exercising control over their working lives.

There was greater emphasis on strategy in the latter period of the second New Left, yet it continued the New Left tradition of poor collective organisation. Perhaps the nearest expression of any perceived coming together of class and social forces was the adoption of the 'broad democratic alliance' strategy of the CPGB at its 1977 Congress, a partial recognition of the influence of Gramsci in seeking a coalition between the working class and its allies. Yet this was too little too late; the CPGB itself was showing signs of terminal decline and division while the rest of the Left was starting to fragment.

The decline of the second New Left became clear around the late 1970s when it become evident – if it wasn't already – that the left would not be the beneficiaries of the economic crisis. The Eurocommunist input which had brought some changes to the CPGB's politics fell away with the defeat of the 'historic compromise' in 1978 which had brought the Italian Communist Party close to power in Italy. Leading feminists meanwhile showed their impatience with the rest of the left and attempted to 'go beyond the fragments', which merely confirmed that the divisions within the feminist movement reflected the rest of the left. And, of course, there was Thatcherism.

THE THIRD NEW LEFT

The failure to go 'beyond the fragments' was not merely a problem for feminism, it was at the heart of the left's overall dilemmas. Moreover, the continuing changes associated with late modernity: for example, the decline of class as an organising principle of beliefs and identity, indicated the wider problem of marrying socialism with an increasingly diverse set of aspirations and concerns. Black politics, along with other movements associated with identity, was becoming by the mid-to-late seventies disconnected from the left; the dispute over 'black sections' in the Labour Party in the mid-eighties being one example of this. The working class itself, seeing its conditions being transformed in a variety of ways, was beginning to show much weaker alignment to its traditional political base. In what should be seen as the defining analysis of the third New Left, Eric Hobsbawm in his seminal Marx Memorial Lecture – 'The Forward March of Labour Halted' – argued that the achievements of the labour movement had come to a halt 30 years previously (ie in the late 1940s/early 1950s), echoing perhaps Raymond Williams' argument about the 'visible moral decline of the labour movement' twenty years earlier. Since this time the character of the working class had undergone major transformation, becoming more heterogeneous, more feminised, with greater demarcation between different trades. This led to greater sectionalism among workers. Despite the rise of militancy in the late 1960s and early 1970s, Hobsbawm argued, this shouldn't be interpreted as an indication of political radicalism. Indeed, he argued that many of the disputes had been 'economistic' in nature – confined mainly to wage struggles – and reflected a growth in sectionalism between different workers on an unprecedented scale, resulting in decreased class consciousness and solidarity. Hobsbawm ended his argument with the following stark warning to the left and labour movement:

> If the labour and socialist movement is to recover its soul, its dynamism and its historical initiative, we as Marxists, must do what Marx would certainly have done; to recognise the novel situation in which we find ourselves, to analyse it realistically and concretely, to analyse the

reasons, historical and otherwise, for the failures as well as the successes of the labour movement and to formulate not only what we would want to do, but what can be done. We should have done this even while we were waiting for British capitalism to enter its period of dramatic crisis. We cannot afford not to do it now that it has. (Hobsbawm, 1981: 19)

Hobsbawm's argument of course appeared initially before the 1979 election, the result of which took him into a deeper analysis of the predicament of the left and 'Labour's Lost Millions' (Hobsbawm, 1983). It follows then that the second defining feature of the third New Left was the significance it attached to Thatcherism and the long-term implications this brought for the future of the left. It was here in the pages of *Marxism Today* that the Gramscian analysis of Thatcherism as a 'hegemonic project' was formulated. With its roots in the organic crisis of British society, its ability to challenge the unresolved contradictions of social democracy, to form a historic block out of the conjunctural opportunities of the moment, Thatcherism had been able to create a new common sense around anti-collectivism and anti-statism, resulting in what Stuart Hall called 'authoritarian populism' (Hall, 1983). Not only was this an indication of the success of the right as a new form of conservative rule, it indicated that a major schism between the left and its traditional constituencies had taken place. The tasks set by the third New Left in the group which had consolidated around Martin Jacques's editorship of *Marxism Today* from 1977 could be described in this way: how can the left reconnect with changing values and popular aspirations? This took them into a deeper analysis of British society and culture eventually leading to the much talked of 'New Times' analysis.

At the heart of this argument was the view that the left was out of touch with the grain of cultural and social change. The third New Left followed its earlier predecessors in emphasising the importance of culture. Here the 'cultural is political approach' defined by Chun (1992: 26), took on a more concrete level. Gone were the more romantic interpretations of the working class as labour movement heroes; here the workers had taken on a variety of identities, as consumers, partners, as individuals. The concerns about the impact of consumerism were not as evident in the third New Left. Although the view of capitalist consumerism was not uncritical, it saw the improvements in living standards such as greater choice and mobility as providing new forms of positive identity. The focus of *Marxism Today* became increasingly cultural, the boundaries between 'the political' and 'the cultural' breaking down all the time, in the style and format of the journal as well as in the nature of its analysis. *Marxism Today* took on an appraisal of trends in consumption, sport, fashion, sexuality and soap operas as well as the more traditional political topics. It even became part of the consumption cycle itself offering 'MT credit cards', mugs, T-shirts and even suggesting, in the late 1980s, a passion for 'designer Marxism'. At times it toyed with the older lefts (including the first and second New Lefts, although its main target was labourism) illustrating perhaps what it perceived to be the massive divide between the culture of the left and that of the people it claimed to represent. This brought much resentment from others on the left, including from those of the first New Left. John Saville, in his survey of the 1988 issues, found *Marxism Today* to be full of 'shallow and superficial trivia', and its general preference – as he saw it – for culture over politics and economics he found 'an exceedingly dispiriting experience' (Saville, 1990: 35–59).

There was, however, a serious political point being made. The left, if you like, had failed to come to terms with the extent of 'the long revolution'. According to Stuart Hall in *The Culture Gap*, while negative aspects of the new consumerism remained, there were positive, even emancipatory sides to the cultural changes which the left needed to address:

> A labour movement which cannot identify with what is concrete and material in those popular aspirations and expropriate them from identification with the private market and private appropriation will look, increasingly, as if it's trapped nostalgically in ancient cultural modes, failing to imagine socialism in twentieth century terms and images, and increasingly out of touch with where people are at. (Hall, 1984)

But it was the pioneering 'New Times' analysis that gave the third New Left its most critical engagement with modernity. First developed between 1988–1989 it was an attempt to analyse the new 'settlements' and then to propose a radical view of modernisation in opposition to that offered by the New Right. Thatcherism according to Hall had pursued a form of 'regressive modernisation': that is it situated its politics in what it perceived (rightly) to be fundamental socio-economic, global and cultural trends of, if not a new epoch, then a very distinctive moment in late modernity. Thatcherism, through its engagement with these 'New Times', or post-fordist economies based on the flexible specialisation of work and the international division of labour, information technology and the rise of consumptions proclaimed the inevitability of the market, the realities of individualism and the end of collective ideologies. Yet, there was an alternative scenario if the left were to engage with the new times: a chance to pursue a radical rather than regressive modernisation.

Essentially this was to be located in a new radical and pluralist politics which took as its theoretical starting-point the new social subject. The experience of the GLC in the mid-eighties gave it a political legitimacy, while the extending myriad of activities going on within civil society gave momentum to an idea of radical pluralism or radical democracy. Here the emphasis on agency is paramount; the decentring of the individual into more fragmented and unstable multiple selves came into sharp conflict with the earlier subjects of the individual-as-worker. As Hall says, 'New Times are both "out there", changing our conditions of life, and "in here", working on us. In part it is "us" who are being "re-made".' But such a conceptual shift presents particular problems for the Left. The conventional culture and discourses of the left, with its stress on 'objective con-tradictions', 'impersonal structures' and processes that work 'behind men's (sic) backs', have disabled us from confronting the subject dimension in politics in any very coherent way' (Hall, 1989: 120).

The end of *Marxism Today* in 1991 meant that many of these influences fragmented. It had not succeeded in providing a strategy for the revival of the left, only the critique that explained its predicament. Yet in retrospect the traditions of the third New Left have had more of a bearing on contemporary politics than was first apparent. Their own contribution towards modernisation had some impact on the Blair transformation in the Labour Party, particularly in the need to break out of labourism, to modernise the party and to situate it in the wider culture. Blair [himself a contributor to *Marxism Today* in its later years], often speaks a similar language of 'projects' and 'moods' and 'civil society' and, at least in some areas such as welfare reform, is not afraid of heresy; he was, after all, the '*Marxism Today* candidate' (Jacques/Hall, 1997). Like *Marxism Today*, Blair took as his defining moment the defeats of the left in the early 1980s and comes across strongly as a strategic politician (Andrews, 1997).

This has led to a common assumption that the 'new times' analysis paved the way for the emergence and success of New Labour: that the modernisers of *Marxism Today*, in effect, had a parental responsibility for the modernising positions of the 'Blair Project' (Freedland, 1998). Indeed one of *Marxism Today*'s later luminaries, Geoff Mulgan, is now a key adviser in the Downing Street Policy Unit, while another, Charlie Leadbeater, was one of the first to theorise New Labour's idea of the 'Third Way'. However, while there may be some close continuities – notably the critique of aspects of the traditional left – key differences can be detected, between the MT'ers and New Labour. These primarily concern the scope of modernisation. For Martin Jacques writing nine months before the election of 1997, Blair clearly had a 'project for the party'; what he lacked however was a 'project for the country': in other words, according to Jacques, there was no vision of how Britain would be a different place or of how the Labour government intended to engage with cultural, social and economic change (Jacques, 1996).

In October 1998 a one-off issue of *Marxism Today* returned to offer its analysis of the first 18 months of the Blair government. The collection of articles from Hobsbawm, Hall and Tom Nairn among others highlighted a deeper, more significant difference between New Labour and the traditions of the New Left as a whole. This was the contrast between the New Left's emphasis on the constraints of 'meta–politics', in which the global economy and its ideological and cultural frameworks remains the barometer for constraining social policy and the possibility of political invention and that of New Labour's 'Third Way', in which the emphasis shifts away from the 'bigger picture' of left versus right and economic conflict to 'modernising' initiatives at the 'micro' level, where pragmatism looks set to replace ideology (Giddens, 1998: Mouffe, 1998).

WHAT'S LEFT OF THE NEW LEFT?

Donald Sassoon in 1996 has argued that it is too early to judge the impact of the 1960s. If we try to analyse the impact of that decade we find contradictory modernising trends, which suggest both a consolidation of New Left traditions as well as a vacuum that could be filled by looking again at the different New Left legacies. The election of the Blair government in 1997 has shown a commitment to modernisation in many areas, notably the move away from the state towards civil society for solutions, a determination to modernise forms of governance and to decentralise power. Here the constitutional agenda of Charter 88, a pressure-group set up by members of the New Left under the influence of the 'Nairn–Anderson' thesis has come to fruition. It is some irony that the more theoreticist leanings of the second New Left should result 30 years later in one of the more practical forms of political modernisation. The Blair government has tried to construct an alternative notion of Britishness, particularly in the wake of the death of Princess Diana, but it has been limited. If *Marxism Today* still had still been around at this time, there would no doubt have been a 'special issue' on the death of Princess Diana, as an indication of the contradictory cultural, national and political themes it raised.

However, while there may be some close links between the modernising projects of the third New Left and the Blair government, there are many differences. Blair's concept of modernisation has accepted much of the neo-liberal framework including a populist endorsement of meritocracy, expressed at a cultural level by the Millennium Dome, 'BritPop' and 'Cool Britannia'. It remains conservative in its view of community, preferring the safety of Middle England as its cultural yardstick by which to measure the possibility of change, and is yet to articulate a convincing vision of a more fluid, culturally diverse, society.

In the spheres of education – particularly higher education – we see more evidence of the 'long revolution' envisaged by Raymond Williams, as we move from an 'elite' to a 'mass' system, with the right to university education now becoming almost a hallmark of citizenship. Yet the institutions of higher education – together with other cultural institutions – are 'over-ripe' for democratic reform. The bureaucratic and technocratic trends taking place within universities are characteristic in many ways of Wilsonite modernisation. For those inspired by the traditions of the New Left much scope exists here for the kind of participative ideals and philosophy of education that characterised the commitment of members of the first New Left to Adult Education in order to challenge the shallow ethos and priorities of the new managerialism.

A combination of demographic, economic and educational factors suggest that it will be women who will shape the social agenda of the next decades. The transformation in the role of women has been one of the most significant social changes of the last 30 years. More evidence has also been produced to indicate greater egalitarianism between men and women of a new generation (Wilkinson and Mulgan, 1997). However, the 'longest revolution', as Mitchell described it over 30 years ago has a long way to go, something made clear by the emergence of communitarian thinking – itself a reaction to the 1960s – and the reassertion of traditional notions of the family.

Globalisation must present the most significant dilemma for the project of 'radical modernisation'. The benefits of a more global culture have brought greater pluralism along the lines suggested by the third New Left and have confirmed perhaps that one legacy of the sixties is the decline of the liberal enlightenment subject, rather than its extension. On the other hand the relentless shifts towards globalisation and the assimilation of politics into economics, confirming in many ways the validity of New Left Marxist critiques of contemporary capitalism, continue to create real problems of democratic control. It is this question of how to rediscover the importance of agency, perhaps the New Left's most recurrent political ideal, which remains central to the project of radical modernisation.

REFERENCES

Anderson, P. (1964), 'Origins of the Present Crisis', *New Left Review* 23 Jan/Feb 1964.
Anderson, P. (1980), *Arguments Within English Marxism*, Verso.
Andrews, G. (1995), 'Young Turks and Old Guard' in *Opening the Books* (eds G. Andrews, N. Fishman and K. Morgan), Pluto.
Andrews, G. (1997), 'Curiosity Free Learning', *New Statesman* August 29.
Andrews, G. (1997), 'Breaking Free: Tomorrow's Intellectuals and New Labour', *Renewal* Vol. 5, No. 1 February.
Archer, R., Bubeck, D., Glock, H. *et al.* (eds) (1989), *Out of Apathy: Voices of the New Left Thirty Years On*, Verso.
Chun, L. (1992), *The British New Left*, Edinburgh University Press.
Freedland, J. (1998), 'The Marxists Return to Pronounce on the Fruit of Their Ideas: Blairism', *The Guardian* September 9.
Giddens, A. (1994), *Beyond Left and Right*, Polity Press.
Gidders, A. (1998), *The Third Way: Renewing Social Democracy*, Polity Press.
Gray, J. (1995), *Enlightenment's Wake*, Routledge.
Gray, J. (1997), *Endgames*, Polity Press.
Hall, S. (1984), 'The Culture Gap', *Marxism Today*, January.
Hall, S. (1989), 'The Meaning of New Times' in *New Times* (eds S. Hall and M. Jacques), Lawrence and Wishart.
Hall, S. (1996), 'New Ethnicities', in *Stuart Hall: Critical Dialogues in Cultural Studies* (eds D. Morley and K.H. Chen), Routledge.
Hall, S. and Jacques, M. (1989), *New Times*, Lawrence and Wishart.
Hall, S. and Jacques, M. (1983), *The Politics of Thatcherism*, Lawrence and Wishart.
Hobsbawm, E.J. (1995), *Age of Extremes*, Michael Joseph.
Hobsbawm, E.J., Jacques, M. and Mutheam, F. (eds) (1981), *The Forward March of Labour Halted*, Verso.
Hobsbawm, E.J. (1983), 'Labour's Lost Millions', *Marxism Today*, October.
Hoggart, R. (1957), *The Uses of Literacy*, Chatto and Windus.
Jacques, M. (1996), 'His Project for the party is a triumph, but what about his project for the country?' *The Guardian* September 26.
Jacques, M. and Hall, S. (1997), 'Cultural Revolutions', *New Statesman* December 5.
Kenny, M. (1995), *The First New Left: British Intellectuals After Stalin*, Lawrence and Wishart.
Kenny, M. (1996), 'After the Deluge', *Soundings* Autumn.
Laclau, E. (1996), *Emancipations*, Verso.
Mitchell, J. (1966), 'Women: the Longest Revolution', *New Left Review*, 40, Nov–Dec 1966.
Mouffe, C. (1998), 'The Radical Centre', *Soundings*, Issue 9, Summer 1998.
Mulgan, G. (ed.) (1997), *Life After Politics,* Fontana.
Rustin, M. (1989), 'The New Left as a Social Movement' in *Out of Apathy* (eds R. Archer, D. Bubeck, H. Glock, *et al.*), Verso.
Samuel, R. (1989), 'Born-Again Socialism', in *Out of Apathy* (eds R. Archer, D. Bubeck, H. Glock, *et al.*), Verso, pp. 41–57.
Sassoon, D. (1996), *One Hundred Years of Socialism*, I.B. Tauris.

Saville, J. (1990), 'Marxism Today: An Anatomy' Socialist Register, *Merlin Press*, pp. 35–59.

Sedgewick, P. (1976), 'The Two New Lefts' in *The Left in Britain 1956–1968* (ed. D. Widgery), Penguin.

Segal, L. (1989), 'The Silence of Women in the New Left' in *Out of Apathy* (eds R. Archer, D. Bubeck, H. Glock, *et al.*), Verso, pp. 114–16.

Steele, T. (1997), *The Emergence of Cultural Studies*, Lawrence and Wishart.

Thompson, E.P. (1960), *Out of Apathy*, New Left Books.

Thompson, E.P. (1963), *The Making of the English Working Class*, Victor Gollancz.

Wilkinson, H. and Mulgan, G. (1997), 'Freedom's Children and the rise of generational politics' in *Life After Politics* (ed. G. Mulgan), Fontana, pp. 213–21.

Williams, R. (1983), *Towards 2000*, Chatto and Windus.

Williams, R. (1958), *Culture and Society*, Chatto and Windus.

Williams, R. (1968), *May Day Manifesto*, Penguin.

Williams, R. (1965), *The Long Revolution*, Penguin.

6 The New Right and the 1960s: the Dialectics of Liberation

Richard Cockett

Like every other decade, there were several stories to the 1960s and those who lived through it emerged with their own narratives, their own singular version of events. What is so striking about the 1960s, however, which marks it out from any comparable era in modern British history, is just how different those narratives proved to be, as if there were two or more tribes living together, side by side, who spent ten years barely noticing each other. On the one hand, the most persuasive and recognisable narrative which has survived through to the 1990s is what I shall call the 'populist' narrative, of the 1960s – as the decade was transfigured into the generic term 'sixties', the age of Carnaby Street, Woodstock, the Beatles, drugs, hippies and the transformation in sexual and moral manners. In so far as the sixties means anything today, it is the populist narrative that matters, particularly to the young – our contemporary pop culture is suffused with elaborate references to the iconic pop stars and songs of that era. For them, as for most people, the sixties has gently subsided into popular imagination as a collage of revolting students, permissiveness and personal freedom.

However, to most people who lived through the 1960s, the above picture would be scarcely recognisable as an account of their ordinary lives. There has always been a debate as to whether 'the sixties' as 'populist' narrative was not in fact, confined to a bedsit in Hampstead and as far as the political classes were concerned, it certainly was. You can trawl all the memoirs and biographies of the politicians of all parties for the 1960s in vain for any reference to the 'populist' narrative; there is sometimes a genuflection towards the Beatles, but that's about it. The 'high political' narrative, as I shall call it, is an unremitting and depressing story of balance of payments crises, devaluation, economic stringency and the twists and turns of the embattled Wilson governments. As for the 'sixties' of modern memory, it might just as well never have happened. Aaron Copland once advised that if you want to know about the sixties, listen to the Beatles. But that will clearly only give you a very partial account as the nearest that the denizens of Whitehall and Westminster ever got to a psychedelic experience was watching the reserves melt away in 1967. Never did a generation of political leaders understand or know so little about the times that they lived through.

Of course, the two narratives occasionally intersected, but usually as broad comedy. In his diaries the comparatively youthful Minister for Technology, Tony Benn, proudly records how he even removed his jacket to observe a student 'debate' at the LSE, only to sound like a diligent anthropologist analysing a newly discovered species of ape.[1] Very few realised that there was a gap to be bridged, let alone attempted to do anything about it. Benn was one on the left who sought to do so, his diaries chronicling his steady dissillusionment with Whitehall-minded, technocratic ethos of Wilsonianism and from 1970 he became increasingly eager to embrace the counter-culture politics of the 1960s to re-invigorate British Socialism in the 1970s and early 1980s. Enoch Powell attempted to do the same for the right, channelling the anger felt by many traditionalists and conservatives (with big and little Cs) at the onward march of multiculturism and the dreaded permissiveness into a new kind of Toryism. 'Powellism', of which more later, was the right-wing mirror of Bennism and both doctrines, if that isn't to dignify two political arguments that were often incoherent, owed much to their authors' different reactions to the sixties. But they were the exception. Parliamentarians could hardly escape registering the anti-Vietnam protests even if they had wanted to, but on the whole their attitude was one of ignorance and hostility, especially on the Conservative benches. Neither is this very surprising; the political mindset of the ruling political class of the 1960s had been forged in the ideological struggles and debates of the 1930s and 1940s, and they merely carried the intellectual battlelines of the so-called 'Devil's Decade' into the 1960s with them. Like the eponymous general, they were busy fighting the battles of previous generations, which is why there is such a clear sense of disjuncture between the politics of desire and the politics of Westminster. It is remarkable that Britain had to wait until 1997 for a Prime Minister, Tony Blair, who was happy to carry the legacy of the 1960s (including the regulation guitar) into high office with him. Mrs Thatcher yearned for the certainties of the 1920s, or even the Victorian era, while John Major harked back to the 1950s Britain of the corner shop and the Great Western Railway. Most politicians fix their political bearings at an early age and seldom change much; a high degree of intellectual inflexibility is a prerequisite for party politics. In this respect, the 1960s was little different from any other decade.

Most politicians and their apparatchiks who were to emerge as the leaders of the New Right by the end of the 1970s (and Powell was never, politically, one of them) shared this political tin ear for the cultural and moral texture of the sixties. In this sense, the sixties had very little impact on them at all. Mrs Thatcher's first marital home was in a flat off the King's Road in the 1950s, and after a suburban interlude the family moved back to a more substantial house in Flood Street, a block away from their old flat, in 1970. The new Minister for Education was obviously appalled by what had happened in the interim, as the prim, middle-class Chelsea of her youth had transformed itself into the epicentre of the cultural revolution. She records in her memoirs: 'Eastern mysticism, bizarre clothing and indulgence in hallucinatory drugs emerged. I found Chelsea a very different place. ... I had mixed feelings about what was happening. There was a vibrancy and talent, but this was also in large degree a world of make-believe. A perverse pride was taken in Britain about our contribution to these trends. Carnaby Street in Soho, the Beatles, the mini-skirt and the maxi-skirt were the new symbols of "Swinging Britain". And they did indeed prove good export earners. The trouble was that they concealed the real economic weaknesses. ...'[2] In this way the sixties could be reduced to the balance sheets of political economy, dismissing any inherent meaning of these events as merely 'perverse'. The criteria for judging the sixties were fixed firmly in another age, another place; 1920s Grantham. Norman Tebbit, another putative member of the New Right, was attempting to get into national politics in the late 1960s, and was finally selected for Epping in 1969. His adoption speech only dealt with the 1960s at one point when, towards the end, he came to the subject of 'Law and Order and the so-called permissive society'. (It is instructive that, even then, the politics of the 'liberation of desire' was seen as a 'problem of law and order'.) Tebbit said: 'Some parts of this permissiveness – I suspect those of sexual morals, particularly – are part of a cycle of fashion, and will turn back before long. Pornography, I think, will become a bore. Exhibitionist and erotic shows will become as passé as the Dancing Years – and Shakespeare will still fill the theatres.'[3] He reflected the view of many Conservatives that the natural hierarchy of values would remain intact, as the natural order of things; the discovery that one of the artistic legacies of the 1960s was that Shakespeare could just be updated and even, in the hands of a new generation of theatre directors, still fill the theatres by becoming sexy was to keep Tebbit in paid employ as the most visible opponent of what he perceived to be the corrupting values of the 1960s for the next 30 years. Like many Tories, he is still wishing the 1960s would just go away, and that society could thus be allowed to revert to the 1950s nirvana of monogamy and hot cocoa. Most New Right Conservative politicians of Tebbit's generation either pretended that the sixties had never happened or that it was just a temporary aberration – to their cost, as they found out in the 1990s.

Essentially, then, the New Right – that cluster of politicians, economists, journalists, businessman and writers who gathered round Mrs Thatcher in the 1980s[4] – conformed to the general political ignorance of the 1960s. They were chiefly concerned with reversing what they saw as the historic and misguided electoral verdict in favour of economic collectivism of 1945 – their intellectual crusade was already well advanced by the 1960s. The New Right that emerged in the late 1970s could claim a long provenance; even by the beginning of the 1960s the sacred texts had already been written, the high priests identified and the foot-soldiers for freedom (as Hayek had dubbed them) had been slogging it out in the academic and political trenches for years. The New Right might only have received its journalistic sobriquet in 1968, but by that time it was already a fully formed intellectual, if not quite political, force. The 'Austrian School' of economists, notably Ludwig Von Mises, had provided the crucial critique of Socialism in the 1920s, Hayek had penned his biblical denunciation of Keynesianism and the 'middle way' in 1944 and Popper's attack on historicism had been published in *The Open Society and its Enemies in 1945.* Hayek's international liberal debating society, the Mont Pelerin Society, had been formed in 1947 and the Institute of Economic Affairs, the fount of so much that was to make up 'Thatcherism', had been going since 1955. By the 1960s, under the evangelical stewardship of messrs. Fisher, Seldon and Harris, the IEA was churning out pamphlets in favour of privatisation and Trades Union reform, the basic gruel of New Right politics. Keith Joseph had begun writing in *The Times* and the *Financial Times,* helped by the impish intellectual dissident Alfred Sherman, on the need for a more 'free-market' approach in government. And in December 1967, Milton Friedman of the 'Chicago School' propounded the ideas of Monetarism, backed by decades of empirical research on the US money supply, to the 80th annual meeting of the American Economic Association. Most of the intellectual ammunition used against the collapsing social democratic consensus in the 1970s was, by then, getting on for 20 or 30 years old – and just as out of date, according to the critics. To the New Right as it was then constituted, the 1960s was important in affirming the follies of economic mismanagement by planning and Keynesianism, but the same could be said of the 1940s and 1950s and would be said of the 1970s. In this sense, the 1960s was no more than another decade's indictment of the ruling politico-economic wisdoms, merely adding further empirical proof against the reigning 'post-war consensus' which neither major political party particularly wanted, but which both found themselves forced to live with, boxed in as they were by the intractable trinity of the Cold War, Britain's post-war impoverishment and the electoral popularity of a burgeoning Welfare State.

So, in an important sense, at the high 'political' level, the sixties was relatively unimportant to the New Right, merely confirming all their gloomiest economic forebodings. In as far as the New Right engaged with the sixties at a 'populist', or cultural level, it was, as we shall see, as a reaction *against* most of what the sixties came to stand for. This was to give Thatcherism its high moral tone, its Gladstonian sense of political earnestness. If she had ever had the time or the inclination to step out of her Jaguar to wander down the King's Road by the late 1980s she would doubtless have been pleased to note her old stamping ground filled with retail outlets like Next and Gap to dress the new *working* class rather than the hippy boutiques of an earlier era. Although the Thatcherite *kulturkampf* took second place to its economics, it was still an important element. In the long run the sixties was certainly to be of considerable importance to both the success, in the 1980s, of Thatcherism, and to its failure in the 1990s. The sixties unleashed various forces which aided and sustained the revolution in political economy in the 1980s, but it also unlocked attitudes and movements which New Right conservatism was antithetical to and would struggle to, and eventually fail, to contain. These subterranean forces at work were little understood at the time and were to take several decades to work their way through society. For the New Right the aberrant decade of the sixties would become both an unintended blessing and a curse.

In short, the contradictory legacy of the sixties of the New Right was a function of the contradictory nature of New Right conservatism, epito- mised by Mrs Thatcher; an economic liberal but a social and moral conser- vative. Such an ideology could work with the grain of the 1960s when it came to the economic aspirations of self-determinism epitomised by the self-made fashion designers and pop-moguls of that era (displaying laud- able amounts of 'vibrancy and talent'), but found itself completely at odds with the aspirations to sexual, moral and political self-determinism which usually went hand in hand with the economic liberalism. If there was a single idea, leitmotif, to the sixties generation, it was personal emancipa- tion, or liberation – but this encompassed the entire variety of human life, economic, social, physical and moral. Theirs was an à la carte liberalism, whilst liberalism for the New Right was strictly a set menu. New Right conservatism tended to view the only valid area for unregulated activity as the economic sphere, but for the rest most of them remained statists, or, at least, entirely static in their opinions. This is, of course, a contradiction that has often been remarked upon. Even before the 1960s was barely over, Samuel Brittain wrote in the *Financial Times* that 'The Non-Muscovite left favours freedom in everything but economics ... the right is sympathetic to freedom only in the economic sphere.'[5] If his formula seems rather exaggerated, that is only because so many on either side seemed to go out of their way to live up to the caricature. This contradictory discourse, economic liberalism and social authoritarianism, has characterised much of twentieth-century conservatism, and the New Right were little different; the St John the Baptist of Thatcherism, Enoch Powell, being a supreme example of a man combining the theology of the economic free-trader with that of the unbending social and moral statist in the same body. The Tories had always promised to 'Set the People Free' after the socialism of 1945–51; Eden had famously declared that conservatism, unlike its rival doctrine, stood for 'liberty of the individual, his right to ... respect for his own distinctive personality'. However, as Martin Francis has written in an essay on the 'Conservatives and the State', 'the Tories were not going to tolerate individualism and diversity if these led to deviance and a challenge to traditional moral authority'.[6] There was never going to be pluralist, post-modern politics under the New Right, despite, as we shall see later, the obvious affinities between a lot of New Right thinking and post-modernism. But in this, the New Right was little different from every other conservative strand.

The New Right were essentially reductionists, wedded to what one critic has described as 'market-fetishism'.[7] Their interest in explaining how society worked in terms of micro-economics led to a micro-focus. This gave the thinkers and politicians of the New Right a wonderful clarity, an unusually clear intellectual cutting-edge, but also rendered them almost totally blind to any other way of thinking about society, and in particular any other framework for thinking about human 'freedom', a lot of which, like the feminist movement or multiculturalism, came directly out of the sixties. In as far as Mrs Thatcher and her acolytes even acknowledged the existence of any of these movements, they were usually hostile to them for the sound conservative reasons enumerated above.

But to take the question of economic liberalism first, how did the sixties help, and even sustain the New Right? The answer has been given in its most extreme and even bitter form by the writer and former record producer Ian Macdonald in his definitive account of the Beatles and the sixties, *Revolution in the Head*. Sam Beer has also given some more refined answers to the same question in his book *Britain Against Itself*[8] in which he characterises the 'populist' 1960s as the 'romantic revolt'. Macdonald's principal thesis about the sixties is that it was a 'reaction of free essence against the restraints of outmoded form...a flood of youthful energy bursting through the psychic dam of the fifites'. Macdonald is surely right in his judgement that the popular culture of the sixties, all stoically ignored by Mrs Thatcher as it washed up on her doorstep in Flood Street, for the first time since the war legitimated individual self-expression and aspirations against the collective restraints of a society that had grown increasingly restrictive, censorious and thus hypocritical since the 1930s. The sixties seemed to make possible a more meritocratic and 'classless' society; whatever the statistics showed, this was the rhetoric and it was repeated so often that the words virtually became cultural artefacts in their own right. With this more meritocratic society went the belief that the individual was responsible enough to make their own choices about the lifestyles that they wanted to lead, and when obstructed in this by the state, the personal, for the first time, became the political. And integral to these beliefs was the growth of affluence and consumerism which have been so well documented and the feeling that the newly wealthy – and in particular, the young, newly wealthy – should be able to keep as much of their money as possible, even (or especially) when they mocked the inherited wealth of the old conservative order with it, an example being John Lennon's psychedelic Rolls-Royce.

Macdonald writes: 'The irony of right-wing antipathy to the sixties is that this much-misunderstood decade was, in all but the most superficial senses, the creation of the very people who voted for Thatcher and Reagan in the Eighties. It is, to put it mildly, curious to hear Thatcherites condemn a decade in which ordinary folk for the first time aspired to individual self-determination and a life of material security within an economy of high employment and low inflation. The social fragmentation of the Nineties which rightly alarms Conservatives was created neither by the hippies (who wanted to "be together") nor by the New Left radicals (all of whom were socialists of some description). So far as anything in the sixties can be blamed for the demise of the compound entity of society it was the natural desire of the "masses" to lead easier, pleasanter lives, own their own homes, follow their own fancies and, as far as possible, move out of the communal collective altogether.'[9]

Thus, although it was the mass hysteria, the screaming girls and fashion-conscious student Maoists who tended to catch the eye of the casual, or hostile, observer, all of which seemed to presage the nervous breakdown of capitalist democracy altogether, to anyone who cared to look just beneath the surface, the economic and aspirational politics of the sixties generation dovetailed perfectly with the older economic liberal traditions of what would become Thatcherism. One such person who was allowed a closer glimpse of rebellious youth than most was William Rees-Mogg, then the fogeyish editor of the *The Times*, complete with establishment lisp, and later journalistic cheerleader for Thatcherism. He was one of the usual suspects from the 'Establishment' (together with, in the tireless search for novelty, a bishop) picked by the young television producer John Birt to interview Mick Jagger on the lawn of a country house for *World in Action* in July 1967. It was one of the more bizarre 'happenings' of the decade, particularly so for Rees-Mogg as, doubtless to the intense disappointment of John Birt, he found himself in surprising agreement with the living icon of the supposed 'counter-culture'. As he later recalled, he was astonished to discover in Jagger a 'right-wing libertarian – straight John Stuart Mill.' For all their posturing and Jagger's own (brief but much publicised) flirtation with revolutionary politics, in essence the Rolling Stones much preferred material accumulation to any sort of politics, and in this they reflected much of their generation. Jagger himself went along with the march on the American Embassy in Grosvenor Square in 1968, but the extent of his radicalism was clearly stated by his own musical response to the turmoil of 1968 in the song 'Street Fighting Man'. The title alone was enough to have it banned by a paranoid BBC, but the lyrics told a different story, which was to lead inexorably to the Rolling Stones corporate rock of the 1990s with the Hell's Angels employed erecting the hospitality suites rather than clubbing members of the audience to death 1969-style:

> 'Everywhere I hear the sound of marching, charging feet / cause summer's here and the time is right for fighting in the street, boy.
> So what can a poor boy do, 'cept sing for a rock n'roll band, cause in sleepy London town / there's no place for a street fighting man.
> They said the time is right for a palace revolution / but where I live the game to play is compromise … .'

The millionaire 'glimmer twins' were still playing the anthemic 'I can't get no satisfaction' at the end of their mammoth stadium tours in the 1990s, as, at one level, the apparent radicalism of the 1960s submerged into the harmless mainstream of contemporary pop. When it came to the crunch, the heroes of the 'populist' 1960s would always prefer to play by the rules of the acquisitive society rather than risk the rewards for their creativity by embracing any one of the varieties of extremist collectivist politics then on offer. By the time that the Stones recorded 'Exile on Main Street' in 1974, they had also been tax exiles for several years.

Tariq Ali quotes 'Street Fighting Man' in his memoir of the 1960s. 'Street Fighting Man' was in many ways a comical account of trying to bring the rock elite of the sixties to a state of revolutionary consciousness, and failing every time. The Beatles were no better from this point of view. George Harrison recorded 'Taxman' in 1966 as the first pop protest against the high levels of Wilsonian taxation and in 1968 John Lennon wrote his own commentary about the quasi-revolutionary situation, 'RevolutionOne'. Written at the Maharashi Mahesh Yogi's Himalayan meditation retreat, the actual writing of the song anticipated 'les événements' of that year by several months but still explicitly condemned the different student politics of the day as 'Minds that hate', and blandly assured his listeners that everything would be 'alright'. His ambivalence towards the whole revolutionary situation was encapsulated in his famous refrain 'You can count me in/out'.

By the time that the Beatles re-recorded the song as the B-side of 'Hey Jude' in July 1968, the ambivalence had disappeared and the line was now firmly 'Count me out', much to the disgust of the radical left. Lennon himself briefly succumbed to Ali's blandishments before settling down to an apathetic millionaire's lifestyle amidst the false security of the Dakota building in New York. As Macdonald wryly remarks, 'Tiananmen Square, the ignominious collapse of Soviet Communism, and the fact that most of [Lennon's] radical persecutors of 1968–70 now work in advertising have belatedly served to confirm his original instincts.'[10] Paul McCartney and George Martin, the Beatles record producer, were both knighted by the Conservative government of John Major, thus belatedly authenticating the inherent conservatism of much of what passed at the time for sixties radicalism. This represented one of the main confusions of the era, as originality was often mistaken for 'radicalism', form for substance.

The sixties brand of economic liberalism occasionally teetered on the brink of something more subversive, but never quite went over the edge. Many of the most prominent entrepreneurs of late-twentieth-century capitalism in Britain were products of the 1960s, such as Richard Branson (who started out in that quintessential sixties industry the music business), Anita Roddick, Clive Hollick or Greg Dyke of the media company Pearson. Ted Turner of CNN provides an example from the United States. They are all capitalists, but what marks them out as different from capitalists of any previous era is that they are all sixties capitalists in that they all have non-economic agendas inherited from the radicalism of the sixties. One commentator had observed of this generation that '... old capitalism ventured into social affairs to protect its business agenda; new capitalism runs business in order to advance its social agenda.... Listen to them talking, and you hear men and women who regard profit and loss not as ends in themselves, but as tools to realise a world vision."[10] These people used economic liberalism for different purposes than their predecessors; Thatcherism allowed them, and indeed encouraged them, to become capitalist entrepreneurs, but they also brought their own agendas from the sixties with them. 'Pure' capitalism, of profit and loss, was no longer privileged above everything else, and, as in the Body Shop, the 'hidden hand' gave way to very direct propaganda. These people, together with the pop 'aristocracy' of Mickie Most, Elton John *et al.* represented the sixties vision of a new meritocracy of self-made men and sometimes women which the New Right advocated and promoted into a social crusade.

In this respect, the sixties pointed the way towards Thatcherism and helped to sustain it electorally in the 1980s. Even if much of the 'populist' 1960s refused categorisation along a straight left/right spectrum, it was united by a radical brand of anti-authoritarianism and, more particularly, a radical anti-establishmentarianism which also informed Thatcherism. Indeed, a lot of the Thatcherites of the 1980s were radicalised by their attacks on the established order in the 1980s, even if their targets then were slightly different. But the mindset remained extremely consistent. Many of the Thatcherites viewed their politics as a crusade against the pettiness, restrictiveness, traditionalism and inertia that characterised the post-war settlement and first started mobilising against it in the early 1960s. This was very much a politics of generational change; it was an analysis that the radical left shared with the radical right in equal measure, articulated by the satire of Peter Cook subverting the cherished myths of wartime endeavour that was in danger of numbing a generation brought up on the 'Dambusters' and the Battle of Britain. If any single moment could be said to have breached the 'psychic dam' of the 1950s, it was Cook's sketch with Jonathan Miller in the 'Beyond the Fringe' show in which Cook, as an RAF officer, invites Miller to go on a suicide mission as a 'futile gesture' to raise morale. In an instant, the high seriousness of stiff-upper-lip military endeavour which everyone had been dragooned into endorsing since 1945 fell away. This was the intellectual landscape of John Osborne's 'The Entertainer'. Indeed, it was the failure of Wilson's governments of 1964–70 to do much about breaking down the social, class and gender barriers to self-advancement that drove many who were ostensibly on the left in the 1960s over to the New Right in the 1970s, including some of Mrs Thatcher's cabinet ministers such as Lord Young.

There they found that Mrs Thatcher, the lower-middle class shopkeeper, was much more eager to upset the cosy assumptions of the haute bourgeoisie than either the Oxford technocrat Harold Wilson or the naval patriot Jim Callaghan. The source of their discontent was summed up in the one word, 'Establishment': the word itself coined in the right-wing *Spectator* magazine in 1954 by Henry Fairlie. Baiting the Establishment became the chief sport of this generation of writers and intellectuals, and the assault burst into full bloom in the early 1960s, brought to a mass television audience by the unlikely figure of David Frost in 'That Was The Week That Was'. (Incidentally, among the scriptwriters on TW3 was Ian Lang, later one of John Major's cabinet ministers.)

In this respect, the skirmishes with the Establishment in the early 1960s established a diagnosis that was to be translated into a more full-blooded political assault in the 1980s. It was a diagnosis pioneered by people who were perceived to be, broadly, on the left in the 1960s – a testimony to the eclectic radicalism of the New Right. There is little that a Thatcherite would have found to disagree with in the old-Etonian Perry Anderson's complaints about British society in his famous essay on 'The Origins of the Present Crisis' in the *New Left Review* in 1964: 'The lasting contours of British society were already visible before the rise of the military–industrial imperialism of the 1880s. Yet it was this ostensible apotheosis of British capitalism which gave its characteristic style to that society, conserving it and fossilising to this day its internal space, its ideological horizons, its intimate sensibility. It is, above all, from this period that the suffocating "traditionalism" of English life dates ... traditionalism and empiricism henceforward fuse as a single legitimating system; traditionalism sanctions the present by deriving it from the past, empiricism binds the future by fastening it to the present. ... A comprehensive conservatism is the result, covering society with a pall of simultaneous philistinism (towards ideas) and mytogogy (towards institutions).'[12] All this would become familiar to the New Right through the pages of Martin Weiner, Correlli Barnett, Bernard Levin, Paul Johnson and others in the 1980s, just as the 'Angry Young Men' of the 1950s, tilting at the same windmills, would join the ranks of the Thatcherite *kulturkampf* for the same reasons. At the same time as E.P. Thompson was organising a group of his colleagues to lead Britain out of its torpor through socialism in the book of essays 'Out of Apathy', so another young historian, Hugh Thomas, was doing the same with his own collection of firebrands in his 1959 edited collection of essays called, simply and pointedly, 'The Establishment.'[13] This is an instructive collection, because many of the authors who thundered against the faceless bureaucrats and time-serving fixers of their day were the same men attacking the same targets in the 1980s. Hugh Thomas, then a historian recently escaped from the establishment clutch at the Foreign Office, later became Chairman of the Centre for Policy Studies and Mrs Thatcher's chief unofficial adviser on foreign policy – and eventually Lord Thomas of Swynnerton. In his preface, he wrote that: 'It is this Victorian England, with all its prejudices, ignorances and inhibitions, that the Establishment sets out to defend. The Establishment is the present-day institutional museum of Britain's past greatness. … To those who desire to see the resources and talents of Britain fully developed and extended, there is no doubt that the fusty Establishment with its Victorian views and standards of judgements, must be destroyed.'[14]

In the pages that followed, Thomas's authors dutifully showed how to take a sledgehammer to the Establishment: John Vaizey to the Public Schools, Henry Fairlie to the BBC, Hugh Raven to the Army and Tommy Balogh to the Civil Service. John Vaizey was an economist who converted to Thatcherism in the late 1970s and who wrote at length as to why his generation became so disenchanted with the social democracy – or just socialism – of their youth.[15] By the 1980s they had added some new targets to their usual list, principally the Trade Unions – absent from any consideration of the Establishment in the 1960s, but which would later be condemned as an archaic, fusty, Victorian institution in the same way as the BBC, the Civil Service or the Judiciary – for powdered wigs read cloth caps. However, once again this dual assault on both sides of the Establishment (the Middle/Upper Class and Working Class Establishments) which characterised at least the rhetoric of Thatcherism also formed part of the appeal of Wilson's new-look Labourism of 1963/4, with his promises to apply the 'white heat of technology' to sweep away the 'restrictive practices' of 'both sides of industry'. The perceived failure of Wilson ushered many into the radical Tory camp as early as the late 1960s.

Although this generation of radicals shared the same diagnosis of an ailing, backward Britain in the early 1960s, those who identified with what became known as the 'New Left' and the putative New Right eventually came to radically different conclusions about what was to be done about the problem. The instruments of redemption were, of course, very different. The left wanted to use the powers of a strong state to bring about a more equal, democratic society, while the right looked to the liberating potential of the free market. The New Left stressed the virtues of 'democracy' as the righteous path to an open society; 'industrial democracy' as much as electoral democracy. Robin Blackburn, one of the most important New Left critics of the 1960s, later acknowledged that both sides were in pursuit of the same goal of personal freedom, and shared the same enemies of Tory paternalism or social feudalism; 'The idea of controlling one's own life, which in 1968 was subsumed into hopes of a complete change of society, showed its negative side. ... Mrs Thatcher was able to give a neo-Conservative twist to this radical individual appeal: instead of controlling your own place of work, it became a question of owning your own home. Common to both was anti-statism.'[16] Except that when it came down to the bottom line of policy-making, it was the New Left which proved as out of touch with the economic aspirations of the sixties as the New Right proved to be with the social and moral aspirations. Just as the New Right were, essentially, playing out the economic battles of the 1940s, so the New Left remained rooted in the political confrontations of the 1950s – and, in particular, 1956. In the end, the egalitarian society of the New Left could only be implemented by effectively insulating Britain from the global economy. A workers democracy would only come about, as the New Left authors of the 'May Day Manifesto' of 1968 admitted, by 'nationalising British privately-held foreign shares and securities. But this implies ... extensive intervention in the banking system and in the capital market ... for import quotas would be established and a total control instituted over foreign exchange'.[17] Thus, at the very moment when Britain was becoming an entrepôt state of fashion, culture, technology and service industries (such as advertising as well as banking), the New Left wanted to condemn the country to the parochial insularity of a siege economy. These ideas eventually ended up as the Bennite 'Alternative Economic Strategy' of 1976, finally defeated as a practical possibility by a Labour Cabinet determined to maintain Britain's role as an outward-looking, internationalist trading nation, even if this meant accepting much of the economic logic of the New Right.

It was out of his concern for the New Left disappearing up the cul-de-sac of economic statism, which seemed to be so out of step with the spirit of the age, that David Collard wrote his seminal pamphlet, 'The New Right; a Critique', for the Fabians in October 1968. He sounded a warning-bell that, in economic thinking, the left, although associated with most of the progressive causes of the 1960s, was being successfully out-flanked by the Right. He was no sympathiser with the economic liberals, but in surveying the work of bodies like the Institute of Economic Affairs, nonetheless argued that 'The New Right must be respected for the quality, consistency and rigour of its approach to the treatment of private industry. In this sense it is rather unfair to lump it together with organisations such as Aims of Industry. The economic vision of the New Right is the economist's model of perfect competition in which rational consumers indicate their preferences to profit-seeking producers by means of prices under conditions of perfect information. This is very far removed from a crude approach on the vested interest of capitalists.'[18] Indeed, at the same time as the May Day Manifesto appeared under the aegis of the New Left, several key figures of Collard's New Right gathered at Swinton College, the Conservative Party's college of the North, to prepare a similarly utopian manifesto for the future. Instead of Raymond Williams, a young journalist called John O'Sullivan took the chair. He was a tutor at Swinton, editor of the *Swinton Journal* and later worked in Mrs Thatcher's policy unit at Downing Street and added the much-needed jokes to her memoirs.

There is no doubt that the young generation of tutors there were all influenced by the heady blend of idealism and optimism that infused the sixties generation. Besides John O'Sullivan, both Stephen Eyres and David Alexander played important roles in converting key sections of the Conservative Party to Thatcherism in the 1970s. The symposium that O'Sullivan organised in the summer of 1968 was entitled 'Intellectuals and Conservatism' and involved several who were to become the leading lights of Thatcherism – Arthur Seldon, Geoffrey Howe, John Biffen, Russell Lewis, David Howell and Michael Spicer. In his editorial in the *Swinton Journal* introducing the symposium, O'Sullivan proclaimed 'the liberal hour' with all the fervour that his fellow activists of the left were contemporaneously ripping up the flagstones in Paris. He wrote of the '…sheer intellectual vitality of economic liberalism. It is scarcely an exaggeration to say that liberalism claims to cure more ills than patent medicine. Are you worried about the world monetary crisis? Flexible exchange rates will ease your mind. Is urban congestion a problem in your town? Enquire about road pricing today. …Now is the time for the Conservative Party to commit itself to this liberal tradition in clear and unequivocal terms.'[19] It would take another 15 years for the party to do so, and even then the scepticism expressed at the symposium about the compatibility of conservatism and such a radical ideology as economic liberalism was never really overcome. However, in the context of the 1960s, it was John O'Sullivan *et al.* who proved to be better attuned to the changing times than their doppelgängers on the New Left.

So the rhetoric of self-determinism, classlessness and meritocracy that permeated Thatcherism was, to a significant degree, a legacy of the generational politics of the 1960s. In this sense, the New Right worked with the grain of the 1960s, with electoral dividends when that generation translated its somewhat inchoate youthful idealism into the hard-headed political action of the 1970s and 1980s. However, in another and equally important sense, Thatcherism was also heavily influenced by a strong counter-revolutionary ethos, directed against what was perceived to be the pathological aberrations of the 1960s – but which many of that same generation who were natural economic liberals regarded as the most hard-won freedoms in social and moral attitudes. As has been noted, the New Right differed little from mainstream Conservatives in regarding most of the social developments of the 1960s as, at worst, reprehensible, or, at best, merely faddish. Thus the New Right was as much a reaction against the 1960s as an embodiment of it. They were, after all, fiscal liberals and conservative moralists, and they could not understand how the one could go quite naturally with the other. Or, to put it another way, they could not allow that the individual was capable of behaving with the same level of self-responsibility in the conduct of their 'private' life as they might be able to exercise in the conduct of their economic life.

In the numerous bibliographies of freedom issued by the New Right from the 1970s onwards, the 'freedoms' insisted upon are overwhelmingly economic. As Chris Tame, one of the most prominent self-proclaimed 'libertarians' of the 1960s, wrote in the forward to a Centre for Policy Studies version of such a bibliography, 'The largest section … is on economics, because of both that subject's importance and that fact that the revival of libertarian scholarship has been most extensively developed (or at least published) in that field.'[20] To the New Right, personal liberty was never really conceived of in any other way, thus ignoring the enormous body of work, principally from the sixties, associated with the post-modernist school, the new sociology, the feminist writers from the late 1960s onwards who all argued for completely different freedoms, freedoms which seemed just as relevant and even more urgent to the 1960s generation as economic liberalism. All this work was usually dismissed by the New Right as being inherently 'collectivist', written, as most of it was, by people identified with the political left. But to the consumers of such thought, these different schools of thought on the left in fact frequently argued for the same sort of autonomy, toleration and responsibility that the New Right could only accept in the economic sphere. Thus most of them never really challenge the notion of a paternalistic state, subscribing to a Victorian ethic of religious, racial and sexual conformity.

The vast majority of Conservatives in Parliament, including those who were to be prominent in the New Right, either voted against the Home Office 'social reforms' of the 1960s, or voted for them on sufferance. Mrs Thatcher, for instance, certainly did not vote for any of Roy Jenkins's reforms to create a new, more humane society. As she records in her memoirs: 'As regards abortion, homosexuality, and divorce reform it is easy to see that matters did not turn out as was intended. For most of us in Parliament – and certainly for me – the thinking underlying these changes was that they dealt with anomalies or unfairness which occurred in a minority of instances, or that they removed uncertainties in the law itself. Or else they were intended to recognize in law what was in any case occurring in fact. Instead, it could be argued that they have paved the way toward a more callous, selfish and irresponsible society.' What she certainly did not intend by voting for them was to provide 'a radically new framework within which the younger generation would be expected to behave'.[21] If the sixties was an era of rapid transformation in sexual behaviour, social attitudes and lifestyles, none of these transformations were ever accepted by the leaders of the New Right. It was, after all, Enoch Powell who sounded the clarion-call against a multi-ethnic, multicultural society, and who became the most unyielding defender of moral and racial intolerance. Even before the end of the sixties, people from the New Right had already become involved in the backlash against what was labelled 'permissiveness'; Mary Whitehouse launched the National Viewers and Listeners Association, and the Black Papers were published to protest against the 'liberalisation' and 'comprehensivisation' of education by the likes of Rhodes Boyson, Dr Dyson and Professor Cox. The Black Papers were of particular relevance, as they were first published as a direct response to the student revolution of 1968 and their authors would go on to have a direct impact on the 'great debate' about education that was launched by Jim Callaghan in his 1977 Ruskin College speech. Thus the discourses of the New Right and most of those radicalised by the sixties remained peculiarly compartmentalised; for the New Right, the feminist movement, environmentalism, the campaign for homosexual and lesbian rights, anti-colonialism and much else just passed them by, or was studiously ignored. Here was the 'liberation of desire', and it became, almost by default, the political preserve of the left – the anti-statist project of the left. But the New Right were, after all, not only economic liberals, they were also Cold War Warriors, nationalists and frequently Christian and for all their interest in the benefits of flexibility that a free-market would bring to working people, they remained remarkably inflexible in their thinking on almost everything else.

There is a profound irony here. The import of much of the rejection of the manners and morals of bourgeois society that characterised the 1960s was essentially post-modern, in the sense that in place of the meta-narratives of the state that the New Right still wanted to uphold (church, family, patriarchy, etc.) the sixties generation, and many on the left, wanted to replace with their own autonomous brand of lifestyle, proclaiming along the way the 'emancipation' of the individual from the constraints of bourgeois culture sanctioned by the state. Yet it was the New

Right that promoted the equivalent agenda in economic terms, which was broadly resisted by the left. What Hayek, for instance, proposed was really a style of 'post-modern economics', rejecting any notion of a grand 'narrative' of economic aggregates, or macro-economics, in favour of what he called a catallaxy. Andrew Gamble has described this notion as follows: 'the most general kind of spontaneous order for Hayek is the market order, which he describes as catallaxy, rather than an economy. The word "economy", derived from the Greek word for household, suggests planning and conscious control. In a catallaxy, no single person is responsible for planning the whole because knowledge is imperfect, fragmented and total.'[22] This is the post-modern economics of the fragmented, atomistic 'Blade-Runner' society, the essence of which had so much in common with the cultural and sociological explorations and 'happenings' of the 1960s, from art to pop music. At its most radical and avant-garde, the 1960s substituted a new mentality of a spontaneous/simultaneous aesthetic, for instance on the Beatles 'White Album', for the older mentality of coherence/development, and for the first time, spread this new aesthetic to the new mass forms of communications such as pop, television, advertising and the press (the *Sun*, for example), all new forms of re-invigorated late-twentieth-century styles of consumer capitalism pioneering a new form of economic aesthetic. However, because the New Right, pop artists, post-modernists and the New Left all existed in their own insulated, self-sustaining universes, with their own grammar, iconography and lifestyles, few ever attempted to make any political or cultural connections. Michel Foucault was one who did, albeit much later. In 1979, in his annual lectures at the College de France, this protean thinker of the French radical left, who had literally been on the barricades in 1968, urged his students to read the collected works of Hayek and Von Mises in order for them to think about 'the will not to be governed'. It was a belated recognition of the way that the Austrian school could be used to describe and further the liberalism of the 1960s, but it remains almost a unique example – and I shouldn't imagine that any of his students took his advice.[23]

This is, eventually, where the New Right fell foul of the 1960s. Even if the new politics of the 1960s described above, where the personal very insistently became the political, was confined to a small minority of people in the 1960s – even if not quite the proverbial bedsit in Hampstead – by the 1980s and 1990s they had virtually become the normal way of thinking for most people under the age of forty – as was brilliantly demonstrated by the success of the BBC drama series 'This Life' in 1996/7. In 1982, Sam Beer, updating his classic, *Modern British Politics* (first published in 1965), wrote in *Britain Against Itself* of the changed social environment which he beheld at the beginning of the Thatcher decade: 'Today, in Britain as in the US, the fighting causes of the counterculture have in great degree been absorbed into the fabric of everyday life for a large part of the society. Consider, for example, how readily people put up with, accept, and where appropriate, practise cohabitation, abortion, homosexuality, pornography, protesters ... undergraduates sitting on University committees, woman doing day jobs traditionally considered men's work, blacks in jobs formerly performed by whites, and, most impressive to the returning foreigner, very little "Sir" and "Ma'm". Shorn of some of its wilder fantasies, the new populism has been institutionalised in political debate ... .' The New Right, by trying to insist on the ethical, moral and sexual code of pre-sixties Britain, was, even before the end of the 1980s, looking tired and irrelevant. And when John Major tried to translate this old morality into a political campaign in the early 1990s with 'Back to Basics', his government merely looked silly, probably the most dangerous adjectival description of all to evoke among voters. What research that has been done, mainly in the United States, shows that the 'baby boom generation' of the 1960s are both economically and socially liberal. An analysis studying young corporate executives in the US concludes that '... baby boom business leaders are taking a fresh look at politics. Neither consistent liberals or Conservatives, they oppose government intervention in both the economy and their personal lives'. To this generation, the politics of Thatcherism, and even more so of John Major, seemed onedimensional; handing out knighthoods to ageing sixties pop stars could not disguise the fact that the New Right ran into a social and moral cul-de-sac just as the left had run into an economic cul-de-sac a generation before.

Timothy Evans, a young activist of the libertarian New Right, in his book *Conservative Radicalism*, makes a persuasive case for a post-modernist conservatism. 'Unlike the young Conservatives of the 1960s or their forebears, the Libertarian right reflects the diffuse patriotic politics of traditional Conservatism. They have little feeling for the nation, the Monarchy and the established order of society. They are post-modern radicals with world-view that attempts to cut across boundaries of geography and ethnicity, class and nationality, religion and ideology ... but freedom does not mean that individuals can impose their will on others.'[25]

This might constitute a post-modern conservatism, but in fact it has so little to do with traditional conservatism, much of which the New Right tried to uphold, that it might as well not be conservatism at all. And in that intellectual conundrum rests the main political dilemma of the New Right and the Conservative Party today. The election of the 37-year-old William Hague as leader is a rather banal attempt to address precisely this issue.

Trying to preserve a traditional state-sanctioned morality within the context of a rapidly changing post-modern catallaxy was always bound to put an unbearable stress on the political programme of the New Right, and so it proved by the early 1990s. The logical consequences of technological, electronic and economic deregulation in the 1980s was always going to be the 'Gaytime TV' and 'This Life' of the 1990s rather than re-runs of the 'Onedin Line'. The ideas and attitudes associated with the populist narrative of the sixties did not go away, as Norman Tebbit hoped they would, but stayed, fructified and, shorn of the hedonsitic excesses of that era, became the mainstream culture of the next generation but two. For them, multi-culturalism, homosexuality, women's equality and consumerism come as naturally as did Queen and Country to earlier generations.[26] The failure of the New Right to acknowledge this eventually made them look as remote and implausible as the left became in the 1970s.

In the end it was the left that put the post-modern jigsaw together, marrying the social and moral legacy of the sixties to the economic liberalism of the post-war era, and New Labour have been the successful and astute beneficiaries of this process. Just as the left was out-flanked by the late 1960s, so a revived and transformed left eventually out-flanked the New Right in the 1990s, or rather leap-frogged over a political generation. The intellectual weaving together of these disparate elements took place largely in the pages of *Marxism Today* in the 1980s under the guidance of Martin Jacques and Stuart Hall. It was in the pages of *Marxism Today* that the remainders of the left which had been radicalised by the 1960s and 1970s dropped the insistence on a collectivist economy, acknowledging that that argument had been lost. The way was thus left open for this New (or Newer) left to bring what had been an often obscure debate about 'rights', 'inclusiveness', 'empowerment' and 'democracy' in the dreary concrete halls of the polytechnics of the 1970s into the mainstream of political thinking, where it found a ready audience among those who no longer shared an automatic deference to or interest in the crown, church, monarchy, and nation – especially after the revolutions of 1989. As Jacques has admitted, *Marxism Today* was long on theory and analysis and very short on policy proposals, and it had to wait for the think-tank DEMOS, founded by Jacques and the sometime *Marxism Today* essayist Geoff Mulgan in 1993, to translate a lot of this new thinking into policy proposals specific enough to be used by a government. Just as Timothy Evans's 'post-modern' conservatism cannot actually be described as 'Conservative' in any sense, even of that most elastic of political terms, to the new politics of 'New' Labour, and DEMOS cannot really be characterised as anything to do with Socialism, or even in the interests of

'Labour' – the old working class. That this is true, and the fact that both parties are now grappling for new definitions and new directions, is to a large extent the social and cultural legacy of the 1960s combined with the legacy of the revanchist capitalism of the 1980s. Tony Blair likes to describe such a new direction as 'the Third Way'. Many scoff that this is too amorphous to be taken seriously, but it at least shows a determination to grapple with the intellectual consequence of those two revolutionary decades, something that Conservatives have failed to do.

The New Right underestimated the legacy of the 1960s, and failed to come to terms with the changes in society that occurred during that much-maligned decade. Theirs was primarily an economic vision of society, a vision which was reinforced during the decade, but the primary importance of the decade for most people was to show how limited a vision that might actually be, and, in the long run it was to undo the New Right.

NOTES

1. See Benn diaries, Vol. 2.
2. Margaret Thatcher (1995), *The Path to Power*, Harper Collins, p. 153.
3. Norman Tebbit (1988), *Upwardly Mobile*, Wedenfeld and Nicolson, p. 80.
4. See my book *Thinking the Unthinkable* (1994), Harper Collins, for a precise definition of the personnel and, where appropriate, principles of the New Right.
5. Samuel Brittan, *The Role and Limits of Government; Essays in Political Economy* (1984), Temple Smith, p. 50.
6. *The Conservatives and British Society, 1880–1990* (1996), ed. Martin Francis and Ina Zweininger-Bargielowski University of Wales Press.
7. Mandela and Polanyi-Levitt, quoted by Radhika Dasai in her excellent analysis of the origins of the New Right in 'Thinking Up Thatcherism', the *New Left Review* (1994), p. 203.
8. Sam Beer, *Britain Against Itself* (1982), W.W. Norton.
9. Ian Macdonald, *Revolution in the Head – The Beatles Records and the Sixties* (1994), Fourth Estate, p. 29.
10. See Macdonald, pp. 223–9 for a full analysis of the social and political background to the Beatles songs of 1968, and Tariq Ail, *Street Fighting Years* (1987), Collins.
11. Trevor Phillips in the *Independent on Saturday*, 8 November 1997.

12. Perry Anderson, *English Questions* (1992), Verso.
13. E.P. Thompson, *Out of Apathy* (1960), Stevens and Sons. and Hugh Thomas, *The Establishment* (1962).
14. Hugh Thomas (ed.), *The Establishment* (1962).
15. See his article in *The Cambridge Review*, 27 April 1981.
16. Quoted by Lin Chun in *The British New Left* (1993), Edinburgh University Press, p. 194.
17. *May Day Manifesto* (1968), ed. Raymond Williams, Penguin.
18. See *Thinking the Unthinkable* for a longer discussion of this pamphlet, p. 157.
19. See the *Swinton Journal*, Summer 1968, and for the background *Thinking the Unthinkable*, pp. 191–4.
20. *Bibliography of Freedom* (1981), CPS.
21. *Path to Power*, pp. 152–3.
22. Andrew Gamble, *Hayek; The Iron Cage of Liberty* (1996), Polity Press, p. 38.
23. See James Miller, *The Passion of Michel Foucault* (1993), Harper Collins, p. 310.
24. Sam Beer, *Modern British Politics* (1965), Faber & Faber.
25. Timothy Evans, *Conservative Radicalism* (1996), Berghahn Books, p. 130.
26. See, for example, 'The Social Survey on Youth' in the *Independent*, 20–21 November 1997.

7 The New Right, New Labour and the Problem of Social Cohesion

Peter Saunders

We are used to thinking about political ideologies in terms of a continuum from 'left' (socialism) to 'right' (conservatism). Such imagery is misleading, however, for there is a third core political ideology of modernity – liberalism – which cannot be located on this continuum. In Britain, classical liberalism withered at around the same time (the late nineteenth century) as modern socialism emerged. Socialism thus displaced liberalism as the antithesis to conservatism, and this probably explains why we have retained the misleading image of politics as a simple continuum between two opposing positions. Since the 1970s, however, there has been a revival of classical liberal thought, both in Britain and in the United States, and this makes it impossible any longer to map the contours of contemporary political debate using a simple left–right continuum. Today, politics are structured around three distinct positions – not a continuum, but a triangle (Figure 7.1).

The defining feature of the classical liberal tradition is its concern to defend individual liberty and its corresponding distrust of the use of state power to bring about collective goals. Any growth in state power tends to

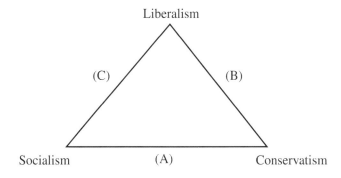

Figure 7.1 The three core political ideologies of modernity

be resisted, even where it commands widespread support and is intended to bring about beneficial improvements in social conditions, for extension of state responsibility necessarily implies a reduction in individual freedom. This concern was clearly expressed in the sociology of Herbert Spencer who spent many years warning his Victorian contemporaries of the dangers posed by their gradual acceptance of increased state intervention in social affairs. Where others saw benign and overdue reform, Spencer saw the looming shadow of state coercion: 'Dictatorial measures, rapidly multiplied, have tended continually to narrow the liberties of individuals' (Spencer, 1982, p. 3). Similarly, Friedrich Hayek warned of the dangers inherent in the renewed enthusiasm for social reform in the 1940s when he suggested at the start of *The Road to Serfdom* that: '... in our endeavour consciously to shape our future in accordance with high ideals, we ... in fact unwittingly produce the very opposite of what we have been striving for' (1944, p. 4). For writers such as Spencer and Hayek, good intentions pave the road to a coercive Hell.

This fear of growing state power sharply differentiates liberalism from both socialism (which seeks to use state power to bring about goals such as greater equality) and conservatism (which seeks to use state power to achieve such goals as the maintenance of a traditional social order). While liberals and conservatives share a common position against socialists on issues to do with private property and wealth distribution, socialists and conservatives take up a common position against liberals on issues to do with individual liberty and the rights of the collectivity. Conservatives and socialists alike talk of the duties and responsibilities which individuals owe to the collectivity, and they justify policies on the grounds that they contribute to the 'common good', even if some individuals lose out. Liberals, by contrast, see the freedom of the individual as paramount and are sceptical of any claim by governments to know better than their own citizens what is and is not in their own best interests.

In practice, of course, governments rarely pursue strategies which consistently operationalise any one of these ideals. Nevertheless, it is only when we clarify the distinctions between them (and in particular, when we recognise that contemporary politics are structured around three distinct positions rather than two), that it is possible to understand the key shifts which have occurred in Britain, and to some extent in other western countries as well, since the Second World War.

For thirty years after the war, British politics was grounded in a broad political consensus. Conservative and Labour governments alike were committed to the basic principles of the comprehensive welfare state, Keynesian economic management designed to maintain full employment, and a 'mixed economy' in which government owned and ran key sectors of industry. Seen in terms of the triangle of ideologies, this period was dominated by a compromise between socialism and conservatism (position 'A' in Figure 7.1, above).

During the 1970s, this compromise fell apart. Keynesian economics led to stagflation with rising unemployment and state-owned enterprises became increasingly sclerotic; attempts by government to govern in co-operation with the powerful trade union movement ended in a wave of industrial unrest and political chaos. Chastened by its failures in government between 1970 and 1974, the Conservative Party in opposition began to search for new ideas and initiatives, and it found them in a return to classical liberal free market principles (see Cockett, 1994).

For twenty years from the mid-seventies onwards, the Conservative Party in Britain pursued a radically new programme which abandoned the old post-war compromise between conservatism and socialism, and which instead sought to link conservatism to the long-neglected principles of classical liberalism (position 'B' in Figure 7.1, above). This self-consciously ideological 'New Right' programme was economically liberal but socially conservative. Its liberalism could be seen in its commitment to reducing the role of government in managing and regulating the economy (eg by abandoning Keynesian demand management, by ending the drift to corporatism, and by privatising the nationalised industries), as well as in its determination to break the monopoly power of the unions. All of this was intended to reawaken a culture of enterprise and individual initiative among the British people (something which conspicuously failed to happen – see Jowell *et al*. 1996).

Alongside this liberal economic agenda, the 1979–97 governments pursued a rigorously conservative social and cultural programme. The powers of government were centralised. Police powers were increased. Uniform national standards of education were imposed across all state schools and universities. Alternative lifestyles were discouraged (eg by banning 'raves', legislating against the promotion of homosexuality, and acting against 'travellers'). Emphasis was placed on the importance of strengthening traditional social institutions including marriage and the nuclear family. National unity and distinctiveness was fiercely defended through opposition to European federalism, Scottish nationalism and Northern Irish republicanism as well as rigorous defence of the Falklands at the time of the Argentine invasion in 1982. These governments also recognised the importance of political tradition through their firm commitment to the monarchy, the established Church and the hereditary Upper House. It was this strongly conservative element in the agenda of Thatcherism (and, across the Atlantic, of Reaganism) which led critics such as Stuart Hall (1983) to define the programme of the 'New Right' as 'authoritarian populism'.

It is one of the paradoxes of the Thatcher/Major years, however, that for all the emphasis placed on national unity, solidarity and continuity, these governments actually presided over a remarkable erosion of social cohesion and traditional morality. On most indicators, the 1980s and 1990s witnessed an increase in social fragmentation and a decrease in social order. In the view of some critics, this was an inevitable result of the pursuit of their liberal economic agenda.

One obvious indicator of growing social fragmentation was the rising crime rate. Despite the increased emphasis on 'law and order', the total number of criminal offences notified to the police doubled between 1979 and 1993. According to the *British Crime Survey*, more than one in ten adolescent males has a criminal record for a non-motoring offence by the age of eighteen, and a staggering 40 per cent of British males have such a record by the time they reach the age of 40. England and Wales today have the highest recorded crime rate in the western world – higher than any other country in Western Europe, and higher even than the United States. The 1997 *International Crime Victimisation Survey* shows not only that England and Wales have more burglaries and more car thefts per head of population than the USA, but also that they have more assaults, robberies and sexual attacks. Only the homicide rate is lower than in America.

Another indicator of the erosion of social cohesion and collective morality can be found in the family statistics (see, for example, Land and Lewis, 1997). Again, despite their official support for the traditional family, the Thatcher and Major governments saw divorce rates escalate to the second highest in Europe (behind Denmark). By the early 1990s one couple was getting divorced in England and Wales for every two getting married, and one in ten marriages was ending within just two years. Meanwhile, the rate of births outside marriage exploded from one in twelve in 1971 to one in three by the mid-nineties. No fewer than 84 per cent of mothers under 20 today are unmarried. Although some illegitimate births are to cohabiting couples, one-quarter are registered in only one name, and half of the remainder are to parents living ats different addresses. Two and a quarter million children are now being raised by just one parent. Of 7.2 million mothers in England and Wales, 1.2 million are raising their child/ren without their father, and one million of these rely on state income support.

The escalation in crime rates and the dramatic increase in the rate of family disintegration both point to the failure of the Thatcher and Major governments to maintain social cohesion. But was social fragmentation an inevitable by-product of New Right policies?

Defenders of the New Right believe not. Rather like defenders of communism who long argued that the theory was right even though the practice kept going wrong, 'New Right' analysts like Charles Murray (1994) believe that the failure to ensure social cohesion should not be blamed on the policies pursued in the 1980s. Murray argues that the rise in criminality can largely be explained by the collapse of the traditional family, and that the collapse of the traditional family is the result of growing state intervention since the 1950s. The problem, in other words, pre-dates Thatcherism by at least two decades.

Critics of the New Right disagree. Writers like Will Hutton (1995) trace the cause of social fragmentation to the emphasis placed in the Thatcher years on values of individualism and competitiveness. It is Hutton's thesis that the Conservative governments of the 1980s and 1990s allowed the market to 'rip through' all aspects of British society, widening inequalities and deepening social deprivation while simultaneously emphasising a 'get-rich-quick' mentality which was relatively unconstrained by any ethic of social responsibility. In his view, it was the growth of inequality and poverty, coupled with the encouragement of greed and selfishness, that was eroding social cohesion (as well as hindering long-term economic efficiency and modernisation), and what was needed to put it right was a renewed commitment to the principles of collective responsibility which the Conservatives had neglected.

It is certainly true that inequality increased in Britain between 1979 and 1997, and that the Thatcher governments in particular emphasised values of individualism and competitiveness, but is this an adequate explanation for why crime rates, divorce rates and other indicators of social fragmentation rose so dramatically during this period?

Hutton's analysis was extremely influential (his book, *The State We're In*, became one of the most unlikely best-sellers of the 1990s), yet in some respects, his critique was misplaced. It was not true, for example, that the poor in Britain became poorer during the Thatcher and Major years, and it is at least debatable whether the number of people in poverty grew as Hutton and others assume. While the income gap between top and bottom certainly widened, expenditure data show clearly that the living standards of the poorest 10 per cent of the population rose in real terms over this period. Indeed, defining the 'poverty line' as an income below 50 per cent of average income, the proportion of the population in poverty fell from

8 per cent in 1979 to 5 per cent in 1995 (Green, 1998; Dennis, 1997). It is still possible, of course, to argue that widening inequalities somehow contributed to social breakdown, but it is difficult to see how social deprivation in and of itself could be said to have caused the increase in social fragmentation which took place during this period.

A further problem with the Hutton thesis is that most indicators of social fragmentation were rising long before Thatcher took office; both crime rates and divorce rates, for example, had been rising since the late 1950s, and both were already at record levels by 1979. Murray's emphasis on the pernicious effects of growing welfare provision seems to fit this chronology rather better than Hutton's emphasis on the pernicious effects of the new economic individualism, for whatever started the ball rolling must have been present from the 1940s/50s, and the welfare state clearly presents itself as an obvious potential factor.

It should also be remembered that the Thatcher and Major governments were nowhere near as indifferent to the question of social cohesion and social responsibility as their critics sometimes implied. Both Thatcher (in her call for a return to 'Victorian values') and Major (in his ill-fated 'Back to Basics' campaign) hoped to balance their emphasis on economic individualism by encouraging a renaissance in the traditional values of charity, compassion and social duty. As liberals, they sought to extend economic freedoms, but as conservatives they were also alive to the need to maintain or restore the old virtues of personal responsibility, emphasising duty over self-indulgence and moral conscience over the pursuit of narrow self-interest. That the boys in red braces in the City of London wine bars paid little heed to this message only demonstrates how difficult it is for any government to direct cultural change, and how unlikely it always was that the values of one century could be dusted down and reinserted into the material conditions of another.

It is by no means clear, therefore, that the neo-liberal economics of the Thatcher/Major years can be blamed for the deleterious social trends of that period. What is clear, however, is that these governments seemed powerless to halt or even slow down developments of which they disapproved. Both Thatcher and Major were undoubtedly concerned by the drift to social fragmentation, but they conspicuously failed to do anything effective about it. The critics may not be correct in locating the fundamental causes of the problem in New Right policies, but they are surely justified in pointing to the impotence of New Right governments in the face of these developments. British society did become more atomised during these 20 years, and 'conservative liberalism' offered few realistic solutions to the problem.

It was the failure of New Right governments to ensure social cohesion and stability which left open to the Labour Party the possibility of forging a new and distinctive politics.

The success of Thatcherite economic reforms (overseas as well as in Britain), coupled with the final collapse of socialism in eastern Europe, had forced the British Labour Party during its long exile from government to come to terms with the legitimacy of large-scale private enterprise and of relatively unregulated and open commodity, financial and labour markets. However, the evident need for a social programme designed to combat the growing disintegration of British society allowed the party to combine its new-found economic liberalism with its more traditional roots in social democratic values emphasising 'social justice' and common citizenship. What emerged was a new politics of 'social liberalism' (position 'C' in Figure 7.1, above).

Like Clinton's 'New Democrats' in the USA, Blair's 'New Labour' Party believed that it should be possible to harvest the benefits of a dynamic global system of capitalism while avoiding the costs of social deprivation and social pathology which have hitherto gone along with it. The strategy for accomplishing this balancing act is two-fold. First, ensure that everybody has a role to play within the social system and that nobody is allowed to abdicate their social responsibility. Central to this first part of the strategy is an attack on 'social exclusion' through fundamental reform of state welfare and an emphasis on the importance of work. Second, ensure that everybody can see that rewards are distributed 'fairly'. This second part of the strategy entails active pursuit of the goal of 'meritocracy' including an emphasis on education as the key means by which individuals can be offered the opportunity to realise their full potential, and a willingness to attack those (such as the much-maligned 'fat cats' of the privatised utilities) whose wealth appears not to be the product of hard work and enterprise. As we shall see, this combined strategy of maximising 'social inclusion' and support for 'meritocracy' is largely consistent with the prescriptions for social cohesion set out by Emile Durkheim over 100 years ago.

To understand the New Labour project for social reconstruction, we have to begin by clarifying why the Thatcher/Major governments failed in their attempts to encourage a stronger sense of social responsibility as a complement to the extension of economic freedoms. The basic reason for this failure was that they thought, wrongly, that they could run history backwards.

Looking back several generations, these Conservative governments saw how economic liberalism had once coexisted with a culture of mutual co-operation and self-help. Believing that this culture had been undermined by the growth of state welfare, they deduced that it could be revived by 'rolling back' the growth of the state. Get government off people's backs, and this generation will develop the sort of self-reliance and social responsibility which earlier generations had exhibited. The reasoning, however, was fallacious.

Dramatic social changes, such as the sudden escalation in divorce rates and illegitimacy rates since the 1960s, clearly have multiple causes. Whether the expansion of state welfare is one of these causes is contentious and debatable, but what cannot be disputed is that welfare provisions have *enabled* these changes to occur (a point made forcibly by many conservatives including Charles Murray and Lawrence Mead). Without welfare support, single parenthood would be economically non-viable for most people, which is precisely why unmarried pregnancy and marital breakdown carried such fears and attracted so much stigma and opprobrium in most social strata in both Britain and America until the 1950s. The extension of state benefits since then has made it easier for men to desert their families (for their wives and children will still be looked after), just as it has made it easier for young women to raise babies without ensuring they have a committed male partner to help them. The economic fear has been lifted, and the stigma associated with divorce and illegitimacy has in consequence all but disappeared. If the deserted family can still get by, why shouldn't the erstwhile father/husband seek to maximise his gratification elsewhere? If the babies can be fed and clothed, why shouldn't young teenage mothers have children on their own if that is what they want? With the state there to pick up the pieces, why shouldn't we all indulge our selfish needs and desires?

What is true of divorce and illegitimacy is also true of other areas of personal and collective morality. It is not that state provision *induces* people to change their behaviour (few young women are tempted to get pregnant with a view to receiving state benefits or even a council flat). It is rather that such provision *enables* people to pursue courses of action which would otherwise have incurred high personal costs. By reducing or even eliminating these costs, state provision makes irresponsible behaviour viable and thereby weakens the traditional norms and sanctions which have hitherto regulated it.

New Right theorists have long recognised this problem. For them, the fundamental problem with state welfare provision is that it 'crowds out' precisely those forms of behaviour which we 'should' seek to encourage and it enables those forms of behaviour which we 'should' seek to deter. It is not just that individuals cease to take responsibility for the consequences of their own actions and come to rely increasingly upon the non-judgemental largesse of the state. It is also that state provision renders pointless those forms of voluntary and communal self-help which foster the bonds of solidarity and cohesion which today seem to be fraying so badly.

David Green (1985) has given one example of how state provision tends to undermine self-provisioning in his work on the history of the Friendly Societies. He shows how the introduction of compulsory state unemployment and sickness insurance in Britain in 1911 led directly to the collapse of the working class friendly society movement. With the introduction of compulsory state contributions, the need for voluntary saving was reduced, and the stimulus for working people to organise together for their common welfare was removed. As a result, the friendly societies, which had evolved as institutions of communal solidarity and support without any prompting from above, simply withered away. As Murray (1988) says, if we want individuals to act responsibly, then we must give them something to be responsible for, and if we want people to come together in thriving communal activities, they must be left with something to do for themselves (see also Berger and Neuhaus, 1977).

New Right analysts and politicians have always understood this. Where they went wrong, however, was in thinking that historical causation could simply be rolled backwards. If state provision had contributed to the erosion of personal responsibility and social cohesion, then, they reasoned, a reduction in state provision would surely begin to re-establish it. Take away the provisions which had stunted communal activity and such activity will spontaneously re-emerge.

The logic, however, was faulty. The culture which sustained and educated ordinary people in the virtues of mutual self-help and social responsibility was the product of an era when nobody expected help from government. The morality governing the behaviour of the respectable working class from the Victorian era through to the inter-war years reflected the common sense of the time, for if people did not assume the responsibility for improving themselves and looking after those close to them, nobody else would. Today, by contrast, common sense tells us that there is no need to live by the irksome rules which governed the behaviour of our grandparents. For fifty years, we have been living by a very different message – one that promises unconditional support whenever we need it, 'from cradle to grave'. In this changed cultural environment, the old virtues have fallen into disuse, and in some cases have even been inverted (see Himmelfarb, 1995 for examples).

It is extremely doubtful whether this could now be reversed. The growth of state provision during the twentieth century undermined a culture based on personal responsibility and communal self-help and replaced it with a 'claimant culture' emphasising political 'rights' to social support. Taking away the state provision will not recreate the old culture, but is more likely to leave people beached in their dependency, thereby provoking festering resentment and social withdrawal. To call, as Thatcher and Major did, for a return to old values is in this sense to misunderstand how culture is reproduced and changed.

The Marxist literature of the 1970s and 1980s probably had a better grasp of this problem than the New Right literature did. In his 1976 work, *Legitimation Crisis*, for example, Juergen Habermas saw that, in the period before extensive state intervention, people had nobody to blame when they fell upon hard times. In the era of the modern welfare state, however, people *expect* government to come to their aid. The welfare state has, he says, undermined the idea of 'natural fate' and has stimulated and sustained 'the demands *that it has placed on itself*' (1976, p. 69, emphasis in original). He goes on to argue that, if the state ceases to meet these demands, the eventual result is likely to be a 'crisis of motivation' as people withdraw from active participation in mainstream society. Rolling back the state, in other words, produces not revitalisation but demoralisation. The emergence of an underclass 'dependency culture' in recent years has begun to look very like this 'crisis of motivation', for it seems that increasing numbers of people have lost the impulse to find work and no longer understand the need to take responsibility for their own lives (see Buckingham, forthcoming).

New Labour seems to have grasped this in a way that the New Right never did. Like Thatcher, Blair is committed to the classical liberal values of enterprise, individual effort and reward for risk and effort. Unlike her, however, he understands that social responsibility will not simply re-emerge once the weight of state dependency is lifted. It has to be encouraged, cajoled and if necessary coerced, for the conditions which originally sustained it have long since been destroyed.

New Labour recognises that a re-imposition of market principles cannot by itself recreate the conditions of social cohesion. Equally, however, New Labour also recognises that simply continuing to expand state welfare is no solution either. Just as the political right has wanted to believe that social cohesion can be achieved by reducing state welfare, so the traditional left has long believed that it can only be achieved by strengthening it, but *both* positions are now understood by New Labour to be fallacious. For 50 years, the Party was convinced that society is held together by giving people handouts. What we are seeing today is the long-delayed realisation that people are held together, not passively by receiving, but actively, by working.

The idea that the post-war comprehensive welfare state functioned as a source of social cohesion was most clearly expressed in Marshall's arguments about the principle of universality grounded in the notion of a common citizenship. In his celebrated essay, Marshall (1964) argued that modern citizens must share equal 'social rights' as well as equal legal and political rights. In the modern welfare state society, in other words, we all have the right to claim social support. Everyone gets treated when they fall ill, everybody's children can go to state schools, and everyone gets cash benefits when they fall on hard times and state pensions when they retire from work. Because we all share in the benefits of the system, the assumption has been that we all owe allegiance to it (or, in Hutton's terminology, that we are all 'stakeholders'). Social cohesion derives from the fact of our shared rights as consumers of state largesse. It is for this reason that writers in this tradition tend to resist mean testing, and are willing to accept a situation where huge amounts of money go to middle-class households which do not need it, for this is seen as the price that has to be paid to keep everybody tied into the system (see Goodin and LeGrand, 1987).

The whole emphasis of this model is on *rights*. The principle of universality does not extend to *responsibilities*, for the model does not expect everybody to contribute. It is true that National Insurance as originally conceived was a system in which individuals established rights to benefits on the basis of earned entitlements, but the National Insurance budget was never ring-fenced from general state revenues and individual contributions were used to pay out current claimants rather than to establish a proper insurance fund. Unlike the old friendly society insurance schemes, therefore, state welfare has generally failed to link contributions to benefits, responsibilities to rights. Far from creating a unified society in which all citizens feel and express a sense of common identity, this system has ended up creating a bifurcated society in which one group pays into the common pool while another group simply draws out.

As I have argued in more detail elsewhere (Saunders, 1993), a system like this is more likely to generate fragmentation than cohesion. There are two reasons for this. The first is that those who are obliged to pay in will feel resentment against those who persistently draw out. In a commercial or truly mutual system of insurance, such resentment is muted because (a) everybody establishes entitlement by paying contributions; (b) benefits are normally paid out only following some calamity which is not the fault of the claimant; and (c) continuing membership is voluntary and 'exit' is readily possible for those who become dissatisfied with the way the fund is being managed. None of these conditions holds in the case of state welfare. Not only is it possible for claimants to have paid little or nothing into the system, but the mere fact of being 'in need' is generally sufficient to establish their claim without further investigation into the circumstances through which the need has arisen. As the old morality of personal responsibility has been eroded, so too has the old distinction between a 'deserving' and an 'undeserving' poor. Inevitably, therefore, the suspicion arises among contributors that funds are being paid out to people who do not really need or deserve support, but the principle of compulsory contributions means that they can do nothing about this. Denied the option of exiting the system, people simply grow increasingly disenchanted and resentful (see Saunders and Harris, 1989).

The second reason why state welfare fosters fragmentation rather than cohesion is that (paradoxically) it encourages individual self-interest. A system of universal benefits is inherently prone to what has been called the 'tragedy of the commons' (Hardin, 1977). In any situation where a large number of people share access to a common resource, the rational, self-maximising individual will seek to make the fullest possible use of the resource in question. Self-restraint will do little to maintain the common resource unless one can be assured that all other individuals are exercising similar restraint, but maximal exploitation of the resource will bring major benefits to oneself while making little impact on the size of the common resource provided others do not follow suit. The consequence is that rational individuals will try to milk the system lest others end up getting more than they do, and the common assets will be over-exploited as a result. State welfare, in other words, encourages ego-ism rather than altruism and is inherently prone to over-exploitation and cheating.

In the language of rational choice game theory, the welfare state is a particularly intractable 'Prisoner's Dilemma' game in which rational indi-viduals are encouraged to cheat even though this is not in their collective long-term best interests. In the 'prisoner's dilemma game', I stand to gain most if I defect (cheat) and you do not. The result is that we are both likely to cheat, yet this is a worse outcome for both of us than if we both play by the rules. In smaller groups (such as the nineteenth-century friendly soci-eties) this problem can be overcome, for all members know each other and are therefore likely to be more willing to moderate their own self-maximising behaviour. As Olson explains, 'Social pressure and social incentives operate only in groups of smaller size, in the groups so small that the members can have face-to-face contact with one another' (1971, p. 62). In larger-scale contexts, however, the dilemma may be irresolvable without imposition of strong rules and surveillance or creation of strong individual incentives to co-operate. Neither condition seems to have applied in the post-war welfare state.

All of this is richly ironic, for socialists have long argued that capitalist free market systems foster widespread resentment and encourage the pursuit of narrow self-interest. We now see that the development of the post-war welfare state has tended to have much the same effect. A system of state welfare which was explicitly set up with the intention of countering the fragmentation of the market by bonding society together has in fact generated conditions which almost inevitably contribute to further fragmentation – a classic example of how unintended (and perverse) consequences can flow from actions intended to bring about quite different results (see Giddens, 1984).

New Labour has come to understand all this. It sees that a free and comprehensive system of state welfare is not the answer to the problem of ensuring social cohesion. Instead, it has begun to search for an answer in solutions which were first put forward over 100 years ago by the French sociologist, Emile Durkheim.

More than any other single social theorist, Durkheim was concerned with the problem of social cohesion in modern societies. In *The Division of Labour in Society* (1933), he identified two main causes of what he saw as the modern malaise of social disorganisation and moral deregulation (what he called 'anomie'). The first was the lack or weakness of any institutional framework expressing to people the importance of the ties of functional interdependence which bind them together. In a modern society with a complex division of labour, we all necessarily depend upon each other for our own welfare for we each perform specialised tasks which allow us to prosper only through extended co-operation with others. Too often, however, we fail to realise how much we depend on others and they in turn depend on us, and like the players in the tragedy of the commons, we focus on how we can maximise returns to ourselves with little regard for how this is likely to affect the whole social order on which we ultimately depend.

In the medieval period, according to Durkheim, the crucial social significance of the occupational division of labour was expressed in the guild system. Individuals belonged to occupational guilds and it was through the interrelation of the guilds that they found a wider common interest and membership in the city and the corporation. In the modern period, however, occupational forms of membership and representation are much weaker and political representation is organised on the basis of relatively meaningless territorial units rather than more meaningful occupational ones. The solution, for Durkheim, is clear – we need to recreate on a national level the sorts of occupationally-based corporations which used to thrive at a smaller scale in medieval times, for only in this way will individuals come once again to realise the importance of co-operation to their own survival.

This is not enough, however, to ensure a properly functioning and relatively harmonious social order. Durkheim argues that a second major source of the anomic conditions characteristic of modernity is the existence of institutional arrangements which prevent the realisation of natural talent. A society need not be equal in order to be harmonious, but it is important that such inequalities that exist are widely felt to be fair and legitimate. This will be the case, in Durkheim's view, only when 'natural inequalities' between people come to be reflected in social inequalities. For this to happen, individuals must all have the opportunity to develop and realise their talents (eg through education), and unearned privileges, such as the inheritance of property, must be reduced or broken down altogether.

Durkheim was writing in the late-nineteenth century, and the prescriptions which seemed sensible then may not necessarily seem sensible or desirable now. We can accept his analysis of the causes of the problem, therefore, without necessarily accepting his identification of the solutions.

The first problem identified by Durkheim is how to guard against excessive self-interest by reinforcing an awareness of functional interdependency. Durkheim was surely right to emphasise the importance of *work* or employment as the source of this interdependence, but his emphasis on corporatist solutions now seems inappropriate. Not only were corporatist forms of organising national solidarity tarnished by the experience of Italian fascism under Mussolini, but weaker forms of corporatism were tried and failed in Britain during the latter years of the period of social conservatism. Between 1962, when the government established the National Economic Development Council, and 1979, when the final attempt at an agreed wages compact with the unions collapsed in the chaos of the 'winter of discontent', government, big business and trade union leaders tried and failed to come to binding agreements which they could impose on their various constituencies (for a review, see Dearlove and Saunders, 1991).

Corporatism thus failed decisively and disastrously in Britain, but its abandonment during the Thatcher years resulted precisely in the sort of moral vacuum which Durkheim had identified. The 1980s was a decade when individuals were seemingly pursuing affluence with little regard to others, and what was lacking was any strong institutional expression of interdependence and social inclusion.

The second problem identified by Durkheim is how to ensure the legitimacy of inequalities. His answer was that an institutional framework was needed which would enable individuals to realise their full potential. Durkheim emphasised that it is not enough that I should recognise how much I depend on others and they depend on me. It is also necessary that I should recognise that others have a right to occupy the positions they hold and that I too occupy an appropriate position given my 'natural' talents and capacities. Both Thatcher (the daughter of a Grantham grocer) and Major (the son of a Brixton circus performer) seemed to understand the importance of this, for both emphasised their view of Britain as an 'open society' in which effort and ability were rewarded. This was not, however, a view widely shared among ordinary people, for as the 1996 *British Social Attitudes Survey* made clear, public opinion through the Thatcher and Major years became increasingly opposed to existing income inequalities, and these governments never succeeded in convincing the electorate that the rich (derided increasingly by opponents as 'fat cats') deserved their good fortune.

To summarise: If Durkheim was right, what is needed for social cohesion, and what the period of liberal conservatism failed sufficiently to provide, is first, a system of social 'inclusivity' based in some way on the occupational system, and second, a system of meritocracy in which social placement depends solely on individual ability and effort. It is these two principles which lie at the heart of New Labour's social liberalism.

One of the sharpest contrasts between the liberal conservatism of the New Right and the social liberalism of New Labour is the latter's concern with social inclusion – a concern that everybody should participate in, and feel part of, a single, cohesive society. This concern has been manifested institutionally in the formation of a new inter-departmental 'social exclusion unit' reporting directly to the Prime Minister. It has also been manifested symbolically in the populism of New Labour rhetoric (notably the tendency to present itself as 'the People's Party'). But most significantly of all, it has been manifested politically in New Labour's commitment to reforming the post-war welfare state.

The core idea of social inclusion is that nobody should be allowed to drift apart from mainstream society. This can mean that escape hatches at the top have to be battened down (one of the new government's first actions, for example, was to abolish the assisted places scheme which allowed bright children from less affluent backgrounds to escape from the state system of comprehensive schooling into the private sector). More often, however, it means that trapdoors at the bottom have to be secured. In particular, people must not be allowed to drop out of employment and live their lives on state benefits. Whether they be the young unemployed, single mothers or able-bodied people claiming disability benefits, those who can work should work.

The Labour Party has traditionally opposed the American principle of 'workfare', in which able-bodied claimants are expected to work in return for benefits, and it has always been deeply distrustful of any attempt to erode the principle of entitlement on the basis of need. New Labour has therefore had to move cautiously, and its policy of 'Welfare to Work' has been couched in the language of enablement rather than coercion. The rhetoric has it that claimants want to work and that the government is simply helping them to do so, although the 'new deal' for the young unemployed has removed any option of remaining on benefit (a move reflecting Lawrence Mead's plea for a strategy of 'help plus hassle'). In reality, New Labour appears to be pursuing a strategy in which work is emphasised as a responsibility which individuals should be obliged to recognise and discharge.

The significance of this switch from old-style citizenship to new-style social inclusion cannot be overstated. Citizenship emphasised rights; social inclusion emphasises duties. Citizenship sought to ensure social cohesion by giving to anyone in need; social inclusion seeks to ensure social cohesion by encouraging everybody to work. Citizenship was passive; social inclusion is active. New Labour's reform of the welfare state is driven partly, it is true, by economic considerations, for the social security budget now accounts for one-third of government spending, and the cost of benefits has increased eight-fold in real terms in fifty years. But more pressing than this economic agenda is a moral one, for the new emphasis on the responsibility to work is part of Labour's answer to the problem of social fragmentation. Like Durkheim, New Labour has come to recognise that social cohesion is grounded in the division of labour, and that moral bonds between people are forged, not through receipt of largesse, but through work. Only when everybody contributes can everybody feel a common sense of membership and interdependence.

Coupled with this new emphasis on the responsibility to work has been a renewed commitment to the principle of meritocracy. In the 1997 election campaign, Tony Blair identified his three priorities as 'education, education and education', and in his speech to the Commonwealth Heads of Government conference shortly after taking office, he proclaimed that, 'The Britain of the elite is over. The new Britain is a meritocracy where we break down the barriers of class, religion, race and culture' (quoted in the *Daily Telegraph*, 25 October 1997, p. 6). The emphasis on education is a recognition that individual opportunity depends increasingly on access to training and the achievement of paper qualifications. The corresponding emphasis on meritocracy reflects a belief that 'social justice' consists not in the achievement of end-state equality, but rather in a system where individuals fill social positions solely on the basis of their ability and their hard work.

As in its commitment to the responsibility to work, so too in its commitment to the principle of meritocracy, New Labour is following a Durkheimian agenda which represents a radical break with old Labour thinking. Old-style social justice emphasised the distribution of resources; new-style social justice emphasises the distribution of opportunities. Old-style social justice was concerned to achieve greater equality of results; new-style social justice is concerned only to ensure that inequalities between individuals have been fairly 'earned'. The emphasis on meritocracy is, in fact, much closer to the sentiments expressed by the previous Conservative administration than those associated with traditional Labour thinking, for John Major too made clear his commitment to the principles of meritocracy early on in his Premiership. The only difference between them is that the Conservatives saw as fair and just certain high earnings (eg those in the City) which New Labour still sees as illegitimate.

Here, then, is social liberalism's answer to the problem which liberal conservatism never managed to solve, the problem of ensuring social cohesion. Where Thatcher and Major believed that a culture of social responsibility would renew itself simply as a result of a shift away from state paternalism, New Labour understands that the problem cannot spontaneously solve itself. Unwittingly taking its cue from the profound insights of Emile Durkheim over a century ago, New Labour seeks to bond us together by emphasising the commitments which we owe each other through our work and by ensuring that hard work and ability are rewarded, thereby minimising the grounds for widespread resentment. The question, of course, is whether this two-pronged strategy will work.

Both parts of this strategy represent a major break with Labour's past, and together they represent much that is distinctive in the new social liberalism. The emphasis on social cohesion through work has displaced the old emphasis on cohesion through welfare, and the emphasis on cohesion through meritocracy has displaced the old emphasis on cohesion through equality of outcomes. The old strategy of welfare-based citizenship and egalitarianism failed because it created resentment and encouraged self-interest. So will the new strategy fare any better?

There are at least two reasons why we might remain sceptical. One is that the United States is on many measures a deeply fractured society, yet this is a country where unemployment is low, where state welfare has always been much less extensive than in Britain, and where the commitment to principles of meritocracy is built into the 'American dream'. If widespread work and a belief in individual opportunity have failed to create cohesion in the USA, why should they be any more successful in Britain?

A second problem is that there may be good grounds for believing that even a genuine meritocracy may encounter severe problems of social cohesion. It is worth remembering that Michael Young's original fable of the rise and fall of a meritocracy ended with a popular revolt against the elitism of intelligence (Young, 1958), for those at the bottom of the heap may be no more inclined to accept the legitimacy of intellectual privilege than the legitimacy of inherited privilege. Indeed, I have suggested elsewhere that a meritocratic system can be self-defeating, for the greater the opportunities available to individuals, the harder it is for failures to accept their fate, and the less likely it is that those who succeed will feel any great benefit or privilege as a result (Saunders, 1996). Meritocracies can breed just as much resentment as any other systems of social inequality.

New Labour's Durkheimian social strategy may well fail to rebuild social cohesion, but it is difficult at the present time to think of a realistic alternative strategy for social renewal. If the triangle in Figure 7.1 really does represent a comprehensive map of modern political ideologies, then it is clear that New Labour has moved to fill the last position that has not yet been tried. Social conservatism's development of a welfare system where resources were allocated purely on the basis of need is today discredited, for in practice welfare dependency and the pursuit of egalitarianism produced not a cohesive society of citizens but a fragmented society of resentful payers and dependent recipients. Equally, liberal conservatism's dream of a return to the small-scale mutualism and market-based co-operation of the nineteenth century must also now be rejected, for the culture that sustained that system of communal self-help has disappeared and cannot be recreated. This leaves only the social liberalism of New Labour with its emphasis on the social duty to work and the individual opportunity to succeed. If this fails to work, then it is difficult to see whence any fourth alternative could arise. As Margaret Thatcher might have put it, it really does seem now that there is no alternative.

REFERENCES

Berger, P. and Neuhaus, R. (1977), *To Empower People*, American Enterprise Institute for Public Policy Research.

Buckingham, A. (forthcoming). 'Is there an underclass in Britain?' *British Journal of Sociology*

Cockett, R. (1994), *Thinking the Unthinkable*, Harper Collins.

Dearlove, J. and Saunders, P. (1991), *An Introduction to British Politics*, Polity Press.

Dennis, N. (1997), *The Invention of Permanent Poverty*, London: Institute of Economic Affairs.

Durkheim, E. (1933), *The Division of Labor in Society*, Macmillan.

Giddens, A. (1984), *The Constitution of Society*, Polity Press.

Goodin, R. and LeGrand, J. (1987), 'Not only the poor' in their *Not Only the Poor: the Middle Classes and the Welfare State*, Allen & Unwin.

Green, D. (1985), *Working Class Patients and the Medical Establishment*, Gower.

Green, D. (1998), *Benefit Dependency*, Institute of Economic Affairs.

Habermas, J. (1976), *Legitimation Crisis*, Heinemann.

Hall, S. (1983), 'The great moving right show' in Hall, S. and Jacques, M. (eds) *The Politics of Thatcherism*, Lawrence & Wishart.

Hardin, G. (1977), 'The tragedy of the commons' in G. Hardin and J. Baden (eds) *Managing the Commons*, W.H. Freeman.

Hayek, F. (1974), *The Road of Serfdom*, Routledge.

Himmelfarb, G. (1995), *The Demoralization of Society*, Knopp.

Hutton, W. (1995), *The State We're In*, Jonathon Cape.

Jowell, R., Curtice, J., Park, A., Brook, L. and Thomson, K. (1996), *British Social Attitudes: the 13th Report*, Dartmouth.

Land, H. and Lewis, J. (1997) 'The emergence of loan motherhood as a problem in late twentieth century Britain' *Welfare State Programme Discussion Paper* No. 134, London School of Economics.

Marshall, T. (1964), 'Citizenship and social class' in T. Marshall (ed.) *Class, Citizenship and Social Development*, Doubleday.

Mead, L. (1992), *The New Politics of Poverty*, Basic Books.

Mead. L. (1997), *From Welfare to Work*, Institute of Economic Affairs.

Murray, C. (1988), *In Pursuit of Happiness and Good Government*, Simon & Schuster.

Murray, C. (1994), *Underclass: the Crisis Deepens*, Institute of Economic Affairs.

Office for National Statistics (1997), *Social Focus on Families*, The Stationery Office.

Olson, M. (1971), *The Logic of Collective Action*, Harvard University Press.

Saunders, P. (1993), 'Citizenship in a liberal society' in B. Turner (ed.) *Citizenship and Social Theory*, Sage.

Saunders, P. (1996), *Unequal But Fair?*, Institute of Economic Affairs.

Saunders, P. and Harris, C. (1989), *Popular Attitudes to State Welfare Services*, Social Affairs Unit (Research Report No. 11).

Spencer, H. (1982), *The Man versus the State*, Liberty Classics.

Young, M. (1958), *The Rise of the Meritocracy*, Thames & Hudson.

8 1968's Unfinished Business – Cultural Equality and the Renewal of the Left

Hilary Wainwright

The spirit of 1968 sometimes seems like an exotic bird: predators seek to kill it and steal the plumage to enhance their own appearance. A shared political characteristic of Margaret Thatcher and Tony Blair is their relish in condemning the legacies of the sixties while selectively deploying its rhetoric for their own ends. Mrs Thatcher destroyed the radical Greater London Council (which put resources and political clout behind ideas seeded by the social movements of the late 1960s and early 1970s). Her policies devasted trade union strength and confidence, another continuity from the sixties. She attacked the democratic, 'progressive' teaching methods that had flourished in the aftermath of 1968. With her mock Victorian family values she sought to contain feminism and stigmatise gay liberation – both gaining new impetus from the cultural firment of this derided decade. Yet at the same time she paraded the plumage of 'liberation', 'empowerment' and 'individual fulfilment'. Similarly, Tony Blair talks 1960's language about 'the third way', 'participation', 'openness', 'new politics' while at the same time presuming private ownership to be a God-given fixture, drastically centralising party power into the hands of his own coteries, closing down debate on controversial issues like the legalisation of cannabis, and receiving business barons in a manner reminiscent of a feudal court.

It is time then, to rescue some integrity for the legacy of 1968. This does not mean a nostalgic dig for treasure buried beneath the detritus of the last 30 years. Rather it requires identifying the possibilities that were opened up. For 1968 was a moment when a repressive culture, already hollowed out, visibly collapsed; before a new cultural order could establish itself, unthinkable alternatives suddenly seemed feasible. State and corporate authority re-stabilised itself but the vulnerability of apparently invincible regimes left powerful impressions on younger generations who witnessed the way that the powerful tottered. Through this process, a genie of cultural confidence had grown among people who had previously accepted a subordinate status; an assertion of cultural equality which could not easily be rebottled.

Which, if any, of the seeds of revolt and of utopia that were sown in the fertile years of 1968 and 1969 have taken root and produced lasting traditions? Which have been distorted by defeat? What innovations and openings have emerged recently that carry on and develop these traditions in new ways?

There is a particular question on which I want to focus. It may be only of personal value but I'll chance it just the same. I believe that a distinctive left, a libertarian left, was born, perhaps reborn, out of the late 1960s. It had roots in the 'new left' that came out of the traumas of 1956 and was associated with E.P. Thompson and also had continuities with earlier non-statist socialist traditions from William Morris to G.D.H. Cole and with the short-lived traditions of cultural equality associated with the French revolution and Thomas Paine. Indeed the continuity that links these varied political phenomena and justifies reference to a distinctive tradition is a shared belief not only in programmes of political and economic equality but also in the need to do away with paternalism and presumptions of cultural superiority by would-be ruling elites – whether political or economic – and to devise methods of democratic self-government. This left has not been morally and intellectually defeated by either the collapse of the Soviet Union or the pressures of the global market. Or to put it more cautiously, the challenges posed by the political bankruptcy of the Soviet bloc and by the increasingly global organisation of capitalist production have been central to its politics from 1968 itself; developments in the past 30 years intensify these challenges but do not put the libertarian left on the intellectual or moral defensive. Its ways of organising have been influenced by the insights of social movements of the last three decades, most notably the women's liberation movement and the radical shop stewards movement of the late sixties and seventies. The experience of the liberated areas in struggles against imperialism, in Africa and Asia, the European peace movement's challenge to the mentality and reality of the Cold War and the doubt cast by the green movement on the uncritically progressive claims for the advance of science, have all shaped its eclectic politics. My question is, what explains the resilience of this libertarian left and is it well founded?

Along with the rest of the left, this diffuse tradition has been severely battered in the past 30 years, beginning with the defeat of radical forces that had gained influence in Labour's shadow cabinet in the final, striketorn years of the 1970–74 Conservative government of Edward Heath. The sidelining of the left was followed by the ignominious defeat of the Callaghan Labour Government and the victory of Mrs Thatcher with all that followed from it: the erosion of union strength, the virtual destruction of local government, the straight-jacketing of education, the inculcation of fear and insecurity, the destruction of any base for opposition or plural politics. The repercussions of the Thatcher years for the libertarian left were so profound that perhaps they have not fully sunk-in. On an international scale too, this left has been weakened by the impact of de-regulation and globalisation on labour and social movements North and South. Its libertarianism is, after all, based on a belief in democratic collectivities and their importance as a basis of social co-operation; if popular democratic organisations are weakened the libertarian left appears utopian, lacking feasible forms of agency.

The libertarian left's belief, however, in the possibility of a social order based on social co-operation, equality and democracy has retained its moral confidence. Socialists from this tradition do not find their foundations to be shaken in the way that many on both the communist and social democratic left feel theirs to have disappeared. Many from these ruling left traditions believed they had no option but to abandon a commitment to socialism or to redefine it as a humanised capitalism. The socialist vision of many leftish western social democrats as well as Communists was closely associated with the model of the command economy. Jack Straw's description of his youthful vision being 'the command economy plus parliamentary democracy'[1] summed up a view shared by many, and shattered by increasing evidence of the failings of economies run by a centralised state. The criticisms made by this kind of socialist of the Soviet model were not primarily of the economic system (the lack of decentralised common and co-operative ownership, accountable economic co-ordination and workplace democracy, for instance) but of the undemocratic, unparliamentary character of the state which ran it. For them, the only alternative to the centralised state, as far as economics was concerned, was private property and the market or some mix of state and private market.

For the libertarian left, the rejection of the Soviet model was more fundamental. The political spirit of 1968 was in opposition to the authoritarianism of Moscow and Peking as much as the imperialism of Washington and London. Our socialism was, from its foundations, shaped as much by our reflections as we protested at the Soviet invasion of Czechoslovakia as by our thoughts as we marched to stop the Americans bombing Vietnam. As a generation frustrated by the bluntness of parliamentary democracy we were both inspired by the original Soviet ideal of participatory democracy and sobered by its fate when the popular participation in local as well as national soviets was subordinated to centralised planning and single party monopoly. The need to combine participatory forms of economic democracy with rules for political pluralism was consequently fundamental to our thinking. But we also learnt directly from our own fraught experiences of participatory decision making, our knowledge of the democratic – and problematic – co-operative models in the areas liberated by guerrilla movements in Vietnam and Mozambique and our involvement or observation of the shopfloor democracy – potential and real – evident in the militant trade unionism of the late sixties and early seventies.

Initially our vision and with it our timetable was somewhat over-optimistic about the power of direct forms of democracy. Harold Wilson's puppet-like stance – whether the strings were pulled by Lyndon Johnson or the City of London – had discredited parliamentary democracy. Events in Paris, along with activity in our own streets, campuses and factories, had given us hope that in some ill-thought-out way, we could bypass this mirage of democratic government with institutions more direct, alert and innovative in meeting the needs of the people.

As quasi insurrectionary hopes gave way to a radical gradualism and as we moved from the flexibility of student life to work in institutions whose bureaucratic routines persisted through lack of a credible alternative, we honed our vague belief in participatory democracy into detailed ideas for the democratisation of every area of public administration from primary, secondary and higher education through to mental health. Through the Institute For Workers Control, some of us collaborated with an earlier generation of radical and free-spirited socialists like Steve Boddington, Ken Coates and Michael Barratt-Brown and a network of left-wing trade unionists who believed in industrial democracy and knew that the creativity and power to bring it about was to be found among workers and their communities. This network of workers and intellectuals led to numerous plans and proposals for democratising nationalised industries, turning medium size companies into co-ops and combining the bargaining power of government and workers to impose some social responsibility on the footloose multinationals.

The women's liberation movement, especially the socialist feminists like Sheila Rowbotham who were part of its origins, made a notable contribution to the feasibly utopian character of the new left in the seventies.[2] As feminists we refused to postpone womens liberation until after the revolution or until a socialist government was elected to office. For women to have even the autonomy necessary to play an active part in working for social change, the conditions of their lives had to improve in the present: women abused by men needed refuge now; mothers trapped in the home by the responsibilities of children needed shared or public childcare now and of a sort over which they had some control. As women gained confidence and a strong collective sense of their needs they took the initiative to make public services such as health, education and transport responsive to women.

Throughout the first half of the seventies these practical schemes, a renewal of the feasibility of democratic socialism, had real popular resonance. The positive alternatives that sprang from these diverse sources were not just academic pipe dreams but the basis of campaigning demands on local government, education and health authorities across the country; they were a radical presence in debates about the future of television and radio; they influenced bargaining strategies and demands on government in industries such as engineering, building, coal and telecommunications.

What we lacked was political representation. When extra-parliamentary activity was at its height this did not seem to matter. The radical left seemed to have its own momentum, even if this was in fact more the product of converging movements with their own concerns rather than being the sign of a single movement with a coherent direction. As Tory cutbacks and company downsizing began to pose new problems for which direct action was not sufficient, and as the impact of radical social and industrial movements began to reverberate through the Labour Party, the libertarian left began to take a wary interest in party politics. Often, they did so in a new way, keeping their social movement or trade union base and attempting to bend the Labour Party to its concerns.

Two moments of political innovation and conflict were the outcome of this collision of extra-parliamentary radicalism and a Labour Left open to new directions. First, the efforts, associated with Tony Benn, to democratise industry and the party itself; secondly, the attempts by Labour Parties, long out of national office, to carry out radical change through the municipality – most famously in London but also in different ways in Sheffield, Walsall and Manchester.

Innovation was inspired by creative convergencies between radical leftists influenced by 1968 and the 1970s and genuine social democrats like Tony Benn and Stuart Holland, radicalised by their government experience under Harold Wilson. The latter group had entered this government as egalitarian and democratic modernisers (not as Clause 4 socialists) and had come up against the hostility of civil service mandarins and City moguls alike, and often in concert. Such politicians, committed as they were to their radical, modernising manifesto commitments turned, sometimes reluctantly, to the organisations of the people in whose interests the policies were intended to be.

In particular, given their concern for industrial modernisation, Benn and Holland turned to the shop stewards movement to make common cause in calling management to account. Tony Benn had long been a critic of old-style nationalisation, quipping that 'Alf Robens plus the Coal Board doesn't equal socialism' (a reference to the chair of the nationalised coal industry when it began a major programme of pit closure and redundancies). His experiences of the energy and intelligence evident among shop floor workers during the work-in to save the Upper Clyde Shipbuilders in sharp contrast to the conservative vested interests at the heart of government, led him enthusiastically to espouse the cause of industrial democracy. He broke away from traditional corporatist relations between government, management and trade union leaders and worked with shop floor representatives on detailed plans for job creation and industrial democracy. The most vivid example was the plan drawn up by the shop stewards committee in Lucas Aerospace, a plan not only for saving jobs but also for converting from the production of missile components to the production of innovative transport equipment, the latest medical technology and innovative energy saving equipment – as the Lucas stewards put it, 'an alternative corporate plan for socially useful production'.

The Lucas workers' plan was one of many but its coherence, technical credibility and the strength of the organisation behind it made it exemplary. It was exemplary of a new approach – in practice if not in theory – to relations between the state, popular organisations and the markets (including the financial markets, in that the Lucas workers prepared plans for democratising pension funds, which make up a major part of the market for capital). The idea of 'a workers' plan' came out of a shared experience of the limits of nationalisation: 'we can't look at it through the eyes of nationalisation 1945 or the eyes of nationalisation in the past ten years. We need to draw up a completely new concept' said one of the shop stewards in the early first discussion of the idea. The 'new concept' built on the old social democratic goal of 'common ownership of the means of production, distribution and exchange' but in the light of experience it involved rejecting the assumption that this necessarily meant 'nationalisation' that is: government ownership, management and administration. No one denied that nationalisation was as another steward put it, 'far, far better than the old set-up – under private ownership. The miners will tell you that. But we have to build on it. It's up to us to look for new forms. If we are going to sit back and leave it to the politicians to carry on, then, well we deserve everything we get'. This self-confidence born of ten years of shop floor strength together with a pride in their combined skills, was the impetus to their innovation: 'to draw up a plan without management. Let us start here from this Combine Committee; after all over the years it has grown and grown', urged a shop steward from the Lucas Aerospace factory near Liverpool. 'The Combine (shop stewards) Committee has the ability not only in industrial disputes but also to tackle wider problems. Let's get down to working on how we'd draw up a plan, on our terms rather than management's to meet the needs of our community'. Which is what they did, drawing on ideas put forward, discussed, and evaluated at Lucas Aerospace factories from Burnley in Lancashire down to Neasden in West London.[3]

Their proposals had implications for government, which was already the company's major customer, as well as for management. Government or at any rate the public sector, would still under the workers' plan be a major customer, but it would be buying products to improve transport services, NHS facilities and energy conservation, rather than military equipment. Their campaigns for the plan involved nurses and doctors, local councillors and an extensive network of people with an interest both in the needs they were responding to and the innovative methods they used. Their plan was resisted by management, some trade union leaders and most of the government, not because of the substantive engineering content – many of its product proposals have since been taken up by other companies – but because of its challenge to established relations of power.

I describe the Lucas workers' initiative in detail because it illustrates in practice distinctive principles which the libertarian left sought to develop and promote, and it illustrates the existence of the spirit of this left in Labour's heartlands. On the one hand it defended, built on and tried to extend the basic principles, and practical achievements of social democratic government (achievements that were already under steady erosion): public provision of welfare, education, health infrastructure, public intervention including conditional subsidies and actual ownership of key parts of the economy, employment protection and a degree of redistribution of wealth. Hence it presumed a legislative framework for success and engagement with the parliamentary process to achieve it. It was not simply a latter day syndicalism. On the other hand, the shop stewards drew on their own practical and technical knowledge – on which after all the company depended – the democratic organisation they had built up over the years and their wider social involvement, from the local council and the health service through CND to projects supporting the Third World, to show a way of democratising this public intervention, making it more effective in meeting social needs.

Thus several years before Margaret Thatcher launched her free market campaign against public services and nationalised industries, exploiting and exaggerating all their inefficiencies and paternalism, there were elements of an alternative embedded in the practice of those who had witnessed in their daily lives both the benefits and the failing of the social democratic state. The Lucas case is just one of the more coherent, well worked out examples of an alternative direction – not yet a model – based on democratising rather than privatising public resources.

The Labour government was impervious to the potential of these shop floor experiments to refresh with a massive dose of democracy the ideal of public industries and provision. But at a local level, a minority of Labour councillors were more responsive. Many of them had indeed been involved in similar experiments over housing, urban planning and community provision. From 1982–86 the Greater London Council managed to confront Mrs Thatcher's mix of freedom rhetoric and centralising reality with a genuinely liberating alternative. With the resources of a small nation state, a large workforce and a wide range of responsibilities, the GLC was able actually to implement ideas campaigned for by the libertarian left in the seventies. The principle drawn from these ideas and partially theorised in an important but undervalued book *In and Against the State*[4] was to defend and extend public resources but democratise their means of management and administration. Many methods of democratising public provision were tried at the GLC. Especially important was the delegation of policy implementation to civic organisations working in close liaison with the Council staff.

A good example would be the planning and development of inner city areas like Coin Street in Waterloo, the hinterland of King's Cross and many parts of London's Docklands: in the 1970s and early 1980s there were forceful and imaginative community campaigns in these areas pressing the needs of local people against the vulture-like interests of property developers. The London Labour Party's GLC manifesto committed the new administration to inner city development to meet the needs of the local communities. It implemented this commitment in a new way. The GLC used its statutory planning powers to ward off the property developers but then, instead of its highly prestigious, expert Planning Department taking over the planning of these areas, the Planning Committee gave grants to coalitions of local community organisations to draw up their own plans, using GLC staff as a resource and source of advice. The plans were then the basis, after negotiation and discussion with interested parties and the GLC's Planning Committee, for the areas' development. The same principles were put into practice in relation to child care, police monitoring, many aspects of economic policy, and policy towards ethnic minorities and women. The logic was not always thought through but it went like this: these are new areas of policy on which local government professionals have very little knowledge. Those with the knowledge and the sense of direction are the democratic community or workplace organisations of the people directly affected. The GLC should support these organisations, including financially, and work with them to elaborate and implement the policy commitments on which the Council was elected. It was an approach which was pragmatic and radical at the same time and productive of results which won the GLC widespread popular support, way beyond traditional Labour constituencies. No wonder the Conservative government felt more worried by what was happening across the river than across the floor of the House of Commons. 'This is modern socialism', said Norman Tebbit at the time, 'and we will kill it'.[5]

And they nearly did. 'They' being not just the Thatcherite Conservatives but also New Labour's children of Thatcher. What they nearly killed was not 'modern socialism' as a complete model, no such thing was, or indeed could have been, fully developed. What they almost put an end to was a messy process by which the egalitarian foundations of the post-war settlement were being built on by a generation with the self confidence and expectations to think that the people could run things themselves in a democratic and co-operative manner with the state as the back up and the publically accountable source of resources. Their liberation of public provision from the mechanical constraints of a social engineering sort of socialism was hijacked mid-journey. It was taken over by people who spoke the language of freedom but in reality provided only the false freedom of money.

Without its own political voice the ideas of the libertarian left were drowned in the cacophony of inner Labour Party conflict. The popularity that built up around the GLC (from an initial low point during which its radicalism was the object of mockery and abuse) provided a brief and incomplete illustration of the potential of the general approach of the libertarian left to provide an answer to the growing appeal of the free market right. Indeed in countries where some variant of a libertarian left had its own voice, Denmark, Germany, Sweden and Norway, for example, the radical right never gained an ideological hold. (Of course there are many other reasons for this including the distinctive strength of Christian Democracy on the right of the political spectrum in these countries and the fact that social democratic principles were entrenched in their written constitutions but the fact that a left alternative to social democracy has had real political legitimacy is undoubtedly an important factor.) In Britain this potential was stymied by peculiarities of both the electoral system and Labour's history as the singular political expression of a unified trade union movement. In the absence of an electoral competitor to its left, the Labour Party as first and foremost an electoral machine, looks over its right shoulder and takes the left for granted. It always gravitates to the centre. And never more so than after four consecutive election defeats.

The result has been a situation in which the left has been locked into a permanently subordinate position within the Labour Party without any other political outlet. In this situation there was little opportunity for new ideas from the left – usually generated or at least influenced by social forces outside the party – to be nourished and promoted in a sustained way. When such ideas did surface in the party, as in the early and mid 1970s as we have just seen, influenced by the radical movements of the time, they become mangled by the inner party power struggle. A vicious spiral of caricature ('loony left', etc), blame (for causing Labour to lose elections), leading to beleaguerment and causing defensive and sectarian tendencies to gain the upperhand. This was one way in which the radical libertarian left lost its momentum in the latter half of the 1980s after the abolition of the GLC and the defeat of the miners' strike.

The defeat of the miners was symbolic of a wider problem for the libertarian left: its ideas depended in good part on the strength and confidence of democratic social movements in the workplace and the community. In the 1970s and early 1980s, the scope and creativity of trade union and other social movements were inter-related. Consider the issue of public housing: self-confident and socialist shop stewards committees in the Direct Labour Organisations of local councils were increasingly open to making common cause with tenants' committees on council house estates in an effort to improve the quality and democratic control over council housing; in some cities, Birmingham, for instance, building workers took up environmental issues, arguing for 'Green Bans' – vetoing by direct action building on certain environmentally precious parts of the town. Such vistas of democratisation opened up partly because of a weakening of the old state and corporate hold on power and partly because of the pressure of a new generation of activists in the unions and the community influenced by the confident, democratic spirit of 68.

New possibilities also depended on there being within mainstream politics a strong commitment to social regulation and intervention. For example, ideas about democratising and materially improving public housing gained momentum, albeit limited, because the ideas of tenants, DLO shop stewards and sympathetic researchers were taken up positively by radical or open-minded Labour councillors. Usually, though, these were in a minority and in the end could achieve very little. A rare example of a formalised relationship between the distinctive power and knowledge of workplace organisations and the legal framework laid down by representative government is provided by the health and safety legislation that was part of the 1974 Labour government's Social Contract. Instead of presuming that state inspectors could police this relatively tough legislation on their own, the legislation delegated powers to Health and Safety Committees based on the workplace shop stewards committees. This way the workers with all their practical knowledge of the risks of the workplace would be able to trigger off the implementation of the legislation. It illustrates principles of delegation and de-centralisation of powers to democratic civic organisations that could be adapted to implement tough and effective regulation on for example, the environment, low pay, sex and race discrimination. In other words strong social intervention in the market does not necessarily mean a greater concentration of power in the state.

The application of this principle in the 1974 Health and Safety legislation was not the result of a thought-through commitment to such a new approach to social regulation. Rather, it was the outcome of the strength of the shop stewards movement and some innovative thinking in the trade union movement. Such creative thinking has tended to wane as shop floor organisations have lost their strength and the self-confidence that it generates. One of the reasons why democratic popular movements are so important for libertarian socialism is the confidence that people gain through the power of their collective resistance and the creativity that can be released as a consequence. The radical republican Tom Paine put this point dramatically in the *Rights of Man* written in the late 18th Century:

It appears to general observation, that revolutions create genius and talents; but those events do no more than bring them forward. There is existing in man, a mass of sense lying in a dormant state, and which unless something excites it to action, will descend with him in that condition to the grave. As it is to the advantage of society that the whole of its facilities should be employed, the construction of government ought to be such as to bring forward, by quiet and regular operation, all that extent of capacity which never fails to appear in revolution.

Tom Paine was arguing against monarchy for representative democracy, which he thought would enable that 'extent of capacity' to be brought forward by 'quiet and regular operation'. But now his appeal points to a damning limit of representative government: while it might, depending on the pluralism and accountability of its structures, ensure the representation of the general opinions of the people, it does not bring forward that full extent of human capacity from which society would benefit. Another way of expressing this is that while representative, parliamentary, democracy presumes formal political equality – universal suffrage, equality before the law, for instance – it can co-exist not only with economic inequality but also cultural subordination. The cultural subordination implied by, for instance, the paternalism of professional social reformers, who presume a cultural superiority to those on whose behalf they are devising reforms; or the benign employer who presumes to know what is in the best interest of their employees. Paine was arguing for cultural equality alongside political equality. Such an intertwining of the two is a part of the radical tradition that has been marginalised in the first 60 or so years of the 20th century. Its revival, connecting it firmly with the socialist goal of economic democracy, is one of the consequences of 1968 – which has indeed been followed by a revival of interest in the late 18th or early 19th century radicals: Paine, Shelley, Wolstencraft, for instance, for whom political égalité and cultural emancipation were inseparable.[7]

The way that this radically democratic tradition was swept aside during the 19th and 20th century by left traditions which turned economic and political equality into goals independent of the cultural capacities of the people, is a pressing study in itself. There is one aspect of the explanation which I would suggest now because it is relevant to understanding the significance of 1968 in reviving the importance of cultural equality for a feasible vision of democratic socialism. It is this: that the marginality of cultural equality in the dominant, and often ruling socialist traditions of the 20th century, is associated with approaches to science, method and knowledge that came to guide the organisations of state and economy during and following the industrial revolution. The struggle associated with the Enlightenment to rid society of the fog of superstition and religious dogma also laid the basis for another kind of domination, in the name of progress: the rule of the all-knowing expert, whether that be the professional politician, civil servant, army general, corporate manage or party general secretary.

A vital element in the new forms of domination which came with the development of science, was the particular philosophy of science that became the orthodoxy of the day, first in the theorisation of natural science and then in the methodology of social science and its application to economic management, technological development, and state administration. It was based on the model of natural sciences which aspired to formulate general laws describing regular conjunctions of events or phenomena. This provided the premises from which science, social as well as natural, was thought to be able to make certain predictions and gain ever more perfect knowledge as discovery of generalisations progressed. Initially this positivistic model had a progressive impact, undermining as it did the influence of religious faith and superstition. However, by the mid-twentieth century it had come to underpin an unduly optimistic faith in scientific production, manipulation and control, and in the capacity of science to move forward, morally, socially and intellectually. When applied to the study and reform of society, it presumed that general (in positivist terms, 'scientific') laws were the only valid form of knowledge. This created the cultural conditions for a separation of the goal of purposeful social change from democratic self-government (in Paine's terms, forms of government that 'bring forward, by quie and regular operation, all that extent of capacity which never fails to appear in revolution'). The people could protest, rebel, cry in pain, but the diagnoses and the solutions were the task of the experts – the professionals schooled in science. As Beatrice Webb, the exemplary social reformer in this school of benevolent experts put it, 'the average sensual man can describe his problem but is unable to prescribe a solution'.[8] Such a presumption stemmed not from prejudice but from a view of knowledge which relegated the knowledge that stems from experience simply to the level of raw material for scientific laws; a source of evidence, in other words, for the constant conjunctures on which scientific laws, according to positivism, are built. Such a minimal, passive role for the social knowledge of the mass of people, tended towards a social engineering model for processes of social reform. A model, in other words, which presumes that the most effective operators of social change, whether a social democratic state or a Leninist party, are acting on society from the outside, without any self-consciousness of the social relations connecting them and the subject of their study. To varying degrees, society was understood as the material, the raw steel. State institutions, in the hands of social reformers, or new state institutions, operated by the revolutionary party, were the engineers working the political machinery to transform the material. They were guided by what they presumed to be a scientific understanding of the material, based on past observance of the recurring patterns of its behaviour, gained through statistical surveys.

A postivistic method also reached into the organisation of labour, first in manufacturing, though latter applied to state administration. F.W. Taylor developed his 'principles of scientific management' in the 1890s and 1900s but they were elaborated in theory and practice for the following half century or, until the workers revolts of the late 1960s made them unworkable. Fundamental to his principles is the assumption that the practical knowledge uitilised by workers in the course of their labour is so simple that there is no obstacle to its codification and centralisation: 'Every single act of the workman can be reduced to a science', he asserts in *The Principles of Scientific Management*.[9] Under his system, 'the workman is told minutely just what he is to do and how he is to do it; any improvement which he makes upon the order given is fatal to success'. His ideas inspired Henry Ford to give mechanised reality in the assembly line to the precise division of labour and machine-like workmanship that his science inspired. In Britain, Fabian notions of planning and Herbert Morrison's model of the public corporation both drew heavily on Taylor in their measures of efficiency and their centralising methods of administration. Moreover in the development of social services, the idea of the standard product was put to social democratic purposes in building the welfare state.

East and West, the late 1960s witnessed a crisis in the practice of social engineering and scientific management just at the same time as philosophy of science and social science was in a state of momentous flux.[10] The confidence that scientific knowledge would show the way reached its political apotheosis in the West in the early to mid 1960s, with the technocratic confidence surrounding both the Wilson government and the Kennedy regime in the United States. In the East a related faith, focused on the command economy, reached its zenith in the mobilisation of Soviet resources to defeat the Nazis in 1944 and complete the country's industrialisation. Significantly, history dealt blows to the confidence of the ruling élites on both sides of the Iron Curtain in quick succession. In the East, the sources were Krushchev's revelations of the crimes of Stalin, followed by the repressed uprisings of Hungary, Poland and then, 12 years later, Czechoslavakia; in the West it was Vietnam, and the defeat by a peasant army and campus revolts of the technologically mightiest army in the world which showed that the methods of the industrial, military and political élites were not only morally flawed but practically fallible.

The movements originating in the late sixties of students, workers, tenants and women were also pressing alternatives to the more everyday legacies of social engineering: the univeristy campuses in bleak parklands, designed with little practical knowledge of students' needs and desires; medical training and hospital organisation developed without knowledge of the particular needs and concerns of women; transport systems worked out as if children and old people did not exist; council housing that gave tenants no power over the colour of their door let alone the efficiency of their repairs; work routines that timed workers' absence in the toilet, and so on.

The movements resisting these and similar indignities and seeking to initiate, not just demand, alternatives echo Tom Paine. They (and the sustained struggles of later years such as the examples mentioned earlier like the Lucas Workers Combine Committee or others like 1984/85 miners' strike) were like a low intensity revolution in the sense that time and time again new groups of people would become involved in struggles through which they found talents and strengths that were surprising even to themselves. This was most dramatic in the case of women – the thousands who became active in the women's movement whether middle-class housewives or night cleaners; the Asian women who created Southall Black Sisters; the women of the mining communities who formed Women Against Pit Closure, these are just better-known examples. In these struggles women both transformed their own lives, became speakers, organisers, writers, poets and in the process created new social forms, some of which have lasted and become focal points of change and support.

The problem, at the nub of Tom Paine's statement, is how the conditions producing this creativity and stretched capacity can be sustained beyond the inevitably limited moments of revolution, resistance or social upheaval. How can the forms of co-operation, mutual encouragement and effective participation produced by such events, enhancing people's self-confidence and bringing out their capacities, become central to everyday economic and political decision making? How could popular participation become endemic to different social organisations rather than exceptional? What are the necessary economic, educational and institutional structures for such regular participation to be possible, realistic and effective? What forms of democratic discipline and social cohesion are necessary for participative organisations to be sustainable, beyond moments of obvious enthusiasm and unproblematic common purpose? Answers to questions such as these would begin to unite once again ideals of political and economic equality with cultural equality.

The libertarian left, in a variety of practical projects, some examples of which I discussed earlier in the chapter, aspired to unite these ideas and in doing so to bring together economic and social reform with democratic self-government, throughout society. It has begun in practice, if not yet in theory, to answer these questions. In a sense its ability to do so was cut short by Thatcherism and the global influence of free market capitalism. This chapter therefore has to have an open-ended conclusion. All I want to do to conclude is to argue that the practical challenge of the libertarian left to the social engineering tradition of social democracy and the command economy, provides at least some tools for an egalitarian and democratic alternative to neo-liberalism. This is important because the hegemony of neo-liberal theory lives on, in Britain and the USA, even though its practice is ripping itself apart.

I have suggested at length in my book *Arguments for a New Left, Answering the Free Market Right*, how the left that was shaped by the social movements that exploded in 1968 holds out the basis for a new left that can answer the appeal of neo-liberalism in the way that the traditional left cannot.[11]

I will summarise these arguments here because doing so demonstrates the innovative character of the left that has been shaped by the social movements of the last 30 years – what I have called 'the libertarian left'. The way in which this left has tools to answer the free market right also helps to explain its resilience in the face of two decades of neo-liberal government.

At the foundations of neo-liberalism's free-market ideology is a theory of knowledge, based on the work of Frederick Hayek which the traditional left has not adequately answered. It is a theory of the limits of social scientific knowledge and the importance of practical knowledge to which I would argue the libertarian left has a distinctive and convincing answer.

The object of Hayek's attack was the social engineering state and the positivistic orthodoxy which I have just analysed (though not in Hayekian terms). The students' and workers' movements of the late 1960s and even more so in consequent movements – most notably the women's, green and peace movements and more recent direct action movements – implicitly challenged this methodology from several angles. They questioned the inevitably progressive character of science and its application, without turning their back on science itself. Also, in their practice and to some extent in their theory, they both valued practical/tacit knowledge and demonstrated the social character of all forms of knowledge, everyday and theoretical. It is this that provides the left influenced by these movements with the tools to answer the neo-liberal justification of its free-market policies.

Underlying the neo-liberal worship of the market is the critique made by Frederick Hayek of both classical economic theory and both social democratic and USSR style socialism (the only kinds of socialism he could imagine). He argued that much essential economic knowledge is not of the law-like, quantifiable or at least codifiable kind that can be easily centralised; millions of economic decisions depend on practical knowledge. This knowledge is frequently tacit, 'things we know but cannot tell',[12] in the words of the original theorist of such knowledge, Michael Polanyi; it is often ephemeral and developmental. It cannot be captured or anticipated by a central brain, however computerised such a centre might be. The connection between social purpose and intention and outcome is broken; we cannot design the social order and it is a 'fatal deceit' to think we can. The only legitimate social order is one, i.e. the unregulated market, arrived at without human design, the haphazard outcome of millions of individual decisions miraculously co-ordinated through the workings of the price mechanism. Not only is this order achieved without conscious intervention but so delicate is its balance, goes the neo-liberal logic, that it would be destroyed by such intervention – however well intentioned its purpose.[13]

In response to these arguments the libertarian left – judging by its practice – would agree about the importance of practical knowledge, though in rather different terms, but strongly reject the idea that the free market is the mechanism that can best make use of the wealth of such practical knowledge. There is an illegitimate leap in Hayek's logic – a leap which provides the libertarian left with the opportunity to trip up the neo-liberals. The leap involves assuming that practical knowledge, as if by definition, is individual. Hayek maintains that, 'all the possible differences in men's moral attitudes amount to little, so far as their significance for social organisation is concerned, compared with the fact that all man's mind can effectively comprehend are the facts of the narrow circle of which he is the centre'.[14] What is significant about this statement is not its recognition of limits on human reason but the dogmatically individual nature of these limits, closing off not only the idea of total rationality and complete knowledge (rightly) but also (wrongly) the possibility of social action to share information and extend the knowledge of individuals beyond their immediate circle.

Hayek's theory of knowledge, the foundation stone of the neo-liberal belief in the unfettered market, completely excludes the possibility that practical knowledge might be shared or socialised. The social organisation of knowledge can take many forms; it does not have to be centralised or even fully codified. Once it is acknowledged that practical knowledge could be social, though in different ways from other, for example, statistical, forms of knowledge, then the possibility exists that the social organisations through which such sharing takes place could influence the character of the market, framing, regulating, constraining it and intervening in it, including in partnership with an elected political authority.

It is in the development of this socialisation of practical knowledge that the vital innovation of recent social movements lies. The theme common to the social movements which shaped this left was a rebellion against authority, both public and private; against the paternalism of those who presumed to know what is good for people: professors of students; men with power of women without it; managers of workers; the state of the people. In their ways of organising and thinking they held out the value of practical and tacit knowledge, testing its insights with those of theoretical knowledge. Their practice is backed up by recent developments in the philosophy of science which have shown the importance of practical knowledge, a central form of knowledge which has tended, in the positivist orthodoxy of most of this century, to be part of 'the empirical' and subsumed under general laws.[15]

A recognition of the distinct importance of practical knowledge and its interaction with theoretical understanding, has immense political implications. It provides a vital foundation stone for thinking through feasible forms of participatory democracy. I explore some of these implications in *Arguments for a New Left*, with the *caveat* that much work still needs to be done: the research agenda of the libertarian left is ambitious though there is much rich practice on which to draw. Whether learning lessons from work with the liberation movements of Asia and Africa in 1968 or from linking with the movements of peasants and casualised workers across the world to resist the Multilateral Agreement on Investment in 1998, the libertarian left has a special contribution to make towards democratic governance in the face of the deregulated global economy. Its alertness to the limits of parliamentary democracy has been sharpened by witnessing both the flaws of even the most meritocratic, representative ruling élites and by directly experiencing the capacities of the people for democratic self-government with all the messy uncertainty which that entails.

NOTES

1. Answer to a warm-up question on 'Any Questions', October 1997.
2. See Rowbotham, Sheila. *The Past is Before Us: Feminism in Action Since the 1960's* (1989), Penguin.
3. See Hilary Wainwright and David Elliott *The Lucas Plan; a new Trade Unionism in the Making* (1982), Alison & Busby.
4. *In and Against the State* The London Edinburgh Weekend Return Group. A working group of the Conference of Socialist Economists (1980), Pluto.
5. Documents from the GLC's Economic Policy Group, including 'The London Industrial Strategy' are available from the Centre for Local Economic Strategies, Whitworth Street, Manchester. See also *A Taste of Power, the Politics of Local Economics* eds Maureen Macintosh and Hilary Wainwright (1987), Verso.
6. 'The Rights of Man', in *The Thomas Paine Reader* (1987), Penguin, p. 277.
7. See E.P. Thompson *The Romantics, England in Revolutionary Age* (1997), Merlin, for a rare and brilliant analysis of these and other themes through the work of Wordsworth, Coleridge and Thelwell.
8. For a discussion of this tradition in the context of British socialism see Fred Whitmore 'British Socialism and Democracy in Retrospect' in *Socialism and Democracy* eds Sean Sayers and David McLellan (1991), Macmillan.

9. *Principles of Scientific Management* (1911), New York, p. 34.
10. Roy Bhaskar's entry on 'Knowledge, Theory of' in 'The Blackwell Dictionary of Twentieth-Century Thought' (1993), Blackwell (eds) William Outhwaite and Tom Bottomore provides a useful summary. Especially important was Thomas Kuhn's *The Structure of Scientific Revolutions* (2nd edn) (1970), University of Chicago Press.
11. *Arguments for a New Left; Answering the Free Market Right* (1994), Blackwell.
12. F. Hayek. 'The Use of Knowledge in Society' in *Individualism and Economic Order* (1949), Routledge.
13. The potential agents of such intervention are understood to be either particularistic interests such as trades unions or an over-bearing, social engineering state; over-bearing private corporations using unequal market power to capture further market power somehow seem to escape scrutiny.
14. F. Hayek. *Individualism and Economic Order* (1949), Routledge, p. 14.
15. See William Outhwaite, *New Philosophies of Social Science* (1987), Routledge, Roy Bhaskar, *A Realist Theory of Science* (1978), Harvester.

9 The Long Sixties in the Short Twentieth Century
Michael Williams

Waiting for the end, boys, waiting for the end.
What is there to be or do?
What's become of me or you?
Are we kind or are we true?
Sitting two and two, boys, waiting for the end.

'Waiting for the end, boys, waiting for the end': such is the refrain of William Empson's hilarious parody 'Just a Smack at Auden' published in 1937 (Skelton, 1964: 64). His direct target was Auden's 'A Communist to Others' (published in 1933) but that refrain highlighted the sense of impending apocalypse that dominated the tone of so much of the literature of the 1930s and raised Empson's own poem above the transient value of mere parody.

The end envisaged in the 1930s was, of course, the impending climactic struggle between reaction and democracy, fascism and communism, modernity and tradition that all could predict and which threatened the survival of civilisation. The same kind of atmosphere surrounded at least the first couple of decades of Cold War and can be sensed in such works as George Orwell's *Nineteen Eighty-Four* (1949) and his friend Arthur Koestler's *The Age of Longing* (1951) which anticipated a Soviet takeover of Western Europe. Only in the early 1960s, with Stanley Kubrick's *Dr Strangelove – or how I learned to stop worrying and love the bomb*, did we begin to shrug off our fears. By 1965, when Barry Maguire topped the US charts with 'Eve of Destruction', that sense of impending apocalypse was fit material for a hit single.

Now that long-impending end seems to have arrived – not exactly with a whimper but certainly not with the bang which so many predicted and feared. The last decade has been dominated by a sense of the end: we are no longer waiting for the end; the end has arrived. This sense of an ending is implicit in the notion of the post-modern which has been present at least since the 1960s but has gathered increasing currency in recent years. The very calendar as the end of the second millennium approaches seems to proclaim it. And it has dominated political debate since the publication of

Francis Fukuyama's seminal article 'The End of History?' published in the American periodical *The National Interest* in 1989 (Fukuyama, 1989), later expanded to book length in *The End of History and the Last Man* (Fukuyama, 1992). Fukuyama was writing as a former US State Department policy analyst turned political philosopher but the very titles of his article and book constituted a challenge to historians to offer their own interpretations of the century – and indeed of the modern age.

I have chosen to focus on the interpretations offered in recent surveys of the century by two British historians – Eric Hobsbawm's *Age of Extremes: the Short Twentieth Century 1914–1991* (Hobsbawm, 1994a) and Robert Skidelsky's *The World After Communism: a Polemic For Our Times* (Skidelsky, 1995). Both are historians of undoubted distinction (Hobsbawm was made a Companion of Honour in the 1998 New Year Honours for services to history) and both also have played an important political role. My title borrows Alan Hooper's notion of the Long Sixties – from 1956 to 1976 – developed elsewhere in this volume – and, of course, the subtitle of Hobsbawm's work. The notion of the Short Twentieth Century has become associated with him since the publication of *Age of Extremes* but, as he acknowledges in an essay published in *Marxism Today* in 1990, it is not his own (Hobsbawm, 1990: 123). He borrowed it from his friend, Ivan Berend, former President of the Hungarian Academy of Sciences and now Professor at the University of California, Los Angeles (personal communication).

The first part of this chapter compares and contrasts the background and intellectual development of Hobsbawm and Skidelsky. For Hobsbawm I have been able to draw on several published interviews as well as frequent autobiographical interpellations and reflections in essays and books written since the 1960s. Skidelsky's presence in his work has been more muted than Hobsbawm's but I was fortunate to have the opportunity to talk to him at some length about his intellectual development as well as the lasting significance of the sixties. The second section turns from the men to their work and looks at their interpretations of the twentieth century and the significance of the sixties. I then argue that political and social changes linking the 1960s and the 1990s can best be understood as moments in a process of democratisation – in what de Tocqueville described in the 1830s as the 'great democratic revolution' that characterised the modern age (Tocqueville, 1835: 9). I conclude with some personal reflections.

Hobsbawm and Skidelsky have both been kind enough to comment on this chapter in draft. I am very grateful for their help. The views are, of course, my own – as are any remaining errors, misunderstandings, or infelicities in tone or expression.

The lives and work of Hobsbawm and Skidelsky are full of fascinating contrasts and parallels. Both are survivors of cultures that were destroyed by the two great cataclysms of this century – of 'the Jewish middle-class culture of central Europe' (Hobsbawm, 1971: 250) destroyed by Nazism, and of the Imperial Russian bourgeoisie destroyed by Bolshevism.

Hobsbawm, as he tells in the opening pages of *The Age of Empire* (Hobsbawm, 1987a: 1–2), was born in 1917 in Alexandria of Jewish parents, his father a British citizen (of Russian/Polish descent) and his mother an Austrian. His parents left for Vienna shortly after the war ended and the young Hobsbawm joined his uncle (also a British citizen) in Berlin after his parents' death (personal communication). It was here in 1931 that he first encountered the Communist movement (Walker, 1994). More than once he has recalled the moment when, as a schoolboy, he saw the newspaper headline announcing Hitler's appointment as Chancellor (Hobsbawm, 1993: 230; 1994a: 4). Not long afterwards Hobsbawm travelled with his uncle to Britain where he studied history with distinction at Cambridge and joined the Communist Party. His fellow-student Noel Annan recalled him as one of two 'formidable marxists': 'astonishingly mature, armed cap-a-pie [sic] with the Party's interpretation of current politics, as erudite as he was fluent, and equipped to have a view on whatever obscure topic one of his contemporaries might have chosen to write a paper' (the other, an Indian, was killed in an air crash while serving as a minister under Indira Gandhi) (Annan, 1991: 254–5). In 1939 he was elected to that most elitist of secret societies – the Cambridge Apostles (personal communication).

For Hobsbawm, the Popular Front of the 1930s was the defining moment in his political evolution. It is the constant touchstone of his political journalism of the 1980s (collected in Hobsbawm, 1989) in which he called, again and again, for 'some way of uniting the majority of the British people which is opposed to Thatcherism' (Hobsbawm, 1983: 67). He gloried in criticisms that he was a 'simple, unvarnished Popular Frontist' (Callinicos, 1985: 155; Hobsbawm, 1984: 81–2). The Spanish Civil War which pitted the Popular Front against fascism was for him 'the only political cause which, even in retrospect, appears as pure and compelling as it did in 1936' (Hobsbawm, 1994a: 160). His lifelong commitment to communism, as he admitted in an interview in 1994, 'wasn't rational. The commitment was … I would almost say religious' (Tyler, 1994). I am reminded of the commitment to communism of Georg Lukács, the greatest representative of the central European Jewish Marxist tradition to which Hobsbawm belongs. At the end of his life Lukács saw his political development (in terms borrowed from Kierkegaard) as one of transition from an aesthetic, through an ethical to an ultimately religious position (Lukács, 1983: 49, 53–4, 151–9). I don't suppose Hobsbawm (who met Lukács while writing *The Age of Revolution*) would be displeased by the comparison (Kadarkay, 1991: 455–6). The whole of his scholarly work – from the early studies in British labour history to the tetralogy concluded by *Age of Extremes* – bears the mark of his political commitment. As he put it himself in an interview in 1978, all are studies in 'the development of capitalism' and 'the nature of popular movements' in response to capitalist development (Abelove *et al.*, 1983: 37).

Skidelsky was born politically and geographically almost at the opposite extreme from Hobsbawm: in 1939 in Manchuria of White Russian exiles. His father was Jewish but took no interest in his Jewish background until late in life when he became interested in Israel. The family had not suffered from the anti-semitism so prevalent in Tsarist Russia; indeed they 'did extremely well and became very wealthy'. Family legend had it that Skidelsky's great-grandfather travelled eastwards across Siberia and was involved in building the Trans-Siberian railway which terminated in Vladivostok where Skidelsky's father was born in 1907. His mother's family supported Kolchak during the Civil War and escaped afterwards to Manchuria whence his father too had fled. The young Skidelsky was interned for some months by the Japanese before coming to England with his parents in an exchange of prisoners in 1942. The rest of the family disappeared into the Gulag when the Red Army marched into Manchuria in the last days of the Second World War. So, as Skidelsky put it – and in striking contrast to Hobsbawm – 'in so far my family were victims of twentieth-century cataclysm we were victims of what took place in Russia and not what took place in Germany'; they were 'victims of Bolshevism' rather than of Nazism. Intellectually Skidelsky understood the horror of Nazi anti-semitism and the whole history of anti-semitism that led to it, but neither formed part of his own cultural experience – which might help to explain the 'detachment and sympathy' which he brought to his biography of Oswald Mosley (Skidelsky, 1975a: 12).

If Hobsbawm may be regarded (like Isaac Deutscher, George Lichtheim, Karl Polanyi and Piero Sraffa – mutual friend of Gramsci and Keynes (Skidelsky, 1992b: 289)) as part of a relatively small 'Red' emigration of the 1930s, then Skidelsky may be regarded as a belated and youthful member of the much more numerous 'White' emigration which, according to Perry Anderson's classic account (Anderson, 1968: 60–5), dominated English intellectual life in the post-war period. Like older members of this 'White' emigration (such as Isaiah Berlin, Karl Popper and Lewis Namier), Skidelsky has sought to reinforce a characteristically

English liberalism and empiricism – in his case, that of Keynes, searching for a middle way – a 'liberal socialism' in his words (cited Moggridge, 1976: 44) – between the ideological extremes of Lenin and Hayek. Skidelsky conceded that his personal background must have had an influence in shaping his views – 'you identify perhaps with eventually a more right-wing view of things' – but he insisted that he had always tried to 'hold some middle ground'. Just as Hobsbawm's work has been marked by an engagement with the Marxist critique of capitalism, so has Skidelsky been preoccupied with Keynes' attempt to save capitalism from itself, from his account of the 1929–31 Labour Government (Skidelsky, 1970), through his biography of that maverick Keynesian Mosley, to the life of the great man himself on which he is still engaged (Skidelsky, 1992a, b).

Hobsbawm and Skidelsky have both played an increasing role as political intellectuals in recent years. Hobsbawm first made a political impact on the wider Left beyond the Communist Party through his famous (and prophetic) Marx Memorial Lecture of March 1978 on 'The Forward March of Labour Halted?' and then through a series of articles in *Marxism Today* during the 1980s (Hobsbawm, 1989). At the time, Hobsbawm was claimed to have had a great influence upon Neil Kinnock's reshaping of the Labour Party. Robert Harris described him as 'Kinnock's favourite Marxist' (Harris, 1984: 236). Reading these articles today, the extent to which they can be seen to prefigure the strategy and themes of Tony Blair's New Labour is much more striking. After Labour's third successive defeat in 1987 Hobsbawm stressed the need for the party to have 'a positive project for the future – a mission for the nation' (Hobsbawm, 1988: 237). What that project might involve was set out more fully in an earlier article: 'Labour will return to office only a party that offers … a New Deal: modernisation – and in a humane and responsible manner'. Labour would have to accept that not everything done since 1979 should be rejected – 'the British economy … *needed a kick in the pants*' (original italics). A modernising Labour government would have to be just as ruthless in its own way as Thatcher. The 'most vital' part of its project would be ensure a better educated workforce (Hobsbawm, 1987b: 209–12).

The resemblance to the Blair project is obvious. Blair's attempts to appeal to 'the nation', to build links with the Liberal Democrats and even Europhile Conservatives, echo Hobsbawm's call for a popular front against Thatcherism. Some of Blair's closest advisers, like Geoff Mulgan, David Miliband and Peter Mandelson, as well as intellectual outriders such as Anthony Barnett, John Lloyd and Charles Leadbeater, and the sympathetic academics organised through the Internet as Nexus, have emerged from a Marxist background, often from within the Communist Party. In a recent interview, Martin Jacques, erstwhile editor of the journal, recalled how Stuart Hall described Blair in 1994 as 'the *Marxism Today* candidate' (Jacques and Hall, 1997). Alex Callinicos was not far short of the mark in characterising Hobsbawm and his fellow contributors to *Marxism Today* as furthering the rightwards evolution of a generation of socialist activists (Callinicos, 1985: 165). But, then, others might reply: what did the Socialist Workers' Party do to end Conservative rule?

Skidelsky has also taken an increasingly prominent role in politics since the early 1980s – though from a very different starting point. If Hobsbawm's politics are rooted in the anti-fascist struggles of the 1930s, Skidelsky's are rooted in the internal Labour Party conflict between the Gaitskellites and the Left of the 1960s. Skidelsky told me that he had little interest in politics when he arrived at Oxford in 1958 but joined the Labour Club and the Gaitskellite Campaign for Social Democracy in his final year in 1960–61. He was 'very excited' to hear Gaitskell – 'a marvellous man' – address the Labour Club. As a research student at Nuffield his thesis (published as *Politicians and the Slump*) was supervised by Anthony Crosland's friend (and Gaitskell's future biographer) Philip Williams. The atmosphere at Nuffield was, he recalled, 'very social democratic; they hoped to be the brains behind the new Labour Government – in which ambition they didn't entirely succeed'. During this time he was close to William Rodgers (Labour Cabinet Minister in the late 1970s and one of the original 'gang of four') and David Marquand (Labour MP from 1966 until 1977 when he followed Roy Jenkins to the European Commission) (Marquand, 1997: 12–20).

By the late 1960s, after trying half-heartedly and unsuccessfully to secure a Parliamentary seat, disillusionment had set in. Richard Cockett describes how in 1968 Skidelsky was involved with Arthur Seldon and Ralph Harris of the Institute of Economic Affairs in attempting to rally support for the dissident Labour MP Desmond Donnelly who, expelled from the Labour Party, fought and lost his seat as a Democrat in 1970 (Cockett, 1995: 179–80). An article in *Encounter* in 1969 lamented a 'general disillusionment with politics' and called for a government of the strong centre capable of rising above party disputes in the service of a wider national interest (Skidelsky, 1969: 25, 34). Skidelsky drifted out of the Labour Party in the 1970s as it approached a 'looming crisis of social democracy'. By 1975 – perhaps under the influence of Mosley whose biography he completed in that year – he was arguing that 'the Keynesian state will be, is already being, replaced by the Corporate State' (Skidelsky, 1975a). A couple of years later he was still anticipating a 'post-Keynesian' rather than a 'pre-Keynesian' resolution to the current economic crisis (Skidelsky, 1977: 40). The turn of the decade found Skidelsky 'looking for a middle way of toughness and tenderness' which the Labour Party under Michael Foot could not provide. Old friendships brought him into the SDP as a founder member in 1981, and admiration for David Owen (who described Skidelsky as 'a close friend' in his memoirs (Owen, 1991: 802)) kept him there until the bitter end. In 1991 he was elevated to the House of Lords where he sat with the SDP until just before the 1992 election when the party lost its last two seats.

Since then Skidelsky has taken the Conservative whip in the House of Lords. He had already admired much of what Thatcher had been doing but 'still believed that an omelette could be made without breaking eggs': in that sense, intellectual conviction was at odds with emotion; he still wished to stand well with people he respected. 'Once the SDP collapsed I was free. Whether I would have gone back to the Labour Party if it had been a Blairite party I can't answer with absolute assurance. When the SDP collapsed it was still a Kinnockite party and I disagreed with too much of what it stood for.' But Skidelsky remains an independent-minded figure – more drawn to tough-minded mavericks ('bold men' as he described them in *Politicians and the Slump* (Skidelsky, 1970: 424)) like Owen – or, dare one say it, Mosley – than to particular parties. He describes himself as 'a Thatcherite Keynesian – although Margaret herself would be appalled by that particular linkage'. *The World After Communism* contains a respectful account of the Marxist analysis of the economic crisis of the 1970s and his biography of Keynes acknowledges the acuteness of the 1930s Marxist Dimitri Mirsky's analysis of the Bloomsbury Group as an intellectual aristocracy which, not being directly involved in the production process, could consider itself as above or outside class (Skidelsky, 1992b: 233–4; 1995: 118–9). In occasional essays and political journalism he sometimes deploys Marxist categories with a facility that might embarrass many socialists. In one place he describes the welfare state as 'designed in the 1940s to protect weakened capitalist economies against the assault of revolutionary socialism' (Skidelsky, 1996a: 38). In another he refers to Britain and the US as adopting 'the Keynesian policy of full employment ... in order to put capitalism in a stronger position to withstand revolutionary assaults, both domestic and international', and to 1960s 'growthmanship' as 'reflecting the view of virtually the whole of the British ruling class that Britain was "falling behind" the more successful capitalist economies like Germany and France' (Skidelsky, 1996b: 48, 57).

As a political figure rather than a historian and biographer he has become best known as Chairman of the Social Market Foundation. Founded originally as a think tank for the SDP in 1989 it was relaunched in 1992 with an orientation towards the social agenda of the Major government. Lewis Baston in his account of the SMF shrewdly remarks that it was well-placed in the early 1990s to occupy ground lost by the more unambiguously right-wing think tanks such as the Centre for Policy Studies and the Adam Smith Institute following the fall of Thatcher and that its turn towards Major largely reflected the fact the Conservatives were in government. He predicted that it might prove to be a rare case of a think tank that would be able to retain its influence with a new government (Baston, 1996: 69–71). Such indeed seems to have been the case. The *Financial Times*'s 'Observer' column reported in September 1997 that the SMF had been included with the Institute of Public Policy Research and Demos in consultations on the revamped Citizen's Charter while the Institute of Economic Affairs and the ASI were left out in the cold. 'Observer' commented that the SMF had 'sashayed effortlessly from SDP to Tory to New Labour' (*Financial Times*, 19.9.97). Recent SMF publications such as Fukuyama's *The End of Order* (Fukuyama, 1997), Frank Field's *Reforming Welfare* (Field, 1997) and Skidelsky's own *Beyond the Welfare State* (Skidelsky, 1997a) have all been directed to the Blair government's key objectives of curbing public expenditure, reforming welfare and remoralising society.

We have seen that Hobsbawm and Skidelsky started out almost from opposite poles in the political spectrum. Both began and have remained political outsiders. Hobsbawm has never abandoned his commitment to communism as a political cause despite its eclipse as a significant social and political movement. Skidelsky remains an unusual (and, I suspect, for some) an uncomfortable figure in the Conservative Party. His biography of Mosley still excites controversy. Unlike many of his friends and former associates in the SDP such as Marquand or Rodgers he has not found his way back into the national coalition that Blair has been trying to assemble. He has little patience with Marquand's ideas for modernising the British state which have aroused such resonance on the left (Skidelsky, 1997b). As Skidelsky put it, he (unlike Marquand) was 'not cradled in the Labour Party'. Nor too, of course, is Blair: 'he's not a Labour boy'. Perhaps that is why Blair has been able to draw on a political strategy and themes mapped out during the worst travails of the Labour Party in the 1980s by a lifelong Communist rooted in a lost central European culture – and why he is prepared to draw on ideas for government from a source headed by a Conservative peer. Hobsbawm stressed the need for Labour to be ready to make hard choices; Skidelsky and the SMF have been mapping out some of the directions in which that those hard choices might take them. From opposing political and ideological positions Hobsbawm and Skidelsky have converged in providing a strategy and themes and then an agenda for New Labour.

So far I have looked at the intellectual and political development of Hobsbawm and Skidelsky and noted the way their trajectories had converged in the contributions each has made to the emergence of New Labour. I now look beyond the personal and the political to their contrasting visions of the twentieth century and the place of the sixties.

Hobsbawm describes the 'structure of the Short Twentieth Century' in striking if uncharacteristically inelegant terms as resembling 'a sort of triptych or historical sandwich'. The First World War marked the breakdown of liberal, capitalist civilisation and the beginning of 40 years of calamity – an Age of Catastrophe in which capitalism 'was shaken by two world wars, followed by two waves of global rebellion and revolution, which brought to power a system that claimed to be the historically predestined alternative to bourgeois and capitalist society, first over one sixth of the world's land surface, and after the Second World War over one third of the globe's population'. During the 1930s the capitalist system faced breakdown and by 1940 liberal democracy had been confined to 'all but a fringe of Europe and parts of North America and Australasia'. So far, all had happened as a Marxist might have predicted.

This Age of Catastrophe which lasted until the aftermath of the Second World War was followed by some 25 or 30 years of exceptional economic growth and social transformation which could be seen in retrospect 'as a sort of Golden Age' which came to an end in the early 1970s. According to Hobsbawm, this Golden Age has been succeeded by 'a new era of decomposition, uncertainty and crisis – and indeed, for large parts of the world such as Africa, the former USSR and the formerly socialist parts of Europe, of catastrophe'. This third period, which he calls the Landslide, showed no sign of ending as he wrote: 'As the 1980s gave way to the 1990s, the mood of those who reflected on the century's past and future was a growing *fin-de-siècle* gloom. From the vantage-point of the 1990s, the Short Twentieth Century passed through a brief Golden Age, on the way from one era of crisis to another, into an unknown and problematic but not necessarily apocalyptic future' (Hobsbawm, 1994a: 6–7). Thus Hobsbawm's vision of the twentieth century, as one would expect from a life-long Communist, is essentially one of disappointment; his vision of the twenty-first clouded yet pessimistic. Elsewhere he has described the twentieth century as a continuing descent into barbarism (Hobsbawm, 1994b). Skidelsky describes *The World After Communism* as a polemic, and at times it reads as an extended response to *Age of Extremes* although he told me that he did not read the book until some time after he had written his own. Whereas Hobsbawm focuses on the internal dynamics of capitalism, especially when describing the impact of the Landslide, Skidelsky focuses on ideas, taking his cue from what he calls, perhaps rightly, Keynes's 'too often quoted passage' (at the end of *The General Theory of Employment, Interest and Money*) that 'the ideas of economists and political philosophers, both when they are right and when they are wrong, are more powerful than is commonly understood. Indeed the world is ruled by little else' (Skidelsky, 1992b: 570). Skidelsky therefore sees the twentieth century in terms of 'the rise and fall of collectivism', which he defines as 'the belief that the state knows better than the market, and can improve on the spontaneous tendencies of civil society, if necessary by suppressing them' and which he condemns as 'the most egregious error of the twentieth century', affecting with varying degrees of severity the liberal democracies of the West as well as Fascist and Communist states (Skidelsky, 1995: xiii). At one point he stresses that 'the collectivist belief system existed independently of the facts of modern life' (67). Elsewhere he devotes a dozen pages to the ideas of mid-century liberal opponents of collectivism – Keynes (heading the list), Beveridge, Popper, Hayek and Schumpeter (70–82).

Within that broad explanatory framework of the rise and fall of collectivism Skidelsky largely adopts the same tripartite periodisation as Hobsbawm. Like Hobsbawm he sees the First World War and the Great Depression as the great watersheds of the early part of the century, to be followed by 'the so-called "golden age" of the 1950s and 1960s – the twentieth-century equivalent of the nineteenth century's "age of equipoise"' (46, 52, xiv). However, he sees the third period (Hobsbawm's Landslide) in terms of the 'shock therapy' needed to correct the 'unbalanced macro-economies' dependent on 'ever heavier state subsidies', a collectivist drift developing during the Golden Age. 'These subsidies were carried to extremes in the wholly state-owned Communist economies, which is why they led to a crisis not in the system but of the system. But they were present in most economies by the end of the 1970s' (140). Skidelsky, unlike Hobsbawm, is bullish about the future: 'The pessimists are a wearying lot. … I am an optimist. I regard the end of Communism, the rolling back of the frontiers of the state, the globalisation of economic intercourse, as the most hopeful turn of the historical screw which has happened since 1914' (xiii).

Whatever their differing perspectives on the century, Hobsbawm and Skidelsky are agreed upon the centrality of the dialectic between

Communism and the capitalist West. For Hobsbawm, the century has been 'dominated by the confrontation between the anti-capitalist communism of the October revolution, represented by the USSR and anti-communist capitalism, of which the USA was the champion and exemplar' (Hobsbawm, 1994a: 143). Only a 'temporary and bizarre alliance' with the Soviet Union enabled the West to defeat Hitler, and the renewal of hostility in the Cold War was an essential stimulus to welfare capitalism. 'It is one of the ironies of this strange century that the most lasting result of the October revolution, whose object was the global overthrow of capitalism, was to save its antagonist, both in war and in peace – that it is to say, by providing it with the incentive, fear, to reform itself after the Second World War, and, by establishing the popularity of economic planning, furnishing it with some of the procedures for its reform' (7–8). Hobsbawm stresses the importance of the Cold War in the economic revival of Western Europe and Japan (239, 275–6). The vogue for planning in the Western economies reflected the impact of the Soviet example (274).

Skidelsky rightly points to the malign role of Stalin in facilitating the rise of Nazism (Skidelsky, 1995: 55) but, as we have seen, he has conceded Hobsbawm's argument about the essential stimulus of the Soviet example in reforming post-war capitalism. In *The World After Communism* he argues that the perceived economic challenge from the Soviet Union in the 1950s and 1960s was crucial in fostering 'the vogue for growthmanship' in the capitalist economies which contributed to the economic problems of the 1970s (Skidelsky, 1995: 11–13). In one of his most eloquent passages, Skidelsky sums up the impact of the Soviet Union: 'The economic imagination of the West has been profoundly influenced by the seeming success and eventual failure of the Soviet model. In the 1930s the gargantuan power of the Soviet industrial machine … provided an irresistible contrast to the idle factories and dole queues in the industrial West. In the Second World War it was the huge Soviet tanks which hurled back the invading Germans in the great tank battles of 1943 that impressed. In the 1950s it was the prodigious growth rates being chalked up by the Soviet economy which … helped frighten industrial nations into "planning for growth". Conversely, the stagnation of the Soviet system after 1970 helped turn the non-Communist imagination against collectivism … . The revival of the free market in the West was built on the decrepitude of Soviet planning' (103). One might add that the decay and eventual collapse of Communism created the opportunity for Reagan and Thatcher to overturn the consensus established in the 1940s and to begin dismantling the Keynesian welfare state. As Hobsbawm remarks: 'the absence of a credible threat to the [capitalist] system, such as communism and the existence of the USSR [has] diminished the incentive to reform' (Hobsbawm, 1994a: 574). Even by its absence the fate of the Soviet Union has had an impact on the West.

So much for Hobsbawm's and Skidelsky's interpretation of the century and the central dialectic between the capitalist West and the Soviet Union. How do they interpret the position of the sixties in this story? Only Hobsbawm has written at length about the social and cultural revolutions of the post-war period (Hobsbawm, 1994a: Chapters 10 and 11). He sets the global student rebellion of 1968 against the background of the unprecedented social and economic transformations of the Golden Age. Key factors were the dramatic movement from countryside to cities throughout the world – 'the death of the peasantry' (289) – and the equally unprecedented increase in student numbers as a result of the growth of occupations requiring secondary and higher education (295). Both of these factors contributed to an unprecedented gulf in experience and expectations between people born before around 1920 and since around 1950 – the so-called generation gap about which so much was written in the 1960s and which must seem incomprehensible to generations born since then (301). The generation gap between parents born around 1920 and children born around 1950 was all the greater for the fact that many political leaders of the time (such as de Gaulle, Macmillan, Eisenhower, Adenauer and Khrushchev) had been born before the century began (325). All of these factors contributed to the global youth culture and the explosion of 1968.

What is unusual about that explosion is that, at least in the capitalist heartland of Western Europe and the US, it involved mainly the beneficiaries rather than the victims of the social and economic transformations of the preceding decades and was directed against the symbols of mass consumption that either had not existed in the 1930s or 1940s or had been available only to a privileged minority. In a sense, therefore, this was a revolt by the generation of whom Keynes wrote in his famous paper on 'Economic Possibilities for our Grandchildren' (Keynes, 1930) when he speculated that the economic problem of scarcity would be solved. The 'strenuous purposeful money-makers' would have carried us all 'into the lap of economic abundance', to be enjoyed by 'those peoples, who can keep alive, and cultivate into a fuller perfection, the art of life itself and do not sell themselves for the means of life'. Then, 'we shall be able to rid ourselves of many of the pseudo-moral principles which have hag-ridden us for two hundred years, by which we have exalted some of the most distasteful of human qualities into the position of the highest virtues'. 'The love of money as a possession' would be 'recognised for what it is,

a somewhat disgusting morbidity', once it was no longer needed to promote the accumulation of capital. Keynes thought that the economic problem would be with us for at least another hundred years (Keynes, 1930:
326–31). Skidelsky was not alone in believing in the 1960s that 'the day
of Keynes' grandchildren had arrived' as a result of the Golden Age combination of steadily rising living standards and increasing welfare provision
with full employment and modest personal taxation.

Skidelsky would be the first to point to the irony that the conviction that
the economic problem had been solved became current just at the moment
when the Golden Age was about to end. In an eloquent passage,
Hobsbawm describes the student rebellion as 'a warning, a sort of *memento
mori* to a generation that half-believed it had solved the problems of western society for good' (Hobsbawm, 1994a: 285–6). Skidelsky, writing
in the immediate aftermath of 1968, saw 'the arrival of youth on the political stage' as 'the beginning of the end' of the consensus of the 1950s
(Bogdanor and Skidelsky, 1970: 13). Far more significant in bringing the
Golden Age to an end was a 'shift in labour's mood', a 'worldwide wage
explosion' triggered by rising inflation which was in turn a product of
declining profitability and declining growth in real wages resulting from a
slowing in the rate of productivity growth. The student rebellion was
important mainly through the stimulus given to working class demands for
higher wages and better conditions (Hobsbawm, 1994a: 301). Skidelsky
would agree. For him too the main reason for the end of the Golden Age
was a slowdown in productivity which contributed to an emerging fiscal
crisis as welfare spending continued to grow faster than the economy itself
(Skidelsky, 1995: 93–4). The crisis of ungovernability of the 1970s was,
in his words, 'labour movement-led', as workers sought to increase real
wages while resisting technological changes necessary to restore profitability. Skidelsky, as we have seen, thought that it heralded the Corporate
State. Hobsbawm, addressing Birkbeck students in January 1975, pointed
to a real prospect for an advance to socialism as a way of resolving what
he described as 'the most serious crisis of this country ... since the post-
Napoleonic period' (Hobsbawm, 1975: 11, 16 – I owe this reference to
Alan Hooper).

A second irony is that the stress on personal liberation that we associate
with the sixties, and which was associated at the time with political radicalism, has turned out to have more in common with the assumptions of
neo-liberal defenders of consumer capitalism than with those of its critics
on the left. Skidelsky reminded me that Samuel Brittan had pointed to this
connection in *Left or Right: the Bogus Dilemma* (Brittan, 1968). Hobsbawm
made a similar point in a famous article on 'Revolution and Sex' which

argued that there was no consistent relationship between sexual permissiveness and political liberation. 'The belief that a narrow sexual morality is an essential bulwark of the capitalist system is no longer tenable'. On the contrary, 'rulers find it convenient to encourage sexual permissiveness or laxity among their subjects if only to keep their minds off their subjection'. Past revolutions may have included libertarian and antinomian elements but far more significant was 'a persistent affinity between revolution and puritanism ... . The Robespierres always win out over the Dantons' (Hobsbawm, 1969: 216–9). The link between sexual freedom and economic freedom in the neo-liberal sense is much more obvious now than it appeared in the late 1960s. After all, Sonny Bono ended up as a Republican Congressman. Richard Branson sold copies of his first paper among the crowds at an anti-Vietnam War demonstration in London. Skidelsky has described Bill Gates as a kind of hippie in the 1960s. Arguably the moral and cultural changes of the 1960s conflicted with the socialism of many of their adherents on the New Left and contributed to the rise of the New Right and the capitalist revival of the 1980s. Perhaps some of the origins of the animal spirits of the boardrooms of the 1980s can be found in the animal spirits of the bedrooms of the 1960s.

In this respect Hobsbawm was quite right to warn in 1971 that the left-wing radicalism of the late 1960s might prove to be temporary and that the radical right might be the main beneficiary of another lengthy period of economic crisis (Hobsbawm, 1971: 256). The comparison he drew was with the wave of revolt which preceded and followed the First World War. The Italian anarchist Errico Malatesta warned about the dangers of unsuccessful attempts to overthrow the bourgeoisie: 'If we do not go on to the end, we shall have to pay with tears of blood for the fear that we are now causing the bourgeoisie' (cited in Stone, 1983: 388). *Age of Extremes* acknowledges that the rise of the radical right between the wars was 'a response to the danger, indeed to the reality, of social revolution and working-class power in general, to the October revolution and Leninism in particular'. In those years, the real danger to democracy came from the right (Hobsbawm, 1994: 124, 112). The same could be said of the decades after 1848: the beneficiaries of left-wing failure were Louis Napoleon Bonaparte, Camillo di Cavour and Otto von Bismarck. As Marx remarked: 'Unless the radicals unite Germany by revolutionary means Bismarck will unite it by reactionary Junker means' (cited in Taylor, 1950: 123).

Hobsbawm has described 1968 as 'the single moment', if there were any, 'in the golden years after 1945 which corresponds to the world simultaneous upheaval of which the revolutionaries had dreamed after 1917' (Hobsbawm, 1994a: 298). The failure of the Left, not only in 1968 but also during the 1970s, opened the way to the rise of the New Right. In 1975 Hobsbawm could argue that 'the capitalists have no ready made solution' to 'the present crisis of capitalism' (Hobsbawm, 1975: 8) and Skidelsky foretold the arrival of the Corporate State. Neither foresaw that Reagan and Thatcher would solve by neo-liberal means the economic problems that a divided and demoralised Left had failed to solve by collectivist means. And freedom was the slogan under which they advanced. As Skidelsky pointed out, the working class was no longer satisfied with 'the utilitarian, standardised social services that were established during the Second World War' when a much wider range of choice had been opened up in other parts of their lives. The climax of the Long Sixties between 1968 and 1976 can thus be seen as a watershed between two epochs in the Short Twentieth Century and, like 1848, as a turning point at which the world failed to turn in the expected direction.

So far this chapter has looked, first, at the intellectual and political development of Eric Hobsbawm and Robert Skidelsky, pointing to a degree of convergence in the strategy, themes and programme of New Labour and then, secondly, at their complementary rather than contrasting perspectives on the century and the place of the sixties within it. We have seen how, as in the decades after 1848 and 1917, the dreams of the Left turned into nightmares as the Right advanced under stolen banners – of nationalism in the 1850s and 1860s, of radical collectivism in the 1920s and 1930s, and personal freedom in the 1970s and 1980s. I now go on to argue that the apparently paradoxical developments of the last third of the century, in which Thatcher and Reagan seemed to benefit from the cultural changes of the sixties, can best be seen as different moments in a continuing process of democratisation.

This notion of democratisation is, of course, derived from Alexis de Tocqueville's notion, advanced in the first volume of *Democracy in America* published in 1835, of a 'great democratic revolution' of which America represented the 'extreme limits' to which Europe was advancing (Tocqueville, 1835: 9). Tocqueville was not the first to see America in this light as the pattern of the future. Hegel in his *Lectures on the Philosophy of History* (first delivered at the University of Berlin in 1818) described the United States as 'the land of the future, where, in the ages that lie before us, the burden of the World's History shall reveal itself'. In his *Aesthetics* he remarked: 'If one wants to have an idea of what may be the epic poems of the future, one has only to think of the possible victory of

American rationalism, living and universal, over the European peoples.'
Both of these passages are cited by Paul Berman, in his recent perceptive
assessment of the sixties, as examples of what he wittily calls 'Yankee
Hegelianism' (Berman, 1996: 309–10). Something of the notion can be
found in Gramsci's notion of fordism as 'an organic extension and intensi-
fication of European civilisation' (Gramsci, 1971: 318) – and, of course, in
Alexandre Kojève and his disciple Fukuyama, with his vision of the
United States as the destination to which all nations are travelling, like
wagons crossing hostile territory (Fukuyama, 1992: 203, 291, 338–9).

When, in the second volume of *Democracy in America* published in
1840, Tocqueville contrasted 'democratic society' and 'democratic man'
with 'aristocratic society' and 'aristocratic man', he had in mind far more
than different systems of political power (Aron, 1968: 187; Siedentop,
1994: 45). Tocqueville's notions of democratic society and the democratic
revolution are best understood as a process of 'levelling' involving the
gradual elimination of civil inequalities and the creation of a common system of values which can be described in terms of a mass society or a classless society. Tocqueville saw this as a process extending over centuries.
Moreover, there is in his account of the rise of industry and the dangers of
a 'business aristocracy' the implication that the process might be put, at
least temporarily, into reverse by the rise of new divisions between workers and manufacturers (Tocqueville, 1840: 557). However, Tocqueville's
notion of a persistent tendency towards equality did not entail the elimination of inequalities of wealth, although he did anticipate an elimination of
gross extremes of wealth and poverty and a gradual spread of property
ownership. The notion of a 'property-owning democracy' has a strong
flavour of Tocqueville about it.

For Tocqueville the democratic revolution involving a gradual elimination of legal and social distinctions and the spread of common values also
entailed growing individualism. Democratic society was a society of competitive individuals: 'equality ... tends to isolate men from each other so
that each thinks only of himself. It lays the soul open to an inordinate love
of material gain' (444). Violent revolution on the French model might be
needed to establish civil and political equality but the resulting spread of
property-ownership and growing individualism would have a profoundly
conservative effect. 'I know nothing', he wrote, 'more opposed to revolutionary morality than the moral standards of traders. Trade is the natural
enemy of all violent passions. Trade loves moderation, delights in compromise, and is most careful to avoid anger. ... Trade makes men independent of one another and gives them an idea of their own importance; it
leads them to want to manage their own affairs and teaches them how to

succeed therein. Hence it makes them inclined to liberty but disinclined to revolution' (637).

Moreover, the democratic society of isolated, competitive individuals, constantly striving against one another to better their positions, is not a happy one. 'In America', wrote Tocqueville, 'I have seen the freest and best educated of men in circumstances the happiest to be found in the world; yet it seemed to me that a cloud habitually hung on their brow, and they seemed serious and almost sad in their pleasures' (536). He explained this chronic dissatisfaction in terms of a formal equality which aroused great ambitions in many people while at the same time frustrating those ambitions because, inevitably, such ambitions could be realised only by a minority, exciting constant envy in the rest. 'That is the reason', he wrote, 'for the strange melancholy often haunting the inhabitants of democracies in the midst of abundance, and of that disgust with life sometimes gripping them in calm and easy circumstances' (537–8). This is the society portrayed by Fred Hirsch (Hirsch, 1977), in constant pursuit of positional goods that, by their nature, can be enjoyed only by a minority, the 'nation of wannabes' portrayed more recently by popular psychologist Oliver James, 'permanently dissatisfied, always yearning for what we have not got' (James, 1997: 27).

This process of democratisation has long been evident to students of popular culture in this country. Richard Hoggart's seminal study of working-class culture in the 1950s, *The Uses of Literacy* published in 1957, is peppered with quotations from Tocqueville. His main argument is that the new commercial culture of mass entertainment has 'unbent the springs of action' (the words are Tocqueville's) among the working class; now, in the 1950s, 'we are becoming culturally classless' (Hoggart, 1958: 169, 342). Differences between the working class and the lower middle class had become 'largely superficial' (343). The new mass entertainment culture tended towards 'a view of the world in which progress is conceived as a seeking of material pleasures, equality as moral levelling, and freedom as the ground for endless irresponsible pleasure' (340). For Hoggart, 'working people' were in danger of being induced 'to accept a mean form of materialism as a social philosophy' that would undermine the achievements of the working class movement and the reality of democracy (ibid: 323). His was essentially a pessimistic vision of the consequences of a democratic society for the traditional socialist values of the Left.

Raymond Williams, writing a few years later in *The Long Revolution* (first published in 1961 and revised in 1965) was more sanguine about the implications for the Left of what he described as 'the democratic revolution' (Williams, 1965: 10). He found comfort in 'a determination not to be

regimented' (321). He anticipated hopefully that this resistence to regimentation would find expression in the rejection of an economic system
that denied to most of the population the autonomy that they enjoyed in
other areas of life and which was inconsistent with the ideals of political
democracy. 'The aspiration to control the general directions of our economic life is an essential element of democratic growth. ... It is difficult to
feel that we are really governing ourselves if in so central a part of our living as our work most of us have no share in decisions that immediately
affect us' (332). Williams looked forward to growing pressure for 'industrial democracy', for a real 'participating democracy', which was bound to
raise issues of ownership that lay at the heart of the socialist vision (339,
343). While he was too acute an observer not to notice the 'visible moral
decline of the labour movement' and the way in which socialism 'has
almost wholly lost any contemporary meaning' (328), he nevertheless
failed to recognise the way in which the resistance to regimentation which
he detected and which was such a hallmark of the 1960s could be turned
by the resurgent Right against the achievements of the labour movement
such as the trade unions and the institutions of the welfare state.

Hobsbawm's main intervention in this debate was, of course, the lecture
published as 'The Forward March of Labour Halted?' (Hobsbawm, 1978).
Tocqueville had pointed to the homogeneous nature of the separate classes
and estates of aristocratic society which would disappear in the course of
the long process which he described as the democratic revolution.
Hobsbawm argued in his seminal lecture that the traditional industrial
working class had lost much of its former homogeneity and sense of class
solidarity since the 1950s. He pointed to 'a growing division of workers
into sections and groups, each pursuing its own economic interest irre-
spective of the rest'. Under conditions of what he described as 'state-
monopoly capitalism' (which others might have described as corporatism)
the bargaining strength of striking workers depended on their ability to
bring pressure to bear on the public and thus to break the political will
of the government. The effect, according to Hobsbawm, was not only to
'create potential friction between groups of workers, but also [to] risk
weakening the hold of the labour movement as a whole' (18). The consequences of this behaviour which, it might be argued, reflected the process
of democratisation analysed by Tocqueville and perceived by the likes of
Hoggart and Williams, were to become all too clear in the next few years,
when Thatcher was able to mobilise sections of the working class in a
struggle against 'the enemy within'.

Another aspect of this process of democratisation can be seen in the
downwards spread of moral values associated with a social elite epitomised

by Bloomsbury in the earlier part of the century. Looking back on his youth, Keynes described his Cambridge and later Bloomsbury friends as being 'amongst the first of our generation ... to escape the Benthamite tradition. ... We entirely repudiated a personal liability on us to obey general rules. ... We repudiated entirely customary morals, conventions and general wisdom. We were, that is to say, in the strict sense of the term, immoralists'. Theirs was essentially a doctrine of an elite. The mature Keynes recognised that the rules and conventions scorned by him and his friends were the foundation of the civilisation of which they were among the main beneficiaries. He was quite aware of the danger for that civilisation of a juncture between their 'libertinism and comprehensive irreverence' and the 'vulgar passions' (Keynes, 1938: 447–50). It might be argued that what has been described as the Keynesian welfare state depended upon customary conventions among the working classes that began to break down in the 1960s.

Skidelsky remarked in conversation upon the coincidence between a democratisation of Bloomsbury hedonism (or immoralism) and the weakening of the British economy in the 1960s. His friend Michael Holroyd's seminal biography of Lytton Strachey, published in 1967, played an important role in revealing the sexual behaviour of Bloomsbury to a wide audience (and in so doing revolutionised the art of biography). I well recall the impression it made, when serialised in the *Sunday Times*, upon a sixth-form friend of mine. Skidelsky thought that the relaxation of moral constraints in the 1960s could indeed be seen as a kind of democratisation of Bloomsbury ideals. As he observed, 'The one thing that really offends a lot of old Bloomsburies nowadays is the idea that their ideas are the common property of the masses – and they really don't like it, because the Bloomsbury idea was really a variant of the old aristocratic idea. The bounds of the permissible for them were just drawn more widely than for others'. However, the consequences of the relaxation of moral constraints upon the working class are much more serious for the rest of society – and for the welfare state devised in the 1940s – than for a tiny elite. One of Skidelsky's (and the SMF's) main concerns today – a concern shared by the Blair Government – is with the consequences of this relaxation of moral constraints for the family and for society as a whole in terms of increased demands upon the public purse. Thus the democratisation of Bloomsbury hedonism in the sixties and after may be seen to have contributed to a growing moral authoritarianism exhibited by New Labour.

This notion of democratisation as a kind of masterkey in understanding the transition from the radicalism of the 1960s to the conservatism of recent decades is not confined to this country. It may be significant that the

American New Left emerged from the Civil Rights movement of the late 1950s and the early 1960s which sought to consummate the process of democratisation in the United States by extending full civil rights to African Americans. Tocqueville himself had commented in 1840 that 'If ever there are great revolutions [in the United States], they will be caused by the presence of the blacks upon American soil. That is to say, it will not be the equality of social conditions but rather their inequality which may give rise thereto' (Tocqueville, 1840: 639). The subsequent transmutation of the American New Left into the so-called 'identity politics' of the Women's Movement and the Gay Movement can be seen as another stage in extending equality.

In Europe the New Left turned to terrorism only in countries like Germany and Italy where liberal democracy had shallower roots than in Britain and France (with the significant exception of Ulster, where the refounded IRA was as much a product of the sixties as were the Red Army Fraction and the Red Brigades). The student rebellion in the streets of Paris in 1968 can be seen as complementing in the social and cultural sphere the process of economic modernisation begun by Jean Monnet and de Gaulle. Perhaps that was why it proved so much more evanescent than in Italy and Germany (and Ulster) where the New Left transmuted into formidable terrorist movements. The process of democratisation found expression in southern Europe in the overthrow of the Greek Colonels and the termination of fascism in Spain and Portugal. The democratic impulse behind the overthrow of soviet power in eastern Europe and the Soviet Union itself needs no underlining. Farther afield the same process of democratisation can be seen in the end of Apartheid in South Africa and the rise of market relations in China.

My purpose in this chapter has been to examine the work of Eric Hobsbawm and Robert Skidelsky as interpreters of their age and as significant influences upon a new political formation – Tony Blair's New Labour. I have suggested that, despite differing backgrounds, their interpretations of the century bear significant resemblances and differences in their perspectives are largely complementary rather than contradictory. Finally I have sought to argue that the apparent paradoxes and ironies of the transition from the political radicalism and moral antinomianism of the sixties to the conservatism and moral authoritarianism of the 1980s and 1990s can best be understood as moments in a process of democratisation charted with exceptional foresight and acuteness by Alexis de Tocqueville.

An earlier version of this chapter ended at this point but Skidelsky challenged me – very tentatively he insisted – to give my own opinion of whether one should start the twenty first century as a bull or a bear. How could I resist the challenge?

Like Tocqueville I am torn between two views of this whole process. His other great work *The Ancien Régime and the French Revolution* describes how '[t]he eighteenth-century Frenchman was ... both better and worse than ourselves'. He had 'nothing of that discreet, well-regulated sensualism which prevails today ... . Even the bourgeoisie did not devote themselves exclusively to the pursuit of material comforts; they often aspired to loftier, more refined satisfactions and were far from regarding money as the sole good' (Tocqueville, 1856: 141–2).

In some ways I regret the passing of the heroic illusions of modernity rather as Tocqueville did 'the outstanding personalities' of eighteenth-century France, 'those men of genius, proud and daring, who made the Revolution what it was: at once the admiration and the terror of succeeding generations' (143). As a boy in the 1950s I regretted having been born too late to fly a Spitfire; as a student in the late 1960s I regretted not having had the chance to fight on the barricades of Madrid or Petrograd. But as a young man in the 1970s I joined the civil service where I stayed for 20 years. And I know that the grandchildren of the militiamen who fought and lost in Madrid are better off – in all conceivable ways – than the great-grandchildren of the Red Guards who fought and won in Petrograd.

Yet today I find something banal in images of heroism drawn mainly from the sports field – televised exclusively on satellite TV and garnished with commercial logos. I was dispirited to read in the *Observer* (22 February 1998) about diminishing numbers of young people volunteering for service overseas in the developing world (even though in all honesty I would not have cared to do so myself). I was saddened to read in the *Economist* (17 January 1998) that 75 per cent of American freshmen consider financial success to be an essential or very important goal of education compared with 41 per cent seeking a meaningful philosophy of life – an almost complete reversal of answers given by students in the 1960s.

Looking back, the generation of the sixties seems to stand on the cusp of history – born and bred in the Golden Age but growing up in the afterglow of the heroic illusions of the Age of Catastrophe and destined to grow to middle age through the Landslide of those illusions, enduring their own sentimental education like Flaubert's protagonists in that greatest of all novels of disillusionment. Now the heroic illusions of modernity have faded and we aspire only to 'a kind of decent materialism' (Tocqueville,

1840: 534) dignified as the post-modern condition. At least in the heartlands of capitalism, and by no means for everyone, we seem to be advancing ever closer to the destination sketched by Tocqueville in 1840, to a world in which '[t]here is little energy of soul, but mores are gentle and laws humane. Though heroic devotion and any other very exalted, brilliant and pure virtues may be rare, habits are orderly, violence rare, and cruelty almost unknown ... Life is not very glamorous, but extremely comfortable and peaceful. Almost all salient characteristics are obliterated to make room for something average, less high and less low, less brilliant and less dim, than what the world had before' (703–4).

In some moods, one is tempted, like Tocqueville, to feel saddened and chilled by the prospect, but perhaps, like him, one should find comfort in the fact that, within what he described as vast limits, humankind is 'strong and free' to fashion a more just society. One should also recall that the French Revolution which excited his 'admiration and terror' may have lain behind him but that the heroic illusions of modernity, with all their unimagined terrors, lay ahead. Who knows what new illusions might succeed the 'decent materialism' of our present sceptical age? Who knows what terrors a new age of faith might bring?

REFERENCES

Abelove, H., Blackmar, B., Dimock, P. and Schneer, J. (eds), *Visions of History*, Manchester University Press, nd (but probably 1983).

Anderson, P. (1968), 'Components of the National Culture', in *English Questions* (ed. P. Anderson) Verso, 1992.

Annan, N. (1991), *Our Age: the Generation That Made Post-war Britain*, Fontana.

Aron, R. (1968), *Main Currents in Sociological Thought* 1, Penguin.

Baston, L. (1996), 'The Social Market Foundation', in *Ideas and Think Tanks in Contemporary Britain: Volume I* (eds M.D. Kandiah and A. Seldon, Frank Cass).

Berman, P. (1996), *A Tale of Two Utopias: the Political Journey of the Generation of 1968*, W. W. Norton & Co.

Bogdanor, V. and Skidelsky, R. (eds) (1970), *The Age of Affluence 1951–1964*, Macmillan.

Brittan, S. (1968), *Left or Right: the Bogus Dilemma*, Secker & Warburg.

Callinicos, A. (1985), 'The Politics of *Marxism Today*', *International Socialism*, 29.

Cockett, R. (1995), *Thinking the Unthinkable: Think-Tanks and the Economic Counter-Revolution, 1931–1983*, Fontana.

Field, F. (1997), *Reforming Welfare*, Social Market Foundation.

Fukuyama, F. (1989), 'The End of History?', *The National Interest*, 16.

Fukuyama, F. (1992), *The End of History and the Last Man*, Hamish Hamilton.

Fukuyama, F. (1997), *The End of Order*, Social Market Foundation.

Gramsci, A. (1971), *Selections from the Prison Notebooks*, Lawrence & Wishart.

Harris, R. (1984), *The Making of Neil Kinnock*, Faber and Faber.

Hirsch, F. (1977), *Social Limits to Growth*, Routledge & Kegan Paul.

Hobsbawm, E.J. (1969), 'Revolution and Sex', reprinted in *Revolutionaries*, Hobsbawm, 1973.

Hobsbawm, E.J. (1971), 'Intellectuals and the Class Struggle', reprinted in *Revolutionaries*, Hobsbawm, 1973.

Hobsbawm, E.J. (1973), *Revolutionaries*, Weidenfeld & Nicolson.

Hobsbawm, E.J. (1975), *The Crisis and the Outlook*, Birkbeck College Socialist Society.

Hobsbawm, E.J. (1978), 'The Forward March of Labour Halted?', reprinted in *Politics for a Rational Left*, Hobsbawm, 1989.

Hobsbawm, E.J. (1983), 'Labour's Lost Millions', reprinted in *Politics for a Rational Left*, Hobsbawm, 1989.

Hobsbawm, E.J. (1984), 'Labour: Rump or Rebirth?', reprinted in *Politics for a Rational Left*, Hobsbawm, 1989.

Hobsbawm, E.J. (1987a), *The Age of Empire 1875–1914*, Weidenfeld.

Hobsbawm, E.J. (1987b), 'Out of the Wilderness', reprinted in *Politics for a Rational Left*, Hobsbawm, 1989.

Hobsbawm, E.J. (1988), 'The Signs of a Recovery', reprinted in *Politics for a Rational Left*, Hobsbawm, 1989.

Hobsbawm, E.J. (1989), *Politics for a Rational Left: Political Writings 1977–1988*, Verso.

Hobsbawm, E.J. (1990), 'Goodbye to All That', in *After the Fall: the Failure of Communism and the Future of Socialism* (ed. R. Blackburn, Verso, 1991).

Hobsbawm, E.J. (1993), 'The Present as History', reprinted in *On History*, Hobsbawm, 1997.

Hobsbawm, E.J. (1994a), *Age of Extremes: The Short Twentieth Century 1914–1991*, Michael Joseph.

Hobsbawm, E.J. (1994b), 'Barbarism: A User's Guide', reprinted in *On History*, Hobsbawm, 1997.

Hobsbawm, E.J. (1997), *On History*, Weidenfeld & Nicolson.

Hoggart, R. (1958), *The Uses of Literacy*, Penguin.

Holroyd, M. (1967), *Lytton Strachey: A Critical Biography*, William Heinemann Ltd.

Jacques, M. and Hall, S. (1997), 'The great moving centre show', *New Statesman*, 21 November.

James, O. (1997), 'Curse of comparison', *Prospect*, October.

Kadarkay, A. (1991), *Georg Lukács: Life, Thought, and Politics*, Basil Blackwell.

Keynes, J.M. (1930), 'Economic Possibilities for our Grandchildren', in *The Collected Writings of John Maynard Keynes: Volume IX, Essays in Persuasion*, Macmillan, 1972.

Keynes, J.M. (1938), 'My Early Beliefs', *The Collected Writings of John Maynard Keynes: Volume X, Essays in Biography*, Macmillan, 1972.

Lukács, G. (1983), *Record of a Life: An Autobiographical Sketch*, Verso.

Marquand, D. (1997), 'Journey to an Unknown Destination', in *The New Reckoning*, Polity Press, 1997.

Moggridge, D.E. (1976), *Keynes*, Fontana.

Owen, D. (1991), *Time to Declare*, Michael Joseph.

Siedentop, L. (1994), *Tocqueville*, Oxford University Press.

Skelton, R. (ed.) (1964), *Poetry of the Thirties*, Penguin.

Skidelsky, R. (1969), 'Politics is not Enough', *Encounter*, January.

Skidelsky, R. (1970), *Politicians and the Slump: The Labour Government of 1929–31*, Penguin.

Skidelsky, R. (1975a), *Oswald Mosley*, Macmillan.

Skidelsky, R. (1975b), 'The future of the state', *New Society*, 2 October.

Skidelsky, R. (ed.) (1977), *The End of the Keynesian Era: Essays on the Disintegration of the Keynesian Political Economy*, Macmillan.

Skidelsky, R. (1992a), *John Maynard Keynes: Hopes Betrayed 1883–1920*, Macmillan (first edition 1983).

Skidelsky, R. (1992b), *John Maynard Keynes: The Economist as Saviour 1920–1937*, Macmillan.

Skidelsky, R. (1995), *The World After Communism: A Polemic For Our Times*, Macmillan.

Skidelsky, R. (1996a), 'Welfare without the state', *Prospect*, January.

Skidelsky, R. (1996b), 'The Fall of Keynesianism', in *The Ideas That Shaped Post-war Britain* (eds D. Marquand and A. Seldon, Fontana).

Skidelsky, R. (1997a), *Beyond the Welfare State*, Social Market Foundation.

Skidelsky, R. (1997b), 'Marquand's missing link', *Prospect*, December.

Stone, N. (1983), *Europe Transformed 1878–1919*, Fontana.

Taylor, A.J.P. (1950), 'German Unity', in *Europe: Grandeur and Decline*, Penguin, 1967.

Tocqueville, A. de (1835, 1840), *Democracy in America: Volumes I & II*, ed. J.P. Mayer, Harper & Rowe, 1966.

Tocqueville, A. de (1856), *The Ancien Régime and the French Revolution*, Fontana, 1966.

Tyler, C. (1994), 'Post-mortem on a bloody century', *Financial Times*, 8/9 October.

Walker, M. (1994), 'Old comrades never say die', *The Guardian*, 15 October.

Williams, R. (1965), *The Long Revolution*, Penguin.

10 The Rise and Fall of an Anti-Racism: from Political Blackness to Ethnic Pluralism

Tariq Modood

INTRODUCTION

Looking back at the issue of 'race' in Britain as it emerged in the 1960s and as it is today the most fundamental question is whether 'race relations' can be understood in terms of a black–white racial dualism. From the 1960s onwards a growing body of political activists, social researchers and equality professionals have answered this question with a 'yes', till by the mid to late 1980s the idea was a racial equality orthodoxy. It is perhaps most succinctly expressed in a sentence from Salman Rushdie:

> Britain is now two entirely different worlds and the one you inherit is determined by the colour of your skin. (Rushdie, 1982)

It has been argued that this recognition of a common racism led in the 1960s and 1970s for Afro-Caribbean and Asian people to come together in common political struggles, to transcend their ethnicities and to forge the anti-racist concept of blackness, the unity in resistance of all those who in not being white suffered racism (Sivanandan, 1987). A major consequence of this act of creating a new political 'black' identity was that as Stuart Hall puts it:

> politically speaking, 'The Black Experience', as a singular and unifying framework based on the building up of identity across ethnic and cultural difference between the different communities, became 'hegemonic' over other ethnic/racial identities – though the latter did not, of course, disappear. (Hall, 1988: 27)

No, they certainly did not. For, as is now increasingly recognised, the ethnicities have struck back; to such an extent that not only has political blackness lost its once dominant position, its hegemony (Ali, 1991: 195), but, as Hall argues, we have seen the end of the essential black subject

168

(Hall, 1992). Indeed, putting it with his usual bluntness, Sivanandan has declared that 'there is no longer a Black struggle in Britain which embraces all the non-white communities' (Sivanandan, 1995).

By uniting all those who suffer from white racism into a single category of *blackness* the race egalitarians of the 1970s and 1980s did provide a sharper political focus and achieved a partial mobilisation of the oppressed groups. But they failed to appreciate that the ethnic pride of various groups, necessary for a confident and assertive participation in a society from which the groups had been excluded and held as inferior, could not be built out of the mere fact of common inequality. Excluded groups seek respect for themselves as they are or aspire to be, not simply a solidarity on the basis of a recognition of themselves as victims; they resist being defined by their *mode of oppression* and seek space and dignity for their *mode of being* (Modood, 1992). Hence, however disappointing it has been to the Left, it is not all that surprising that most Asians have not positively embraced the idea of themselves as 'black' (Modood, 1988, 1994a) and that many Muslims have mobilised around a Muslim rather than a 'black' identity (Modood, 1990, 1992). The narrow focus on colour – racism and the development of a unitary non-white political identity has not only been politically short-sighted but, as will be argued below, has obscured important dimensions of racism.

If you will accept a crude distinction between an 'inside left' (the left inside the Labour Party) and an 'outside left' (the left beyond the Labour Party), it would be fair to say that the idea of political blackness, whatever its specific origins, was very much developed by the 'outside left' in the 1970s, but came to be part of the vocabulary and politics of the 'inside left' in the 1980s, especially in London, in Black sections, and in metropolitan local authorities, a combination perhaps best exemplified in Ken Livingstone's GLC (Shukra, 1993). It is therefore perhaps not surprising that criticism of this later form of political blackness should first appear among the 'outside left' (Sivanandan, 1985; Gilroy, 1987, 1992). To be sure it was not a criticism of political blackness *per se*, and nor was the criticism all of a piece. It was a criticism of what was taken to be a spoilt form of political blackness. Spoilt because it was, variously, a politics of careerists jumping onto a bandwagon, overly bureaucratised and professionalised, with little appreciation of the historical and global liberation struggles, out of touch with the communities it claimed to represent and collaborating with state structures it ought to be opposing, while at the same time steeped in dangerous appeals to culture and ethnicity (Sivanandan, 1985; Gilroy, 1987, 1992). At about the same point in time I too began to develop a critique of this form of political blackness. The central idea was that political blackness cannot do justice to the oppression and aspirations of Asian people (Modood, 1988, 1994). What I would like to do here is to point to some developments since the 1960s which I think help to explain why racial dualism no longer fits the facts, if it ever did.

ECONOMIC DIVERSITY

Despite the persistence of racial discrimination, the ethnic minorities in Britain are reversing the initial downward mobility produced by migration and racial discrimination.[1] All ethnic minority groups, however, continue to be employed and to earn below the level appropriate to their educational qualifications and continue to be grossly under-represented as managers in large firms and institutions. Moreover, while the Chinese and African Asians have achieved broad parity with whites, the Indians and Caribbeans are relatively disadvantaged, and the Pakistanis and Bangladeshis continue to be severely disadvantaged. The qualifications, job-levels and earnings spread in 1994 are roughly what one would have predicted from the spread of qualifications in 1974, if racial exclusion was relaxed but not absent. Those groups that had an above-average middle-class professional and business profile before migration seem to have been able to re-create that profile despite the occupational downgrading that all minority groups initially experienced. The progress of ethnic minorities has also depended on their studying harder and longer than their white peers, and their working harder and longer in their jobs. The high representation of most of the Asian groups in self-employment may represent the same phenomenon. Certainly, self-employment has been critical to the economic survival and advancement of some groups, and to narrowing the earnings gap with whites. There is severe and widespread poverty amongst Pakistani and Bangladeshi households, with more than four out of five having an income below half the national average – four times as many as white non-pensioners. This is related to their poor qualification levels, collapse of the Northern manufacturing industries in which they were employed, large families, poor facility in English amongst women, and the very low levels of economic activity among women.

While many Caribbean people seem to have escaped from disadvantage, others are probably worse off in some ways than their equivalents 20 years ago. Young black men are disproportionately without qualifications, without work, without a stable family life, disproportionately in trouble with the police and in prison. Many young black women are in work, with earnings higher than white women's; but others are disproportionately likely to be lone parents, unemployed and in social housing – with all that implies for poverty. While for most groups disadvantage may be diminishing across the generations, this is less clearly the case for Caribbeans.

In the 1960s, it just about made sense to portray all non-white groups as uniformly disadvantaged in terms of educational, economic and professional opportunities. Today, with some minority groups, such as the African Asians and the Chinese, being among the highest academic achievers, and others, such as the Pakistanis and the Bangladeshis, continuing to be in intergenerational poverty, the idea that British racism would produce a common class position for all non-whites is unsalvageable. Race and class continue to interact but as much in making possible various forms of social mobility as in creating underclass formations. All non-white groups for the time being are still under-represented in the top jobs, but some of them have successfully re-created their pre-migration middle-class character. Moreover, not all those in poverty have given up their middle-class aspirations, as evidenced for example in the number of Caribbean women and South Asian men and women university students from working class homes (Modood and Acland, 1998).

DECLINE OF AN ATLANTOCENTRIC PERSPECTIVE

One of the most important developments has been to do not with class but with what we mean by 'race'. Here, Britain has been moving away from an Atlantocentric perspective. What I mean by an Atlantocentric model is the conceptualisation of the black–white relationship in the Atlantic rim as the paradigm of race relations (Modood,1993). The historical core of this model is the slave trade triangle, and the modern political core consists of the US civil rights movement, anti-apartheid, the urban and equal opportunities programmes that arose in response to riots and the prospect of social breakdown in the inner cities. In this way the Atlantic triangle could be said to be widened from Liverpool to West Africa – Virginia to London – Soweto to Los Angeles. As such it represents, of course, a valuable political force with much to its credit. Yet the conceptualisation of British race relations in Atlantocentric terms, even if it once seemed plausible, is currently faced with three problems. The first is the non-Atlantic character of the majority of non-white Britons. According to the 1991 census two of the three million people in Britain of non-European origins have origins from outside the Atlantic triangle, above all from the Indian sub-continent. They bring with them cultures, solidarities, communal authorities, aspirations, emnities, memories, including a colonial relationship of subordination, which is quite different from the Atlantic pattern.

The second flows from the first. Events outside the Atlantic world, outside of its intellectual and political frame, are now impinging on domestic British race relations – in fact more so than the race relations events within other parts of the Atlantic area are affecting Britain. Khalistan, Kashmir, and Khomeni; the Gulf War, the destruction of the mosque at Ayodha and the fate of multiculturalism in Bosnia; all have a greater influence on British race relations than the fortunes of the ANC in South Africa, Jesse Jackson or the riots of Los Angeles. In 1989 the chairman of the influential US congressional black caucus brought a large delegation to London to support the launch of a parallel organisation at Westminster; it has sunk without a trace. The Ayatollah Khomeni, without leaving Teheran, was able to inspire and possibly fund the creation of a 'Muslim Parliament' in London launched in 1992, which has repeatedly been able to capture the media headlines and, for better or for ill, colours majority–minority relations in the UK.

The third reason for the declining relevance of the Atlantocentric model is Britain's increasing integration into European political structures. If the principal Atlantic racial line is that of black–white, in Europe the fault-line Europa–Islam is equally if not of more importance in understanding contemporary prejudice and racism. I think it is already the case in Britain now, as it has been in Europe for some time, that the extra-European origin group that suffers the worst prejudice and exclusion are working-class 'visible' Muslims. As about two-thirds of all non-white people in the European Union are Muslims, Islamophobia and the integration of Muslims have rightly emerged as key race relations issues.

ETHNICITY UNPRIVATISED

Minority ethnicity, albeit white ethnicity, has traditionally been regarded in Britain as acceptable if it was confined to the privacy of family and community, and did not make any political demands. Earlier groups of migrants and refugees, such as the Irish or the Jews in the nineteenth and the first half of the twentieth century, found that peace and prosperity came easier the less public one made one's minority practices or identity. Perhaps for non-European origin groups, whose physical appearance gave them a visibility that made them permanently vulnerable to racial discrimination, the model of a privatised group identity was never viable. Yet, additionally, one has to acknowledge the existence of a climate of opinion quite different from that experienced by the earlier Irish or Jewish incomers.

In the last couple of decades the bases of identity-formation have undergone important changes and there has come to be a minority assertiveness as described in the Introduction, above. Identity has moved from that which might be unconscious and taken-for-granted because implicit in distinctive cultural practices to conscious and public projections of identity and the explicit creation and assertion of politicised ethnicities. This is part of a wider socio-political climate which is not confined to race and culture or non-white minorities. Feminism, gay pride, Quebeçois nationalism and the revival of Scottishness are some prominent examples of these new identity movements which have come to be an important feature in many countries in which class-politics has declined. Identities in this political climate are not implicit and private but are shaped through intellectual, cultural and political debates and become a feature of public discourse and policies, especially at the level of local government. The identities formed in such processes are fluid and susceptible to change with the political climate, but to think of them as weak is to overlook the pride with which they may be asserted, the intensity with which they may be debated and their capacity to generate community activism and political campaigns.

CULTURAL RACISM

British race relations policies and anti-racisms have been premised on the assumption that the problem is of an exclusionism typified by the notice that some landladies in the 1950s and 1960s put in their front windows: 'No Coloureds'. The imagined solution to this exclusionary tendency is symbolised by the black and white handshake that serves as the logo of the Commission for Racial Equality. But neither the problem nor the solution were ever quite so simple. The 'No-Coloureds' racism was not unitary: racists always distinguished among the groups they rejected, and while the likelihood of someone who discriminated against one group discriminating against other groups probably was high, the culturally constructed grounds of rejection varied depending upon the immigrant group.

The latter have over time developed to a point where colour-racism may continue to be a constant but the different brands of racism have separated out from each other. For example, white people who are racists towards some ethnic groups can yet admire other ethnic groups because of, for example, aspects of their subcultural styles:

Most typically, of course, many White working-class boys discriminate positively in favour of Afro-Caribbean subcultures as exhibiting a macho, proletarian style, and against Asian cultures as being 'effemi-nate' and 'middle-class'. Such boys experience no sense of contradic-tion in wearing dreadlocks, smoking ganja and going to reggae concerts whilst continuing to assert that 'Pakis Stink'. (Cohen, 1988: 83)

Les Back found these insights confirmed in his ethnographic study of a large South London council estate in 1985–87 (Back, 1993). He observed among the young Whites on the estate a 'neighbourhood nationalism', side-by-side and in tension with a British nationalism. While the latter was understood as a preserve of Whites, the former was based on racially mixed groups of friends and the prestigious position of black youth cul-tures and styles in the area, and embraced blacks as well as whites. The Vietnamese on the estate were, however, excluded from both these local patriotisms and therefore incurred 'the full wrath of the new racism which defines "outsiders" in terms of "cultural" difference' (228).

Cultural-racism is likely to be particularly aggressive against those minority communities that want to maintain, and not just defensively, some of the basic elements of their culture or religion; if, far from denying their difference (beyond the colour of their skin), they want to assert this difference in public and demand that they be respected just as they are. Some of the early researchers on racial discrimination in England were quite clear about the existence of a colour and cultural component in racial discrimination, and yet thought the former much the more important. A leading study in the 1960s by W.W. Daniel, for example, concluded:

> The experiences of white immigrants, such as Hungarians and Cypriots, compared to black or brown immigrants, such as West Indians and Asians, leaves no doubt that the major component in the discrimination is colour. (Daniel 1968: 209)

This was further confirmed for Daniel by the finding that West Indians experienced more discrimination than Asians, and he takes the view that people who physically differ most from the white population were dis-criminated against most and therefore, he argues, 'prejudice against Negroes is most deep-rooted and widespread' (209). In contrast, he thought that lighter-skinned Asians suffered from some discrimination for cultural reasons, but that this would tend to decrease for British-educated second generation Asians. While his prediction appears, on the surface, reasonable, it overlooked the increasing significance that cultural-racism was to play in determining attitudes to ethnic minorities.

The annual Social Attitudes Survey, which began in 1982, has consis-tently recorded, as have other surveys, that the English think there is more extreme prejudice against Asians than against Afro-Caribbeans. The differences, initially minor, have tended to widen. The most recent evidence shows that young white people are half as likely again to express prejudice against Asians as Caribbeans (Modood *et al.*, 1997: 352). It was also found that all ethnic groups believe that prejudice against Asians and/or Muslims is much the highest of all ethnic, racial or religious prejudices (Modood *et al.*, 1997: 133–4). Part of the explanation for the failure of Daniel's prediction may be found in Michael Banton's observation that:

> the English seemed to display more hostility towards the West Indians because they sought a greater degree of acceptance than the English wished to accord; in more recent times there seemed to have been more hostility towards Asians because they are insufficiently inclined to adopt English ways. (Banton, 1979: 242)

Since that time there has been a significant growth in black–white sociability and cultural synthesis, especially among young people. This is evident in the high esteem in which black cultural styles are held in high prestige, in the hero-worship of successful Black 'stars' in football and sport, music and entertainment (Boulton and Smith, 1992), and in how black–white marriage and cohabitation has become quite common in a way that has not occurred in the United States. Of those born in Britain, half of Caribbean men, and a third of women have a white partner at any time (compared to about 10 per cent of South Asians) (Modood *et al.*, 1997). It is particularly important to note that this sociability is not necessarily in a colour-blind assimilationist, 'passing for white' context in which racism is ignored. For some young people it can take place in ways in which black ethnicity and anti-racism are emphasised – or, indeed, are the point. Black persons can be admired not in spite of, but because of, their blackness, for their aesthetics, style and creativity as well as for their anti-racist resistance: for example, at a typical performance of the controversial black nationalist rap band, Public Enemy, more than half the audience will be white.

COMPETITION BETWEEN IDENTITIES

There have been attempts to form a single 'black' constituency out of the non-white settlers and their British-born descendants. Such attempts have sometimes seemed promising. But they have yet to succeed and it is not obvious that they will ever do so. For example, only a fifth of South Asians, with no significant age or class differences, ever think of themselves as 'black' (Modood *et al.*, 1997: 295). This is not an Asian repudiation of 'the essential black subject' (Hall, 1992) in favour of a more nuanced and more pluralised blackness, but a failure to identify with blackness at all. Hence, the last few years have seen the growing use of a plurality of identities to form pressure groups and coalitions to win public resources and influence and the emergence of open competition between them.

While some groups assert a racial identity based on the experience of having suffered racism, others choose to emphasise their family origins and homeland, others group around a caste or a religious sect as do Hindus such as the Patels or Lohanas, while yet others promote a trans-ethnic identity like Islam. Yet the competition between identities is not simply a competition between groups: it is within communities and within individuals. It is quite possible for someone to be torn between the claims of being, for example, 'black', Asian, Pakistani and Muslim, and also having to choose between them and the solidarities they represent or having to rank them, synthesise them or distribute them between different areas of one's life – and then possibly having to reconcile them with the claims of gender, class and Britishness.

The important contrast between groups was that religion is prominent in the self-descriptions of South Asians, and skin colour in that of Caribbeans. Although younger people are generally less connected to a religion than their elders, they still think religion is important to how they lead their lives. This is changing the character of religion in Britain, not just by diversifying religion but by giving it a greater public policy significance. Interestingly, the minority faiths are beginning to side with the Church of England against those who say multiculturalism requires a severing of the ties between religion and the state (Modood (ed.), 1997).

THE FUTURE OF ANTI-RACISM

In the three decades from the 1960s to the end of the 1980s there have in fact been two different anti-racisms, an earlier and later version. The early response, for example, in the shape of Campaign Against Racial Discrimination (CARD) in the 1960s, influenced by the US Civil Right Movement and the leadership of Martin Luther King Jr, was to deny the significance of the black–white dualism by arguing that we are all the same under the skin. This colour-blind humanism gave way, again first in the United States and more slowly in Britain where it only became prominent in the 1980s, to two forms of colour-consciousness. One form consisted in the recognition that the socio-economic disadvantage of non-whites and structural bias against them in all the institutions of a white society meant that monitoring by colour was essential to identify discrimination and measure inequalities and whether any progress in their elimination was being made.

The second form of anti-racism consisted in raising black consciousness, in getting black people to emphasise their blackness and pride in their roots, in solidarity with other black people and their struggles and in organising as black people in mutual self-help and collective empowerment (Malcolm X, 1966; Cleaver, 1968; Blauner, 1972). This movement was, in effect, to create a black identity or a black political ethnicity. The result was that the racists' dualism of people into black–white was accepted, even sharpened by racism-awareness, but reinterpreted. When this American anti-racist movement was pursued in Britain, there was a problem. For in Britain there was also a second dualism, a West Indian–Asian dualism. Despite the different political and cultural histories that this cleavage represented, British anti-racism, having accepted the first opposition between black and white, continued to deny any political or anti-racist significance to this second division (Modood, 1997).

The growing calls to revise and update anti-racism by pluralising the concept of political blackness are to be welcomed (eg Hall, 1988: 28; Jasper, 1993; Parekh, 1994: 102). An element of this project depends on the argument that a 'black' political identity does not compete with or replace other identities, for example, 'Asian', for, it is argued, different identities refer to different aspects of a person's social being or are emphasised in different situations, say, one in politics, the other to do with culture. As no one has yet given this idea any content, I am unsure as to what is being proposed. Who, for example, is to decide what is a political situation and what a cultural one? As a matter of fact, most of the minority of Asians who think of themselves as 'black' do not think so in relation to specific contexts but to what they perceive as a pervading fact of social existence (Modood *et al.*, 1997: 295–7). Moreover, is 'blackness' really available to Asians when some of the most thoughtful and acclaimed contributions to the development of 'blackness' are not about downgrading the cultural content but increasing the reference to African roots and the Atlantic experience (eg Gilroy, 1987, 1993)? Can political blackness, emotionally and intellectually, really hope to replace an ethnic blackness, with all its powerful resonances and appeals to self-pride, with a notion that is supposed to unite in certain limited contexts for pragmatic purposes? It is because I think that 'blackness' has so much of the history, sorrow, hopes and energy of descendants of African enslavement in the Atlantic world that I do not think that it can be turned into a politics that is neutral between different non-white groups. It cannot have the same meaning or equally give strength to those who can identify with that history and those who cannot.

There is in racial discrimination and colour-racism quite clearly a commonality of circumstance among people who are not white. It is partly what gives sense to the term 'ethnic minorities' and to suggestions for a 'rainbow coalition' (Modood, 1988: 402). The question is not whether coalitional anti-racism is desirable, but of what kind. My personal preference and commitment is for a plural politics that does not privilege colour-identities. We must accept what is important to people, and *we must be even-handed between the different identity formations*. Political blackness is an important constituent of this pluralism, but it can't be *the* over-arching basis of unity. The end of its hegemony is not without its problems and dangers, but is not to be regretted. A precondition of creating/recreating a coalitional pluralism is the giving up of the corrupting ideal of a solidaristic monism.

Indeed, one has to go further and have a sense of society that is more than just a coalition of non-whites, or, even, a coalition of the oppressed. One such sense of society is the idea of multicultural Britishness. The 1980s saw the promotion of a chauvinistic and ungenerous form of Britishness, for example, in some of the coverage of the Falklands War, in the Christian nationalism of the Education Reform Act of 1988, and in Norman Tebbit's 'cricket test'. Consequently, some anti-racists and social theorists wrote off nationalism as an inherently monistic, 'essentialist' and quasi-racist idea (for example, Gilroy, 1987; Anthias and Yuval-Davis, 1992). This was an over-reaction, and I am pleased too see that pluralistic notions of nationality and citizenship are now being elaborated (Parekh, 1990, 1998; Kymlicka, 1995; Miller, 1995).

It is clear that what is often claimed today in the name of racial equality is more than would have been recognised as such in the 1960s. The shift is from an understanding of equality in terms of individualism and cultural assimilation to a politics of recognition, to equality as encompassing public ethnicity. Equality is no longer simply about access to the dominant culture but also not having to hide or apologise for one's origins, family or community but expecting others to respect them and adapt public attitudes and arrangements so that the heritage they represent is encouraged rather than contemptuously expected to wither away. The challenge today is twofold. Firstly, to devise and pursue a pluralised concept of racial equality that focuses policy on the variously disadvantaged circumstances of some minority groups without assuming that all the ethnic monorities are worse off than the white population (Modood *et al.*, 1997). Secondly, to reach out for a multicultural Britishness that is sensitive to ethnic difference and incorporates a respect for persons as individuals and for the collectivities to which people have a sense of belonging. That means a multiculturalism that is happy with hybridity but has space for religious identities (Modood, 1998). Both hybridity and ethno-religious communities have legitimate claims to be accommodated in political multiculturalism; they should not be pitted against each other in an either-or fashion as is done all too frequently (by for example, Rushdie, 1991; Waldron, 1992). The emphasis on a new Britishness is particularly worth emphasising because there are people today who want not just to be black or Indian in Britain, but positively want to be black British or British Indians. They are not so much seeking civic rights against a hegemonic nationality as attempting to politically negotiate a place in an all-inclusive nationality.

Such political demands create argument and debate and unsettle identities, sentiments, symbols, stereotypes, etc., especially amongst the 'old' British. Yet, despite some wild rhetoric, it should be clear that the politics of ethnic identity is a movement of inclusion (at least from the side of those excluded) and social cohesion, not fragmentation. Translated into policy it could be a contribution to a renewal of British nationality or national-rebuilding of the sort exhorted by Prime Minister Blair, especially in his Labour Party conference speech of September 1997 (Jacques, 1997). The idea, as mistakenly once supposed by Salman Rushdie and quoted at the start of this chapter, that Britain is 'two worlds' of black and white, has rightly given way to a more sensitive awareness of plurality. But it is a plurality that aspires to be not just 'in' Britain but 'of' Britain.

NOTES

1.   The evidence for the factual claims in this and the next four paragraphs is to be found in Modood *et al.*, 1997.

REFERENCES

Ali, Y. (1991), 'Echoes of Empire: Towards A Politics of Representation', in *Enterprise and Heritage: Cross Currents of National Culture* (eds J. Cromer and S. Harvey), Routledge.

Anthias, F. and Yuval-Davis, N. (1992), *Racialised Boundaries*, Routledge.

Back, L. (1993), '"Race" Identity and Nation Within An Adolescent Community in South London', *New Community*, 19: 217–33.

Ballard, R. and Kalra, V.S. (1994), *The Ethnic Dimension of the 1991 Census*, University of Manchester.

Blauner, R. (1972), *Racial Oppression in America: Essays in Search of a Theory*, Harper and Row.

Boulton, M.J. and Smith, P. (1992), 'Ethnic Preferences and Perceptions Among Asian and White British Middle School Children', *Social Development*, 1(1): 55–66.

Cleaver, E. (1968), *Soul on Ice*, McGraw Hill.

Cohen, P. (1988) 'The Perversions of Inheritance: Studies In The Making Of Multi-Racist Britain', in *Multi-Racist Britain* (eds P. Cohen and S. Bains), Macmillan.

Commission for Racial Equality (1990), *Britain: A Plural Society*.

Daniel, W.W. (1968), *Racial Discrimination in England: a Penguin Special based on the PEP Report*, Penguin.

Donald, J. and Rattansi, A. (eds) (1992), *'Race', Culture and Difference*, Sage.

Gilroy, P. (1987), *There Ain't no Black in the Union Jack*, Routledge.

Gilroy, P. (1992), 'The End of Anti-Racism' in *'Race', Culture and Difference* (eds J. Donald and A. Rattansi), Sage, originally published as a Runnymede Trust lecture in 1987.

Gilroy, P. (1993), *The Black Atlantic: Modernity and Double Consciousness*, Verso.

Hall, S. (1988), 'New Ethnicities', in *Black Film, British Cinema* (ed. K. Mercer), also in *'Race', Culture and Difference* (eds J. Donald and A. Rattansi), Sage, 1992.

Hall, S. (1992), 'The Question of Cultural Identity' in *Modernity and its Futures*, (eds S. Hall and T. McGrew), Polity Press.

Jacques, M. (1997), 'The Melting Pot That Is Born-Again Britannia', The *Observer*, 28 December, pp. 14–15.

Jasper, L. (1993), 'Shades of Blackness!', *Black To Black*, Issue No. 2, 1990 Trust.

Jones, T. (1993), *Britain's Ethnic Minorities*, Policy Studies Institute.

Kymlicka, W. (1995), *Multicultural Citizenship*, Oxford University Press.

Malcolm X. (1966), *The Autobiography of Malcolm X*, written with Alex Hailey, Hutchinson and Collins.

Miller, D. (1995), *On Nationality*, Oxford University Press.

Modood, T. (1988), '"Black", Racial Equality and Asian Identity', *New Community*, 14(2).

Modood, T. (1990), 'British Asian Muslims and The Rushdie Affair' *The Political Quarterly*, 61(2), 143–60; also in *'Race', Culture and Difference* (eds J. Donald and A. Rattansi), Sage, 1992.

Modood, T. (1991), 'The Indian Economic Success: A Challenge To Some Race Relations Assumptions', *Policy and Politics*, 19(3); also in Modood, T. (1992), *Not Easy Being British: Colour, Culture and Citizenship*, Runnymede Trust and Trentham Books.

Modood, T. (1992), *Not Easy Being British: Colour, Culture and Citizenship*, Runnymede Trust and Trentham Books.

Modood, T. (1993), 'The Limits of America: Re-thinking Equality in the Changing Context of British Race Relations', in *The Making of Martin Luther King and the Civil Rights Movement* (eds B. Ward and T. Badger), Macmillan.

Modood, T. (1994), 'Political Blackness and British Asians', *Sociology*, 28(4).

Modood, T. (1997), '"Difference", Cultural Racism and Anti-Racism' in *Debating Cultural Hybridity* (eds P. Werbner and T. Modood), Zed Books.

Modood, T. (ed.) (1997), *Church, State and Religious Minorities*, Policy Studies Institute, 1997.

Modood, T. (1998), 'Anti-Essentialism, Multiculturalism and the "Recognition" of Religious Minorities', *Journal of Political Philosophy*.

Modood, T. and Acland, T. (eds) *Race and Higher Education*, Policy Studies Institute, 1998.

Modood, T., Beishon, S. and Virdee, S. (1994), *Changing Ethnic Identities*, Policy Studies Institute.

Parekh, B. (1990), 'Britain and the Social Logic of Pluralism' in Commission for Racial Equality, *Britain: A Plural Society*, London.

Parekh, B. (1994), 'Minority Rights, Majority Values', in *Reinventing The Left*, (ed. D. Milliband), Polity Press.

Parekh, B. (1998), 'National Identity', The Kapila Lecture.

Rushdie, S. (1982), 'The New Empire Within Britain', *New Society*, 9 December.

Rushdie, S. (1991), 'In Good Faith' in S. Rushdie *Imaginary Homelands*.

Shukra, K. (1993), 'Black Politics and Ethnicity in Britain', British Sociological Association Conference on 'Research Imaginations', University of Essex, April.

Sivanandan, A. (1985), 'RAT and the Degradation of the Black Struggle', *Race and Class*, XXVI(4).

Sivanandan, A. (1987), *A Different Hunger: Writings on Black Resistance*, Pluto Press.

Sivanandan, A. (1995), 'Interview', *CARF*, February/March.

Waldron, J. (1992), 'Minority Cultures and The Cosmopolitan Alternative', *University of Michigan Journal of Law Reform*, (25), 3 & 4.

11 From Berkeley to Blair: a Dialogue of the Deaf?
Anne Showstack Sassoon

TRAJECTORIES PERSONAL AND POLITICAL

Thinking about the past provides the occasion, for those of us who have lived it, not only to analyse political, social, and economic developments, or cultural trends, but our own growth and development, or lack of it. Noticeably absent, however, from most political or intellectual discussions is self-interrogation. This is not surprising given the vulnerablity that this can expose. There is a strange pretence that we have always been what we are now. Convincing intellectual and political argument, whatever the content, wears the clothes of infallibility. By convention academic and political legitimacy and authority are rooted in certainty, which is required both of those in leading roles, and, it is expected, of those who accept such leadership. A parent–child relationship is constituted in which little if any change and development is expected of either part.

Reflective modes of debate run the risk, of course, of self-indulgent narcissism. Such narcissism is neither useful nor attractive and only rarely interesting. There should be a place, however, for reflecting on personal trajectories as one, even if a small, contribution to producing some of the questions which can inform wider discussions. Private trajectories, of course, are not representative or even pre-figurative of wider truths, but they can provide insights into wider phenomena. What follow are some explorations and conjectures, no more than that, which grow out of trying to learn from rather than take for granted the widespread opposition to Blair and New Labour of the generation of the left whose political culture is rooted in the 1960s. Those of us who, while not endorsing every aspect, feel comfortable with Blair's political project because we see it as expressing many of the aspirations and criticisms of mainstream politics going back to the 1960s, are few and far between. We are oddballs, or at the very least non-conformists.

DISSENT FROM THE POLITICS OF DESPAIR

The fact that some of us have gone in another direction from this 1960's left 'mainstream' does not feel, at least, like movement to the 'right' or weary accommodation to a supposed neo-liberal hegemony. How is it possible that some of us dissent and look to the future if not with confidence at least with hope? A new political generation is in power which has both been influenced by and rejects its elders. Those elders, my contemporaries, in turn, lacking recognition, refuse to believe that any of their ideals can become reality. This is in part because a lifetime of oppositional politics is deeply conditioning. It is also because the collapse of communism, the challenge of globalisation, and nearly 20 years of neo-liberal hegemony in the US and Britain have contributed to undermining the real capacities and the political legitimacy of state intervention and much of the expertise and professional practice associated with it. It needs to be reiterated that New Left criticism and the contradictory effects of welfare state provision have also played their role in undermining the postwar consensus. This alienation, particularly evident in demoralised state sector professionals, has lead to no little political despair as the symbols and much of the content of the left politics of decades gone by have been relegated to the scrapheap. A still younger generation in their teens and twenties were delighted to be rid of the Tories. Rebranding Britain without any need for exhortations from above, they are engaged in their own opposition to parental figures. They are probably only interested in political relics from the past as artefacts.

REFLECTIONS, EXPLORATIONS, CONJECTURES

I grew up in the United States before coming to this country in 1966. The 1960s were the period of my secondary and university education. From a political perspective, my life spanned joining the Young Democrats at 16 and helping to elect John F. Kennedy in 1960, when that was a radical thing to do in Orange County, California, to attending the University of California, Berkeley from 1962–66 during the period of mobilisation around civil rights, the free speech movement, and the Vietnam War, and coming to the LSE just before it erupted at the end of the decade. There I studied the work of Antonio Gramsci and Marxist theory more generally, the history of the working-class movement in Europe, the Russian Revolution, and Italian fascism. Along with new-found friends from the British student left, I shared anti-Americanism, dismissed Labour politics because the British government supported American intervention in Vietnam, and was inspired by a heroic image of the working class. Recently I re-read some of my own work from a decade later, and I was struck by how the easy use of leftist language, for example, reference to 'the masses', conveys the impression of certainties long gone. However, this represents only one aspect of how many of us felt. Inspired by many different sources, for example, not only Gramsci but Trotsky and later Althusser, there was enormous excitement about going beyond cold war dichotomies and 'free world' complacency to engage with racism, sexual discrimination, and poverty and to feel that new spaces were opening up and that a different future was possible. We may have started, in my case, with Kennedy's New Frontier but we ended up using the forbidden language of Marxism, forbidden, that is, by associating it only with the worst excesses of communism. We felt we were overthrowing the patriarchs as we criticised the assumptions of both 'sides'. We did not think we were embracing old dogmas, even if we may have argued dogmatically to the dismay of our elders.

As paradoxical as it may now seem, we employed the words of old-fashioned Marxism, and many of the songs and symbols of the Old Left, of our elders, to condemn what we had inherited. Depending on which political uniform we adopted, the style varied, but our arguments and practices were adorned by different combinations of Marxism–Leninism, vanguard party, barricades, spontaneity vs leadership, reformism vs revolution, utopia, freedom against authority, feeling vs rationality, youth vs age, sexual freedom vs sexual inhibition. Some of us, eventually, adopted the language of Gramsci to try to rethink left politics in terms of possibilities rather than guarantees. Indeed, this is the sense of a beautiful essay by Stuart Hall who has provided such an important role model, of integrating what is useful in Gramsci, Althusser, and more recently Foucault, to engage with what is new rather than to try to force reality into old schemas.[1]

We went on, some of us, to try to understand what challenges historical development poses to our very way of thinking. This has, of course, taken a wide variety of forms, especially under the impetus of the collapse of communism in Eastern Europe and of traditional Social Democracy. Reactions have varied from complete rejection of the past to clasping desperately to what are considered eternal verities. The biggest challenge of all, however, is to build on what is useful from the past while ridding ourselves of what is holding us back from the growth and development necessary to negotiate transitions as the construction of better futures rather than merely the destruction of the past.

We have inevitably to move on. Yet in doing so we also have to recognise that the present and future are inevitably built upon elements of the past, and that the very attempt to destroy it undermines our personal and political capacities. But if this recognition, however, is to be constructive, it must be something very different from defending the indefensible, from holding on for dear life because of the fear of loss, understandable though this may be before a better future takes concrete form. We have to acknowledge loss, to grieve for what is dead, and to face the future courageously, not as political heroines or heroes, but as naturally anxious human beings. It is this tension between what is lost, what remains, and what will or can be that delineates not only our human condition but social and historical progress, in the sense of moving forward, on a voyage of change.

LONG SHADOWS OF LOSS AND DESTRUCTION

Recently I have been reflecting on how the perception of time changes at different points in the lifecycle. In this context I have thought about the difference between growing up in the postwar period in the United States compared to in Britain, and about how little I understood at the time. The following has struck me. The experience of the war was so recent in the 1960s that both what was said and what was left unsaid or repressed in the postwar period must have cast a long shadow even over those developments which were new and different. In Britain, unlike in the US, the physical destruction and consequent rebuilding of cities and the construction of new towns, however much we might now be critical of what was built with eyes and needs formed by a later period, must have had a major impact. The demand to remake society, and support for the postwar settlement, must have related to what people saw and experienced daily. The consensus around the welfare state reflected the desire not to go back to the social and economic conditions of the 1930s. But this consensus must also have been buttressed by a sensation that society was improving. This was not false ideology or the product of social engineers or modernist writers but was rooted in the daily lives of millions of people. Not only was decent housing urgently needed, but getting rid of the rubble and filling in empty spaces would have reminded people daily that life *could* improve. This impression must have been reinforced by the experience of full male employment, along with the continuing participation of married women in the paid labour force, and reforms in health, education, and other social provision. There was 'good' and 'bad' in this, but the 'new' was literally, concretely, no pun intended (!), the stuff of everyday experience.

The lacunae wrought by war were filled, in private lives as well as the physical fabric of society. But ambivalent feelings were undoubtedly aroused. We can also understand why, in the face of postwar changes, a certain conservatism emerged as a reaction to the disruptions and terrible human and material losses of the Second World War. It is true that the return by many women to more traditional family roles and the dismantling of nurseries after the war were reinforced by the arguments of psychologists and sociologists which became embedded in the professional expertise of social workers, teachers, and others about what was 'normal' and 'good' for children and families. These arguments, which Denise Riley has analysed so well in her book *War in the Nursery*,[2] can certainly be criticised. But both their acceptance at the time and their continued persistence in British political debate, so different in most other European countries, must be explained by something more than the influence of experts.

Large-scale change never takes place unless it also corresponds to needs in the lives of millions of people who never experience such transitions merely as victims of policy or of ideology. There never was, and never can be, a complete return to the past. Women never simply go back to their pre-war lives even if they do not continue all of their wartime roles. Long shadows were undoubtedly cast by the terrible disruption of the war years. Sudden death and loss of homes and possessions, separation and physical dislocation marked the lives of millions of people of different generations in Britain, and to an even greater extent those in occupied Europe, witnessed by British troups at the end of the war and reported in the news broadcasts of the time. Moreover, it is likely that guilt caused by surviving, so well known by Holocaust survivors, was a widespread phenomenon in the population at large.

Death, destruction and loss were, of course, also accompanied by new freedoms. Untraditional paid work brought greater economic freedom, and women enjoyed wider cultural and sexual horizons, not least because of the influence of American troops. Food parcels from America, jazz and American movies and G.I. brides probably all contributed to the British love–hate relationship with the US. But millions of women also experienced heavy, multiple burdens as they laboured to look after themselves and their children, keep house, contain the fear of death, and find some laughter and enjoyment in difficult wartime circumstances. Is it really surprising then that many felt that what they wanted after the war was a husband in full-time work earning a wage to cover household needs, the so-called 'family wage' so much more common then than now, a washing machine and a hoover, a comfortable home, perhaps a house with a garden, eventually a car, and some paid work for an element of financial independence?

FREE OF FEAR, FREE TO CRITICISE

We now have the luxury, which many of us began to enjoy in the 1960s if not earlier, of being free from the fears and the deprivations of the depression, a defining moment for several generations of Americans in the same way as the war was for the British, to criticise materialism while enjoying affluence and new educational, professional, and political possibilities. We are right not to feel guilty about this. But having closed our ears to endless parental stories of earlier deprivations and why we should be grateful to previous generations, as well as having experienced the effects of so many silences about loss and fear of loss, perhaps we can now also begin to appreciate the impact of the context of our parents and grandparents on public policy and political projects.[3] We can continue to enjoy memories of the excitement of discovery while recognising that the new worlds of years gone by were neither perfect ideals nor suitable any longer for changed circumstances. We can continue to adhere to many of the aims of the past, and still admit that some were neither possible nor perhaps even desirable in the light of further understanding. We can seek better means of obtaining what is still desirable but not yet reached while also building on new insights to aim at new and better goals.

At the end of the century it is often hard to appreciate fully what the achievements of abortion and homosexual law reform and anti-discrimination legislation represent. The beginning of the end of deference in Britain including the flowering of youth culture was related to the expansion of educational opportunities and an improvement in living stan-dards. These and other changes have represented truly major advances. They are not undone because we now can also recognise their limitations. We may now be critical of some of the effects of much urban regeneration from the 1960s. Of course 'people should have known better'. But any mature analysis would recognise that what is no longer considered accept-able, or 'progressive', could still have constituted an advance at the time. If we place Britain in a wider European context, we can acknowledge that, for example, Le Corbusier's modernist housing for workers was a good deal better than the conditions that millions of people had endured up to then. Separate kitchens – isolating as they may feel now – were an improvement on living in a one-room slum. It is important to avoid, to use an inelegant term, 'presentism', that is, condemning the past from today's standpoints. What was a reasonable decision because of contemporary understandings and widespread demands would not be reasonable today in changed circumstances and with the benefit of hindsight.

Criticism of the past should bring humility about the present and help us to avoid both old and new mistakes. But attempts to destroy the past is dis-abling and the mirror image, I might add, of holding on for dear life and against all odds to what we know and what is familiar however problem-atic it may be.[4] Our taken-for-granted 'common sense' derives in large part from previous experience. What was once exciting and new comes to be internalised and transforms what appears 'normal' and 'natural'. A deeply conservative cynicism about whether change is possible can develop, even when change is taking place all around us, because we fail to historicise and relativise past and present.

WHAT CELEBRATION OF 1968? OR
TEN YEARS IS A LONG TIME

Indeed, the past looks different at different points in time. This can be illustrated by focusing on what for many encapsulates the 1960s politically: 1968. That year represents what many people consider the political high point of the decade, the culmination of student militancy in the US and student movements in the UK and elsewhere, the May events in France, the Prague Spring and the Soviet invasion of Czechoslovakia, and so on. Yet compared to ten years ago, my impression is that very little is being said about 1968. This is probably a result of how much has changed in the last decade, not only the fall of communism, but also the undermining of a neo-liberal hegemony if not its disappearance, and the emergence of a centre-left politics which claims to be radical. Re-reading what I wrote for an Italian left journal, *Rinascita*, on the British reaction to the twentieth anniversary of May 1968, it struck me that despite many differences, some observations may still be relevant. I noted that given the political significance of 1968 in countries like France and Italy, it would have been easy to misread the media coverage which the anniversary engendered in Britain. This included television and radio programmes, several major books and therefore lengthy book reviews, newspaper articles, magazine inserts, even a festival of nostalgia and celebration. But a word of caution before we romanticise the past. What was significant about this interest was not so much the *content* which focused above all on the French May, but what these activities had to say about Britain in 1988. First, and by no means least, the men, and it was mainly men, who made the programmes, wrote the books, and organised debates were the generation who lived 1968 as a life event in its way as significant as the second world war for another generation.

There was a mixture of nostalgia, a feeling of lost youth and unfulfilled promises, the memory of sexual adventure. Questions were asked about what it had all meant. The sensation that nothing was the same afterward and that things changed and yet so much remained the same or was worse with the Right in power combined with an enormous ambivalence about lost illusions and about impossible yet marvellous utopias. Of course, all these could be dismissed as the musings of 40 somethings expressing their mid-life crisis in a public way and transferring a cycle of personal change on to a political dimension. And yet, the very fact that they were, and many still are, in positions of power as intellectuals who controlled and influenced the media or held academic positions was itself a significant outcome of 1968 and a comment on Britain both ten years ago and now.

DIALOGUE OF THE DEAF

We can understand the relative silence about 1968 today and the alienation of the 1968 generation better if we consider the following. Ten years on there has been a significant displacement with Blair in power, oppositional politics, the only kind of politics most of us know, detached from engagement with concrete programmes of reform, in a moment when it is impossible to return to pre-1979, and there are many reasons for not doing so. We confront a younger and different generation in the corridors of power who find it difficult if not impossible to articulate anything good about the left politics of a previous generation. A dialogue of the deaf ensues. The oldies have their political antennae tuned to another station whose music they recognise. They shut their ears to new accounts of a world that has changed so much compared to their youth. They do not even hear the argument that achieving social justice requires a different story line if there is to be a happy ending. And just as new worlds are opening up in Britain, the desire for the solutions of times past, so long repressed under the impact of 18 years of Conservative governments, explodes but remains unanswered by those in power.

And yet, rather like in the post-war period, but for different reasons, there are huge silences almost as if fantasy fears reality. In the leftist opposition to the government, who speaks, as we used to do, of poverty traps caused by the workings of the benefit and tax systems? Where are the demands for full employment? Why, we used to ask, was money spent on unemployment benefits when people – usually meaning men – could be working, spending money, and paying taxes? Demands were made for new opportunities for women to be in formal paid work, and for the provision of good child-care as a precondition for making women's rights a reality. After all, it was said, women were not only mothers. No one, we used to say, should be stuck on benefits. Of course, much of this was itself oversimplified. It took time to incorporate a richer understanding of the pleasures as well as the responsibilities of parenting, to put men into the equation, and to make some progress in incorporating the needs of the disabled and of the elderly. Yet what is striking is how much is being repressed. This is caused, I think, by widespread ambivalence about change and personal growth, which after all always implies loss as earlier states of being disappear.

This is certainly true of a generation of intellectuals whose world view changed forever after 1968 and who occupy important spaces, however constrained, which have formed significant threads of the fabric of Britain under Thatcherism. It was easy in 1988 to see only those aspects of a complex present which seemed to negate the hopes of 1968: the BBC was under increasing government pressure; the universities had to defend themselves by showing how they could succeed according to the logic of the market; the moral panic associated with AIDS led to a new attack on homosexuality, and the possibility of restrictions imposed on abortion. Ten years ago there was a tone of self-criticism, of 'how could we be so young and naive', a painful cry of personal and political crisis, a feeling of impotence and dismay or adolescent defiance. In 1998 now that we once more have a Labour government, howls of betrayal drown out any soul-searching as 18 years of opposition to the Conservatives appear unrecognised by those in power. Yet if we listen carefully to the ways in which that crisis was expressed in 1988 and think about it with a sensitivity formed by the needs of the present as much as the experience of the past, there is much we can learn from this ten years old 'celebration–mourning' of 1968.

PASSING THE TORCH TO WOMEN

It is not a reductive or simplistic feminism in 1988 to note that the voices we heard and therefore the message we received were masculine. This was not surprising. After all the best known protagonists of 1968 were almost all male. Women were present and were active, but it was not women's historical moment, even if, according to these 1988 commentators, it made our moment possible. And in 1988 this was a theme voiced by men on the left who, in what was in large part a romanticised and idealised view, made a ritual bow in the direction of feminism which, it was said, had continued to pursue the promises and aspirations of 1968. Feminism was granted (rather than having seized) responsibility for putting the personal on the political agenda. It was women above all who demanded an authentic politics rooted in subjectivity and reflecting the need for autonomy and self-fulfillment, and carried on questioning old roles and old authorities, above all traditional definitions of gender and sexuality. Most importantly, it was said, feminism had undertaken that historical task contained in the promise of 1968 to break with the old, to re-think society from a new perspective, to ask unasked questions, to speak the unspeakable.

Yet women of the 1968 generation know something which goes beyond a ritual gesture to what is presented as a last hope delegated to 'the others', that is, which is voiced as a delegation rather than as part of an assumption of shared responsibility. We know the pain, the effort, the exhaustion, the wounds, the disorientations, the resistances, the repetitions and the search for reassuring structures which have been part of this break with the old. We also know the excitement accompanying this growth, this experiencing life as process rather than structure, this leap into the future – without any guarantees of an endpoint, for there is none. Having experienced the fear of the unknown, we can understand if men hesitate before a similar process yet we can still be angry confronted by this abdication and delegation. We also recognise the exhaustion of juggling roles and trying to perform, made to measure, for what structurally and to a considerable extent also culturally is still, in the main, a man's world.

ASSUMING RESPONSIBILITY FOR A CHANGE

It should also, once more, be pointed out that perhaps the politically most significant immediate effect of the anti-authoritarianism, anti-statism, and the general critique of the corporatist consensus of post-war politics was the victory of the new right which was determined and able to make that break which neither the new nor the old left managed and yet prepared the way for. We cannot ignore the fact that Blair and New Labour and the support for New Labour in the last election and afterward are related to that failure. Why has the right always tended to be so much better at understanding an epoch than the left? Perhaps because the new right, itself one of the products of what Gramsci might have described as a long-term organic crisis, of which 1968 was another manifestation, learnt the lesson taught by one of the theoretical fathers of conservatism, Edmund Burke, that history is process and that institutions have no choice but to change to ensure social continuity. But the lesson is not just one of conservation. If the aim is radical change and renewal, and the establishment of legitimacy for a new political project, one which cannot simply be overturned by the next government, change not must not only be shaped in a progressive direction through public policy promoted from on high but must be based on widespread consent and reflect needs articulated from below.

The right learned to articulate and to respond sufficiently to demands to organise and maintain a social basis of consent in order to shape and manage its version of a modernising project. Many on the left, meantime, dazzled by the rapidity and apparent fragmentation of change, continued, and continue, to clasp the life-raft of the old. In fact, the past never disappears completely but has to be integrated because it serves inevitably as the basis of the new, however radical or, as we once said, revolutionary. Yet so often what is truly novel is obscured by the energy expended holding on to the old or, on the contrary, seeking a clear break, abandoning the project altogether. Will the left be able to learn to look at the new and to analyse the past without simplistic schemas? Will renewed interest in the 1960s provide the occasion for doing so which the celebration of 1968 ten years ago failed to do?

But New Labour also bears some responsibility. A hand might be held out to those of good will who could, if encouraged, make a journey of discovery and contribute to renewing the country. Social creativity and social entrepreneurship, so praised by the gurus of New Labour, often imply untidy, messy and unintended outcomes which are stepping stones to new problems as well as new solutions. A celebration of diversity as a distinguishing mark of new brand Britain, and a recognition of the social worth of providing care, both of which have roots in 1960s politics, could create connections outwards and across political generations to the benefit of the government and the society. Social consensus and social creativity could both be enhanced. If the older political generation of 1960s leftists does not respond because of problems of identity and recognition, perhaps a younger, more open and more energetic generation will.

NOTES

1.   Stuart Hall, 'The problem of ideology: marxism without guarantees', in *Stuart Hall. Critical Dialogues in Cultural Studies*, (eds D. Morley and K.-Hs. Che), Lawrence and Wishart, 1996.

2.   Denise Riley, *War in the Nursury. Theories of the Child and the Mother*, Virago, 1983.

3.   Recent reflection on how relieved refugees from continental Europe must have been to arrive in Britain before and after the war, and British intellectuals to have avoided Nazi occupation has made me understand much better than earlier a generation of intellectuals whose

view of Britain was above all of tolerance and pluralism. Of course, this reinforced a certain British complacency and self-satisfaction about the British political system in the 1960s which we criticised so vehemently. As 1960s leftists were not shy of pointing out, both the literature on British politics, forever stressing British continuity and supposed lack of profound social cleavages, in implicit contrast to France, and mainstream political debate in the 1960s appeared blind to the history of class conflict, imperialist domination, and racism.

4. This is exemplified in the exchange between Christopher and Peter Hitchens, 'Oh brother, what a time', The *Sunday Times*, 1 March 1998.

12 Crafting a New Social Settlement*
Paul Hirst

Modern industrial societies have little to hope for in common. At the top of the pile individuals may expect a big bonus or at the bottom they may dream of winning the lottery. But we no longer have collective imagined futures that are capable of mobilising and inspiring masses of people. The reason for that is that we appear to have no viable methods of how we might govern our affairs to improve them. The models that we have relied on for the better part of the century have worn out. Those of the centre left faded with the discovery that it was far from easy in the long run to manage the economy to provide full employment and steady growth. Those of the right are dying as people recoil from the true consequences of unregulated markets and overwhelming corporate power.

State *dirigisme* and *laissez faire* are both discredited. The other form of governance, that made state action effective, and the current desperate return to *laissez faire* unnecessary, was corporatism. Yet after a heroic period in which in many countries it helped to stabilise economies after the oil-price inflation of 1973, it too has become less effective. We shall return to the reasons for the failure of corporatism below.

The point is that the social changes that undermined corporatist governance as a 'third way' between state intervention and the market have created the conditions for the appearance of a new model, associative democracy. Associative democracy aims to devolve as many tasks of governance as possible – in economics, politics and welfare – to self-governing voluntary associations. The claim is that by deepening and extending democratic control, more effective because more local and, therefore, better informed decisions will be made, thus improving economic and social governance. This model is both radical and practical. It is also capable of attracting support from across the political spectrum from those who reject the decayed orthodoxies of the right and the left. It is the best option for continuing the negotiated co-ordination of market economies of corporatism and the social solidarity made possible by welfare states.

---

* This essay first appeared in *New Times*; the editors wish to thank the journal for permission to publish it here.

The classic form of governance through negotiation and bargaining is corporatism – the regulation of capitalism through co-ordination by organised interests at national and at plant level. Industry, organised labour and the state co-operated in order to secure sustainable commitments by each of the parties. Corporatism has been one of the most effective institutional supports of the large-firm economy in the post-1945 advanced world. But it has been threatened by economic and industrial changes that have made it more difficult to bargain through centralised organised interests.

Divisions of labour and forms of manufacturing organisation have changed radically since the early 1970s. The workforce has differentiated as a consequence of the decline of standardised mass production. Such changes have led to a blurring of the blue/white collar boundary in changing structures of skill. Unions are now less representative of labour as a whole and less able to centralise bargaining around the common interests of the labour force. At the same time, the structures of 'the firm' have been changing rapidly. Increasingly, highly-centralised top-down control has been abandoned in favour of more responsive forms of organisation able to cope with changing demand, rapid innovation, and the flexible production of a wide range of goods. Decentralisation, de-merger, the growth of inter-firm partnerships, and relational sub-contracting, weaken the classical managerial line of command and also mean that the interests of industry are more and more difficult to represent through national business federations.

The new forms of negotiated governance – networks, partnerships, trust-relationships that are emerging after the decline of national corporatism – are more specific and more evanescent, less capable of being synthesised into a 'model' on a national scale. The state too is less of an effective corporatist partner than it was in the era of the post-1945 great boom. States have fewer capacities to determine macro-economic conditions and thus have less to offer labour and business in exchange for their compliance.

The decline of corporatism and the weakening of Keynesian demand management strategies have limited the scope for distinct national responses to changing economic circumstances. Not only have general models of governance ceased to be effective guides to political actors but their embodiment in distinctive 'national' models is now increasingly under threat. Until recently, specific national capitalisms could be held up as models to the laggards in industrial performance and economic governance – West Germany, Japan and Sweden being the most often cited examples. The Swedish combination of comprehensive welfare, active full-employment policies, centralised corporatist bargaining, and highly concentrated internationally competitive industrial companies has clearly 'unravelled', even though popular support for welfare institutions remains strong. Germany and Japan are both increasingly seen as problematic models suffering from weaknesses and constraints that are systemic rather than conjunctural.

The problem now is that models at every level seem less applicable. This is not to say that there are no new forms of governance and no specific experiences from which others can learn. There are a great many examples of institutional and organisational innovation. Firms are engaged in many evolving experiences of partnership, of building networks, of creating new working practices, and of seeking new relationships with customers, suppliers and employees. Governance through negotiation continues to develop in many forms at local level: new relationships between companies, local authorities and public agencies, worker groups, and local associations and activists.

Thus the problem is not that nothing is happening in the creation of new forms of governance. It is that such changes are specific to definite localities, evanescent, and subject to constant revision. They are thus difficult to generalise or to learn from – in part because they are processes rather than a settled architecture of institutions. Models of the old kind offered firms, societies and states that were seeking to catch up, the chance to do things by numbers, to copy institutional designs and practices. Keynesian demand management was available to any medium-sized state with a large enough public-sector and a competent civil service. 'Fordism' was an ideal–typical model of industrial efficiency that could be copied and adapted to local circumstances by mediocre firms.

Models also meant that much of society was following the same script; that fact ensured a degree of uniformity and an ability to grasp the prevailing institutional architecture. Such simplicity had significant advantages – societies where institutions are localised and rapidly changing, are hard places for all but the most talented and adaptable to live in, and difficult for outsiders to break into. They make accountability above the level of the local difficult and common standards all but impossible.

Those who hanker after the uniform governance of the nation state, for social democratic fairness and common standards of life, and for settled industrial routines, will find this new and evanescent world threatening. We cannot go back to such uniformity in governance, but we need to go beyond a situation where the only certainties are perpetual learning and institutions that exist only in evolution. A world of examples cannot create an economic and political system. A patchwork world of this kind is also unlikely to be a successful or sustainable one. Modern societies need to sustain broad-based prosperity. If this cannot be had by the old social-democratic national state-based strategies then we must find new ones, adapted to less stable and standardised production regimes but which will have similar effects.

In the absence of new models, the old ones persist – increasingly inaccurate and pernicious in their effects. A good example is our unthinking use of liberal notions of a democratic state in a market society, with a clear division of public and private spheres, and of 'civil society' as a realm of voluntary action and private freedom. Yet this liberal architecture is a gross misdescription of the structure of modern societies.

There is now no clear divide between the public and the private spheres, between democracy and markets, public and private choice. In fact modern societies are dominated by very similar large organisations on both sides of the formal public–private divide: business corporations, big public bureaucracies, quangos, and many intermediate kinds of organisations. These are in the main weakly accountable to those to whom they provide services.

The space between the public and private spheres is crossed by a wide variety of large governments, which are neither answerable through democratic elections nor through the market choices of consumers. Much of private life is dominated by large corporate businesses. We thus are faced with a post-liberal organisational society in which the fundamental relationship on either side of the public–private divide is that between a service provider and its clients, and in which the old liberal relationships of citizens and representative government, sovereign consumer and neutral market mean less and less.

For most purposes people are confronted by organisations, and even though those organisations directly affect their interests they have very little to say in how they are run. The institutional architecture of a post-liberal society is so different that conventional economic liberal measures to boost accountability are no longer effective: downsizing government simply shifts the government functions of large organisations from one formal constitutional site to another, from public to private, or public to quasi-public; and attempting to restore the role of 'markets' is not to remove individuals from the scope of governance, but to shift the agencies that perform the functions from state to corporate bureaucracies.

Responding to the institutional architecture of a post-liberal society requires that schemes for democratisation and reform cross the boundary between civil society and the state, that they explicitly tackle the broader issues of the governance powers of all organisations and not confine their remedies to government and to the state. Civil society needs to be made 'public', its organisations being accepted as governing powers over which citizens with significant affected interests should have a say proportionate to their involvement and the risk to their interests. Thus organisations – state and non-state – need to be treated as political, not merely administrative or private, and the relevant publics given a greater direct role as organisational 'citizens'. If supposedly private organisations are governmental, then many public bodies and government agencies are now structured as if they were private corporations.

Traditionalists respond to this by seeking to reassert the power of the nation state. They claim that such a state, democratically accountable and imposing common standards, can check the slide away from national uniformity and common citizenship. They fail to realise that the state is weaker in certain dimensions than it was, but is ever more over-extended in providing a diverse range of services and seeking to regulate an ever-widening range of contingencies. As such it is too overloaded to act as an effective democratic overseer and too enmeshed in trying to rationalise its own activities to offer a check to the growth of private and quasi-public managerial power. Indeed, elected politicians and career officials are eager to assert corporate models of management in the public service; the paradox is that they are often the ones that business has been abandoning in practice as it tries to become flexible and responsive.

Unaccountable private government is currently able to grow unchecked – in the major financial markets, in media empires, in major corporations – because its actions are presented as non-governmental, as the private actions of free citizens in civil society. Privatisation and marketisation are failing to confront the problems of modern public management, while reducing equality and fairness in the provision of public services. Yet social democracy has not enjoyed a real renaissance in response. It depended on an economic-governmental conjecture that cannot readily be put back together again. The range of modern public services is too wide and too diverse to be delivered to everybody in the same way. Social democratic and Christian democratic welfare measures and social provision reinforced national political identity, civic consciousness and a spirit of public service – they thus provided some of the social foundations for an effective mass democracy. A measure of cultural and social homogeneity is essential to democracy. One has to be sufficiently like one's fellow citizens to trust them with legislative power over one.

The capacity to reform and to renew the welfare system is central to our ability to find a new substitute for social democracy. Currently the centre-left has little to offer in this direction; it is in thrall to the right. The welfare state and democracy are intimately linked. One cannot build new forms of democracy without ensuring a measure of social security. Thus the decentralisation of sovereign power has to be coupled with a welfare system and set of public services that is itself decentralised, but which ensures common minimum standards of provision. This can only be achieved by maintaining public funding and common minimum entitlements. An associationalist welfare system would combine public funding related to individual membership of voluntary bodies providing services with citizen choice over providers. Public funding and common basic minima are essential in order to sustain an adequate level of welfare and a suitable range of services for all. Public entitlements and choice need to be combined, not driven apart as economic liberals who seek to privatise welfare provision wish to do. The provision of services through publicly funded voluntary associations in which individuals can choose and can craft the specific services they want is compatible with the common basic entitlements that were central to classical social democracy.

Indeed, it is probably the only way social democratic aims can survive. Unless individuals in a more differentiated society have choice and will consume the public services they pay for in the way that they want to, then public welfare will degenerate into poor relief. This advocacy of 'targeting' welfare services, concentrating them on the poor, has begun to capture socialist parties. It is a political disaster, that will promote the worst kind of social differentiation – creating services that only the desperate will consume through want of other choices but which all have to pay for.

A decentralised society can be a diverse one, but it cannot be a polarised one. A new democratic welfare system based on provision through self-governing associations requires an adequate minimum of common security. A society divided between the poor and the excluded and the rest will promote centralisation and repression, not localism and choice. Thus diversity in provision, where all can choose the services they want and the well-to-do can top up a common sufficient minimum, may actually be the only route left to a relatively fair and not grossly unequal society. Taxpayers thus will get the services they want, and will be more likely to be willing to contribute to services they consume. Associationalism is a way to crack tax aversion on the part of middle-income people.

Associative democracy provides new and clear models of governance that are applicable in the political system, in economic life and in welfare services. Associationalism does not do this by proposing the replacement of the existing social order with an entirely new alternative. Rather it is a supplement to existing institutions that has the capacity to transform their workings rather than to supplant them. Associationalist governmental means can be added piecemeal and iteratively to existing institutions in an ongoing reform process. Thus it has the gradualist and reformist potential of social democracy, but adapted to new conditions.

Associative democracy aims neither to abolish representative government nor to replace market exchange with some other allocative mechanism, rather to free the former from the encumbrance of an over-extended and centralised public-service state and to anchor the latter in a complex of social institutions that enables it to attain socially desirable outcomes.

Associationalism responds directly to the problems of how to democratise a post-liberal organisational society, since it aims to promote governance through democratically legitimated voluntary associations. The conversion of public and private corporate hierarchies into self-governing bodies answerable to those whom they serve and who participate in them, would thus answer to the greatest democratic deficits of our time – organisational government without consent and corporate control without representation.

The great advantage of associative democracy is that it offers a coherent model to guide reform initiatives across specific organisations and localities. It provides a means to link-up and to systematise local experiments. Suitably applied, associative democratic concepts provide a coherent and sufficiently loose-textured model that can help to convert many local experiments in decentralisation, democratisation, and negotiated governance from one-offs into contributions to a move towards a new style of social governance.

Index